ONE
GOSPEL
FOR ALL
NATIONS

One sign of an excellent book is the number and variety of people with whom one is eager to share it. Again and again as I read *One Gospel for All Nations*, names of colleagues came to mind—pastors, Bible teachers, evangelists, seminary faculty, missionaries, heads of agencies, missions mobilizers, and cross-cultural workers in many different fields. In short, I would commend this book to anyone who wants to understand the Bible more fully or to communicate its message more clearly to others, locally or internationally. For those working in honor/shame cultures in particular, Wu's work is essential reading.

David W. Bennett, DMin, PhD
chief collaboration officer and teaching pastor
The Lausanne Movement

The context of missions has changed. The pivot from the Gutenberg galaxy into the digital galaxy has taken place. How do people from different cultural worldviews make sense of the one true Gospel? A deep examination of the Scripture is required. Wu's book calls us into a serious reflection in the work of contextualization and meaningful presentation of the Gospel. Wu offers a timeless perspective that is both theological and practical. I highly recommend your attention to *One Gospel for All Nations*.

Rev. Samuel E. Chiang
executive director, International Orality Network

Many studies talk about contextualization in theory, but Jackson Wu wants to help equip missionaries and Christian workers to do it well. Wu gives his readers a model for contextualization that seeks to let the whole biblical narrative speak with a specific cultural accent, while at the same time interpreting and critiquing contemporary contexts through the lens of Scripture. But the real strength of this book comes when Wu shows us how his model works out in practice, as he beautifully retells the biblical story for Chinese people. Jackson Wu deserves thanks for a balanced and engaging contribution to our understanding and practice of contextualization.

Dean Flemming, PhD
professor of New Testament and Missions, MidAmerica Nazarene University
author of *Contextualization in the New Testament*

With honor and grace, Wu tackles the tough question of how the gospel may be understood and communicated to every culture. In this spirited and creative work, Wu begins with a biblical foundation, using the framework from the Scriptures to develop a clear and practical method for understanding the gospel and understanding cultures. He challenges narrow and short-sighted models, encouraging theologians, missionaries, and all Christians to get practical. In *One Gospel for All Nations*, he forms a clear, relevant, and timely challenge to communicate truth to every people. Throughout, he proposes a model that remains biblical faithful and culturally meaningful, so every nation can hear and understand the gospel."

Mark M. Overstreet, PhD
vice president of T4 Global

It is easy to announce that "all theology is contextualization" or that "contextualization is complicated," but it is another to do the actual work of contextualizing. In Wu's book, we get not only theory about contextualization but a practical model for working out the most significant theme in the Bible: gospel. Entering into this book is to enter into recent biblical discussions about the gospel and missiology's theories about contextualization. Wu even takes us to the heart of the matter when he shows what gospel looks like in the Chinese culture.

Scot McKnight, PhD
professor of New Testament, Northern Seminary
author of *The King Jesus Gospel*

A practical book by a practical theologian who takes seriously the integration of biblical theology and missiology in relation to the gospel so that proclamation remains biblically based yet culturally calling.

Tom Steffen, PhD
emeritus professor of intercultural studies
Cook School of Intercultural Studies, Biola University

ONE GOSPEL
GOSPEL FOR ALL
NATIONS

A PRACTICAL APPROACH TO
BIBLICAL CONTEXTUALIZATION

JACKSON WU

WILLIAM CAREY
LIBRARY

One Gospel for All Nations: A Practical Approach to Biblical Contextualization
Copyright © 2015 by Jackson Wu

Unless otherwise indicated, all Scripture quotations are from the ESV® Bible (The Holy Bible, English Standard Version®), copyright © 2001 by Crossway, a publishing ministry of Good News Publishers. Used by permission. All rights reserved."

Italics within scripture quotations indicate emphasis added.

Published by William Carey Library
1605 E. Elizabeth St.
Pasadena, CA 91104 | www.missionbooks.org

Melissa Hicks, editor
Brad Koenig, copyeditor
Hugh Pindur, graphic design
Rose Lee-Norman, indexer

William Carey Library is a ministry of
Frontier Ventures
Pasadena, CA 91104 | www.frontierventures.org

Printed in the United States of America
19 18 17 16 15   5 4 3 2 1 BP300

Library of Congress Cataloging-in-Publication Data

Wu, Jackson.
   One gospel for all nations : a practical approach to biblical contextualization / Jackson Wu.
      pages cm
   Includes bibliographical references and index.
   ISBN 978-0-87808-629-0 -- ISBN 0-87808-629-3 1. Missions. 2. Christianity and culture.
3. Witness bearing (Christianity) 4. Evangelistic work. I. Title.
   BV2063.W8 2015
   261--dc23
                              2015001107

Special thanks is given to Enoch Wan who granted permission to use four previously published articles, which have been revised for the sake of this book. Chapter two uses "We Compromise the Gospel When We Settle for Truth—How 'Right' Interpretations Lead to 'Wrong' Contextualization," *Global Missiology*, vol. 2, no. 10 (Jan 2013). Select portions of chapters three and four draw from "Contextualizing the One Gospel in Any Culture: A Model from the Biblical Text for a Global Context," *Global Missiology*, vol 3, no. 10 (April 2013). The main arguments of chapters eight and nine first appeared, respectively, in "Biblical Theology from a Chinese Perspective: Interpreting Scripture through the Lens of Honor and Shame," *Global Missiology*, vol. 4, no. 10 (July 2013) and "The Gospel with Chinese Characteristics: A Concrete Example of Cultural Contextualization," *Global Missiology*, vol. 1, no. 11 (October 2013).

Contents

Figures

Foreword

It is not a matter of *whether* we will contextualize the gospel. It is only a matter of whether we will do so faithfully or unfaithfully. Although the word "contextualization" is recent, coming into popular usage over the past three or four decades, its practice and reality have always been present as essential to the Christian faith. Unlike the Qur'an, which sees truth as timeless divine oracles, or the Western Enlightenment tradition that believes truth to be found in unchanging and eternal ideas, the Bible understands truth to be the mighty acts of God in history, authoritatively narrated and interpreted in Scripture, as the true story of the whole world in which all people are invited to find their place.

The mightiest act of God and fullest revelation of himself and his purpose for the creation has been disclosed in the person and work of Jesus the Christ, especially in his death and resurrection. Truth is a person along with the historical events surrounding him that have irreversibly changed the course of universal history. Sin and evil, death and demonic power, sickness and injustice, poverty and pain—in fact all that corrupts the very good creation of God—have been defeated at the cross of Jesus. A new world has begun in his resurrection. This is good news that must be made known to all peoples. Communicating these events in life, word, and deed in the various cultures of the world *demands* contextualization, a message *faithful* to what God has accomplished in Christ and *relevant* to the various contexts so that it is seen and heard as good news.

The cross-cultural contextualization of the gospel took place very early as the gospel moved from its Jewish home into the pagan environment of Roman culture. Jesus the Jewish Messiah is proclaimed as Jesus the Roman Lord, a title associated with the Roman emperor (Acts 11:22). The fresh Gentile form of the gospel that subsequently took shape in Antioch began to spread throughout the Roman Empire. This riled up those who believed that the covenant with God must take the form of the divinely authorized culture of Israel. And the ensuing stir led to the council at Jerusalem, where once and for all it was made clear that Gentiles could become part of the end-time gathering of eschatological Israel, not simply as proselytes in the Jewish community, but as fully gentile believers who did not need to surrender their cultural identity (Acts 15:17; cf. Isa 63:19). God's people had been transformed into a multicultural community that must embody the gospel in every cultural setting, and this meant that from this point forward all cultures must be brought to the cross to be affirmed and judged.

But this movement from a Jewish to Gentile form of the faith can be seen not only in the story narrated in Acts. It is also evident in our very New Testament canon. Jesus proclaims the good news of the kingdom (Mark 1:15; Luke 4:43), a theme that captured the imagination of the Jewish people and expressed the fulfillment of the Old Testament story. This theme of the kingdom dominates the ministry of Jesus as he gathers the lost sheep of Israel and is the central motif of the synoptic gospels.

However, when we turn to the gospel of John, written a little later, the word "kingdom" disappears from its pages. Instead, the dualistic categories of Greek culture take its place—heaven and earth, soul and body, word and flesh, light and darkness, life and death. Eternal life rather than the kingdom is the good news. John masterfully communicates the gospel of the kingdom in new terminology as a message that answers the longing of the Greek, while at the same time critiquing its idolatrous worldview. The pagan categories are filled with new meaning and good news is made known. And so it continues today, the gospel moving from culture to culture.

Jackson Wu understands this contextual impulse of the gospel well. He is aware that we have no option but to contextualize if we are to be faithful. He is aware that to avoid the task with an appeal to an Enlightenment view of truth masquerading as the absolute biblical truth may well lead to unfaithfulness. As he says: "If we do not take contextualization seriously, we open ourselves up to various dangers, including cultural and theological syncretism." And so he offers us this book as a guide to help us make our way through the complicated issues of today.

Over the past century the issue has become even more urgent. The church has exploded in the Southern and Eastern parts of the globe dwarfing the

Western church. The question of how to hold fast to one gospel while at the same time seeking many faithful cultural forms in the various nations and cultures of the world is as pressing today as it ever has been. It is one of the burning issues of the day for the Christian church and Wu joins the conversation seeking biblically faithful answers.

But there is a deluge of literature on the subject as Wu himself acknowledges. So why should one take up this book amidst many other offerings? I suggest four reasons.

The first is the one that Wu himself notes: he is not only interested in describing contextualization but offering concrete and helpful guidance on how to contextualize the gospel. It would be a mistake to conclude, therefore, that this means he has simply opted for pragmatism in the face of complex issues. In fact, what one sees in the book is precisely what should happen: sound biblical and theological reflection in the context of practice. As he seeks to answer the concrete question "how do we contextualize the gospel?" he thinks more deeply and not less.

This leads to a second reason: Scripture guides and shapes his reflection on contextualization. It would seem that this should be a given, but sadly when one reads the vast body of literature on the subject, it becomes clear—with superb exceptions, of course—that hard work in the text of Scripture is not a priority. Two things are noteworthy in this book. On the one hand, faithful contextualization will never succeed if the text of Scripture is understood in a fragmentary way. And this is often the default option in both the liberal and evangelical camps since the Enlightenment. Wu understands this and throughout treats the Bible as the one true story of the world. On the other hand, this does not keep him from a close reading of many different texts. He does not remain at 30,000 feet but lands on specific texts and interacts with the details of Scripture.

Wu's commitment to the Bible comes from within the evangelical tradition where scriptural authority is held in high regard. But this does not lead him simply to uncritically adopt Western evangelicalism. It is precisely his commitment to Scripture that leads him to criticize his own tradition at a number of points: evangelical models of contextualization that simplistically separate an unchanging gospel core and a changing cultural husk; a reductionist gospel characteristic of American individualistic culture; and a narrowing of truth to propositions aligned with our Enlightenment heritage. At each point he follows Scripture and the fruit is a more nuanced and faithful understanding of contextualization.

The third reason to pick up this book is that Wu understands well how deeply our cultural situation will shape our reading, communication, and embodiment of the gospel. It is often the case that when one gives priority to Scripture, it is at the expense of a deep understanding of the profound shaping impact of culture. The fear is relativism. The problem also moves in the opposite direction: a recognition of the pervasive forming influence of culture leads one to abandon scriptural authority and move toward relativism. To understand how to be faithful in contextualization, it is necessary to hold fast to both: Scripture must be given priority because it is the word of God and is truth for all peoples, all places, all times. Yet God's people are a multicultural community and the understanding and embodiment of the gospel in every setting is profoundly shaped by each cultural context. Wu understand both of these things and struggles with how *one* gospel can *faithfully* take *many* cultural forms.

There is a final reason to take up this book and read. Wu understands both the Western and Eastern contexts. Paul believes we can only grasp the riches of the gospel "together with all of the Lord's people" (Eph 3:18). We are all blind to dimensions of the gospel that come from the limitations of our cultural and theological traditions. We all have an "implicit gospel" and an "explicit gospel" shaped by our cultural prejudices. We need the eyes of others to help us see this. Our brothers and sisters in different contexts can offer needed enrichment and correction. I believe that there must be at least a threefold dialogue: a dialogue with Christians from other confessional traditions, with Christians in other historical eras, and with Christians in other cultural settings.

Today there is need to foster the last of these. We in the West can learn from our brothers and sisters from the South and from the East. The problem is, of course, how is it possible for us to hear their voices? It takes someone immersed in both Western and non-Western cultures who can communicate in ways we understand. That is why there are two kinds of Christians who are a gift to the Western church today. The first are Third World Christians who have had a Western education but have not been swept into a Western worldview. The second are missionaries from the West who have a deeply bicultural and bilingual experience. It is these brothers and sisters that we must welcome because they straddle non-Western and Western cultures. They have the gift of new eyes to see our cultural blind spots that distort the gospel. Jackson Wu is such a person. Born and educated in North America, he has lived a long time in China, spending over a decade struggling with the complexities of that culture. This experience has given him new eyes to see many issues important for struggling with the question of contextualization.

The struggle to contextualize the gospel in China that makes up the third section of the book will offer some new perspectives. If we are willing to listen to an unfamiliar telling of the biblical story and fresh ways of approaching a culture that is not our own, both in critique and in affirmation, we will be in a position to hear the gospel speaking to our own context in a new way.

At its very heart, contextualization struggles with two unavoidable and urgent questions. The first is concerned with the gospel and the many cultures of the world: How can we be faithful to one gospel without falling into ethnocentrism *and* embrace plural expressions without falling into relativism? The second is concerned with the gospel and various aspects of a particular culture: How can we be faithful to the gospel without becoming irrelevant *and* be relevant to the culture without becoming syncretistic? Ethnocentrism and relativism, syncretism and irrelevance are all bars that imprison the gospel, evaporate its power, and weaken the church's mission. Jackson Wu has given us a sound book that will help us struggle with these questions in a way that is faithful to the Bible. His simple and clear writing style, his diagrams, charts, and appendices, and his key points at the end of chapters will also help in this important quest.

No one will agree with everything written in this book. The complex subject matter of contextualization makes that an unlikely possibility. Yet for the one who is willing to read and listen, there is much wisdom in its pages. May this book be used by God to enable his people to be more faithful to the gospel revealed in Jesus the Christ.

Michael W. Goheen, PhD
Vancouver, B.C., Winter 2014
director of theological education, Missional Training Center, Phoenix
author of *The Drama of Scripture*

Introduction

BIBLICALLY FAITHFUL AND CULTURALLY MEANINGFUL?

Imagine this was the first gospel presentation you ever heard:

Many years ago, the first human couple had big problems. In order to gain wisdom, they listened to a snake and ate fruit from a tree that God had put in their garden. Consequently he became very angry. Because that first couple had an unfortunate fruit fixation, God should now send all people to hell.

However, God loved the world. Therefore, he told a small nation in the Middle East that he would bless both them and the world if they would listen to him. If they would circumcise themselves and kill innocent animals, God would not punish them. In the process of blessing the world, God conquered many nations, even allowing innocent children to die.

As a way of saving the world, God eventually sent his own Son, Jesus, so that he could be wrongly condemned and executed instead of us. If fact, we are all criminals because we have broken laws. We should die. We need God to be our copilot.

Yet Jesus today can live our hearts if we would believe that we cannot earn our salvation. Jesus said, "If anyone comes to me and does not hate his own father and mother and wife and children and brothers and sisters, yes, and even his own life, he cannot be my disciple." If we would just accept God's great love for us, we could go to heaven when we die.

This example is an obvious caricature of the message many people "hear" when someone preaches the gospel to them. Unfortunately, it all too accurately describes reality. At some level, this is exactly how a lot of people understand the gospel when they first hear it. The story sounds strange and fragmented.

We all can agree the above summary distorts certain aspects of the biblical story. On the other hand, fewer people would object to many of the individual statements, if taken in isolation. In other words, the above presentation gets a number of facts correct. Yet the hypothetical evangelist frames the story entirely wrong. Themes and emphases are lumped together in a way that makes the message sound like foolishness (and *not* in the sense Paul means in 1 Corinthians 1). Not surprisingly, people everyday reject the "gospel" they hear. They do so not because they have hard hearts; they refuse to believe a message that, from their perspective, lacks any significant meaning. It is very possible to proclaim the truth and yet still be wrong.

A gospel presentation is more than the sum of its sentences. It is a story, not a system. The gospel is a declaration, not a mere doctrine. The gospel found in the ancient biblical text remains relevant in every cultural context. Yet how do we make sense of all this? There seems to be a tension. On the one hand, we want to be biblically faithful to the ancient Scripture. On the other hand, how does one understand, communicate, and apply the gospel within a contemporary context? Maybe we should ask a different question.

Are we biblically faithful if our gospel message is not culturally meaningful?

We Need More than Principles

Do we really need more books about contextualization? Perhaps not. In fact, that is one reason I've written this book. A lot has been written "about contextualization." Many people have tried to explain contextualization— what it is, why it's important, and what its potential dangers are. Those are important topics for sure. However, we need to move the discussion beyond principles. It's time to get more practical. What do we need to do?

While a number of other (important) books are descriptive, this one is *prescriptive*. It is helpful to do case studies and examine what other people have done. Evangelicals have done a good job emphasizing key ideas that should guide contextualization. Nevertheless we still need to make progress. Specifically, we need to think about how to *apply* those principles. Practically speaking, *how do we contextualize the gospel?*

This may sound too ambitious for one book. Regardless, this is what the church must strive to do if we are to preach the gospel in a biblically faithful and culturally meaningful way. This book certainly won't answer every question someone might have. Yet it does provide a starting point for further conversation. It suggests an approach that is practical but not pragmatic. I hope to give a perspective that is realistic without being overly simplistic.

Why can't people agree on an "evangelical method" of contextualization? I want to mention at least one possible answer to that question. Simply put, people struggle to reconcile the relationship between the Bible and culture. Everyone would agree that both are critical. Still, affirming their importance doesn't tell us what to do. How do people know when they have confused the biblical text with the cultural context (i.e., syncretism)?

Because evangelicals are committed to the authority of Scripture, they want to avoid this danger. While trying to be biblically faithful, one can fall into another, more subtle problem. One can be content to present a true message that is practically irrelevant to his or her listeners. At one level, the Bible is never "irrelevant." Yet, if I said, "耶稣作弥赛亚" to someone who didn't know Chinese, the message would amount to gibberish, even though I just said, "Jesus is the Messiah!" Even if I used English, someone may wonder, "What in the world is a messiah?" This is just one way we might compromise the gospel by settling for what is merely true. I'll talk more on this in chapter 2.

Context Is King

"*Context is king.*" This is one of the first rules a seminary student learns about biblical interpretation. The phrase simply means that the biblical context determines the Bible's meaning. We cannot force our personal assumptions and opinions into the biblical text. Context is king and *not* a seminary professor, a theological tradition, nor any human culture.

It is a bit easier, however, to recite the rule than to apply it. The problem is apparent. Every single modern reader lives in a culture quite foreign to the Bible's original context. This creates a challenge for anyone who wants to be faithful to Scripture. It is possible for our theology to reflect one's own cultural assumptions rather than that of the biblical authors. If so, what are the implications for evangelism? How do we bridge the historical and cultural gaps?

We face a very practical question. When it comes to preaching the gospel, *which* context is king? The ancient biblical world? Literary context? The interpreter's culture (or subculture)? How about the cultural context of our listeners? If we are honest, finding an answer is far more difficult and sobering than one might expect.

"Christ Is King"

At this point, someone may make an objection by saying, "Oh, you are making this all too complicated. All we need to do is proclaim Jesus Christ and him crucified. We don't need to bring in a lot of Old Testament, Jewish history." In response, I would simply ask, "What do you mean by the word 'Christ'? Is that a family name?"

According to Acts, the gospel can be summarized in this way: Jesus is the Christ (cf. Acts 5:42; 9:22; 17:3; 18:5). The word "Christ" is a Jewish title routinely carrying royal connotations. Likewise, the four Gospels center on the message of Jesus' identity as Israel's "Christ." (See Michael F. Bird, *Jesus is the Christ: The Messianic Testimony of the Gospels.*) The "Christ" is Israel's King (cf. Mark 15:32; Luke 23:2; Acts 17:3,7). How can Gentiles, whether ancient or modern, make sense of this message if they do not grasp the significance of Israel's story?

We immediately find ourselves faced with a question. How are we supposed to preach an ancient Jewish gospel to modern Gentiles? The tension only mounts when we recall that Acts is a letter between two Gentiles, Luke and Theophilus (Acts 1:1). After all, Luke's account is thoroughly "Jewish." One could simply look at the teachings given in Acts 2–4; 7; 13 as examples. He does not simply edit out all the Jewish history and replace the title "Christ" with "King."

On the one hand, saying "Christ is King" is redundant. On the other hand, the declaration that Jesus is the "Christ" carries with it a vast and critical backstory. In fact, grasping the significance of the "Christ" necessitates an entirely different worldview. This particular king is far more than the hope of a single nation. In the Christ, God fulfills his purposes *for the world.*

The gospel proclaims, "Christ is King." This announcement is relevant for every culture of the world. Christ is King over every context. The gospel transcends culture, yet is revealed to men and women within specific historical cultures.

How do we communicate and apply this ancient gospel within a contemporary setting?

Preaching the Gospel When Context Is King

To resolve these tensions, theologians and mission strategists often discuss a concept known as contextualization. Although people have used a range of definitions to explain "contextualization," evangelicals tend to agree on a number of foundational principles. For example, a good contextualization will attempt to present a gospel message that is faithful to Scripture and meaningful for contemporary culture.[1] However, there remains a great need to develop practical models that demonstrate *how* Christians might actually apply these principles. This book offers a practical approach to contextualizing the gospel in any culture.

Contextualization brings into conversation a number of voices from diverse fields—such as Old and New Testament studies, systematic theology, history, anthropology, and others. Missiology—the study of missions—draws upon all these areas of study. The typical missionary has no time to keep up with all the scholarly debates that could possibly be relevant for his or her ministry. How then do we simplify something so inherently complex as contextualization? This book is written with these questions in mind.

I hope this book serves as a bridge between multiple contexts. At first it seems that missionaries only have two cultures to think about—their home culture and the culture in which they serve. In fact, the picture is far more complex. For example, missionaries themselves are also influenced by countless other subcultures, whether that of their family, denomination, or mission agency, to name a few. The same could be said about those whom missionaries serve. Regional, religious, and tribal influences affect the way they understand and respond to the gospel. To make matters more difficult, Christians face the challenge of preaching a gospel that is found in the Bible, whose authors come from a myriad of ancient cultures.

Nevertheless this book was written with the conviction that the Bible is God's authoritative revelation and *that* gospel must be proclaimed to all nations. The Bible transcends any one specific cultural setting. Likewise, the one true gospel of Christ is relevant for all cultures. Yet these facts do not imply that theology, particularly the gospel, should be turned into some abstraction. The Bible tells what God has done for the entire world, for those with flesh and blood who live in time and space. How then do we understand, communicate, and apply biblical truth in such a way that upholds absolute truth yet makes sense to people who have limited, culturally relative perspectives (including us)? Contextualization seeks to maintain this balance.

Moving Beyond Principles and Problems

In section I, the first chapter answers the question, "What is contextualization?" This chapter surveys the most common views people have concerning contextualization. Ironically, it seems to be a concept that everyone agrees is important, yet no one quite agrees on what it is and how to do it. Most evangelicals have regarded contextualization as a form of communication or application of a doctrine or biblical text. Examples include gospel "bridges" and "redemptive analogies."

Nevertheless I suggest that evangelicals have overlooked a critical, even foundational, aspect of contextualization. Contextualization fundamentally begins when we interpret the Bible. I have argued this point more thoroughly elsewhere.[2] The contextualization process has already started even before we try to communicate or apply the gospel. Not only do we need a new *perspective* on contextualization, we also need a *practical* model for actually doing it. This book attempts to address both of these needs.

It is important to understand that "all theology is contextualized theology." We all interpret the Bible from a cultural perspective. We all live within particular social contexts. Contextualization is both inevitable and essential. Therefore, Christians need to intentionally consider the influence of culture on their theology. If we do not take contextualization seriously, we open ourselves up to various dangers, including cultural and theological syncretism. Since contextualization fundamentally concerns the interaction between culture and

the Bible, I suggest that we distinguish between two types of contextualization—exegetical contextualization and cultural contextualization.

Chapter 2 explores a fundamental problem that undermines efforts to
contextualize the gospel. The challenge is more subtle than choosing between
right/wrong and truth/error. Instead we may confuse the biblical author's
original meaning with a correct application or implication. Even if we teach
right doctrines, we may stress points that are neither the author's emphasis
nor meaningful to the contemporary listener. Consequently it is possible to
compromise the gospel by settling for truth.

Getting Practical about Contextualization

Section II is the heart of the book. It develops a *firm* but *flexible* model of
contextualization suitable for *fluctuating* cultures. A contextualized gospel
presentation should be faithful to Scripture and meaningful to the local
culture. There are two features that distinguish this approach. First, it begins
with biblical theology and not simply systematic theology. Second, it takes
seriously the influence of the reader on one's theology. In other words, it
reckons with the fact that we all come to the text with limited and culturally
biased perspectives.

The section spends a significant amount of time examining various biblical passages in order to ensure that our contextualization model is rooted in
biblical exegesis. At times the reader may get overwhelmed either in details
or by the quantity of texts. Yet one should keep a few points in mind. First,
God inspired the entire biblical canon. Therefore, we want to be careful that
we not settle for a select few verses that serve as proof texts for a theory that
we have already presupposed. Rather, a holistic view of contextualization
requires a well-rounded biblical theology. Second, a person's mind is not
easily changed when he or she is accustomed to thinking a certain way for a
long time. This is particularly true when considering a model that supposes
to help people contextualize the gospel in a way that is both biblically faithful
and relevant for any culture.

Therefore, this section appeals to the "Bereans" who might read this book.
In Acts 17:11 Paul found that the Jews in Berea "were more noble than those
in Thessalonica; they received the word with all eagerness, examining the
Scriptures daily to see if these things were so." I wince at the thought that

any reader could possibly "take my word for it" when I make claims about the gospel and biblical theology. Therefore, the exegesis in these chapters is more thorough than some readers will be accustomed to finding in other missiological literature.

Although I will examine some texts multiple times, this is not needless repetition. Each chapter presents a distinct set of ideas. Therefore, it is necessary that we revisit a number of key passages in order to discern and apply different aspects of biblical truth to our model of contextualization.

How can we affirm only one gospel when the Bible contains a diversity of gospel presentations? Chapter 3 explains by highlighting a critical observation. The biblical writers have a distinct way of framing their gospel presentations. In particular, at least one of three interconnected motifs serves as the context for other gospel-related doctrines. These three themes are derived from the grand narrative of Scripture and include creation, covenant, and kingdom. Without exception, these three themes decisively shape the biblical authors' gospel presentation. The gospel is a particular story that demands a firm framework, even if there is flexibility in how one specifically explains the message (i.e., points of emphasis within that framework). If this framework does not shape our contemporary gospel presentations, we are not preaching the gospel as the biblical writers understood it, even if we do teach many correct and important doctrinal truths.

Within this framework, how do we answer the question "What is the gospel?"? Chapter 4 explores the various biblical passages that explicitly use language like "gospel" and "preach the gospel." Although we cannot limit our understanding of the gospel to such passages, they nevertheless should be foundational in shaping our understanding of a gospel presentation. The chapter argues that the biblical writers consistently answer four key questions when presenting the gospel: "Who is Jesus?" "What does he do?" "Why does he matter?" and "How should we respond?" These questions are not random. In fact, there is a basic logic and priority to these questions that should shape the way we preach the gospel today.

Chapter 5 balances the previous chapter by explaining the diversity inherent to gospel preaching. A person presents the message according to a certain set of organizing principles that emerge from one's cultural and personal perspective. These principles often go unrecognized and serve as a filter that determines our *implicit gospel*. An "implicit gospel" refers to the subtle message we don't realize we are preaching. We may consciously intend to emphasize a given point yet do so from such a perspective that we implicitly give prominence to other ideas. For example, a stereotypical Western gospel presentation especially highlights the *personal* relationship with God, individual diversity, identity based on differences, God as judge, and the law as the metaphorical language of right and wrong. Though reading the same book—the Bible—a possible "Eastern" presentation might stress the group, harmony or unity, identity based on similarity to others, God as Father or King, and could employ honor/shame language to discuss morality. It is possible that our "implicit gospel" has greater influence on our listener than does out "explicit gospel."

Chapter 6 explains the entire process of contextualization, drawing together the content from previous chapters. We need a model that is both firm and flexible. The chapter uses simple illustrations to demonstrate the relationship between a gospel's framework, various biblical themes, and the surrounding cultural context. In the second half of the chapter, I lay out four stages necessary for fully contextualizing the gospel. Stated in brief, we need to (1) *identify* how the Bible frames and explains the gospel, (2) *interconnect* cultural themes corresponding to the biblical gospel, (3) *interpret* the Bible using a cultural lens, and (4) *infer* the gospel's significance for the local culture. The rest of the chapter elaborates on this process so that the reader can reproduce it in his or her own ministry setting.

What Does It Look Like?

What does contextualization look like in practice? The book's third section offers a few concrete examples of contextualization that illustrate the model proposed in the prior chapters. Genuine contextualization occurs from within a certain cultural vantage point. To guard against abstraction, I first use contemporary Chinese culture as a context from which to demonstrate the two types of contextualization discussed in section I. Additionally, I go on to explain what this contextualization model means for our ministries, whether strategy, training, or our character. Finally, this section defends the use of culture in developing biblically faithful theologies.

Chapter 7 uses Chinese culture as a context in which to demonstrate what a contextualization looks like in practice. This chapter retells the grand biblical narrative from a Chinese perspective. It shows how an "Eastern" perspective highlights certain aspects of the biblical text otherwise unnoticed or underemphasized in traditional Western theology. In short, the chapter gives an example of "exegetical contextualization" (first introduced in ch. 2). After a brief introduction to Chinese culture, the entire biblical story is retold in six interconnected episodes that emphasize more "Eastern" themes. At the same time, the reader will find this reading more balanced than traditional accounts that generally skip from Genesis 3, ignoring Israel, and focus squarely on Paul's epistles.

The eighth chapter then provides an example of cultural contextualization, by which one uses the Bible to critique a contemporary culture. As a result, one gains a more critical and balanced perspective on a given culture, like China. If one imagined a gospel with Chinese characteristics, what would it look like? I offer one suggestion that focuses on the parent-child relationship within modern China. Among the false gospels found within China, family, face, and fortune together serve as a sort of "trinity" that steers people away from the truth. We are called to preach the gospel in a manner that is faithful to the text and meaningful for the context; in so doing, many Chinese people, who are now enslaved to various cultural expectations, will be set free to become slaves of righteousness and children of our heavenly Father.

Contextualization is not an isolated aspect of Christian ministry. It is holistic and systemic in its influence. Building on the prior discussion in the book, chapter 9 explores other potential implications for ministry strategy and training. It also highlights many of the obstacles to contextualization. This chapter gives a number of suggestions that readers can develop and implement after finishing the book.

A Few Lingering Questions

Can we really use contemporary cultures to interpret Scripture (as ch. 10 argues)? It is not enough to say that cultures influence our understanding of Scripture. We need to learn *how*. The chapter suggests a simple albeit counter-intuitive idea: by learning more about modern cultures, we gain insight into the biblical world. One author puts it this way—a multicultural view is more objective than a monocultural worldview. Naturally, we find that contextualization is the critical point of intersection between theology and missiology.

These ideas require a bit more nuanced argument than is needed for other chapters. This is why I leave this discussion for the last chapter in the book. Some will not be interested in such issues; however, many readers no doubt will want greater elaboration about the relationship between culture and Scripture. In many ways, this chapter is an apologetic for the previous content in the book. It also poses a number of ideas that readers could develop for contextualizing the gospel in their own ministry setting.

Finally, I offer a few tools in the appendices that I hope will prove helpful in applying what you learn in the main sections of the book. We can apply what we have learned about contextualization to the various ministry tools that already exist. Accordingly, I have included an evaluation form for assessing any gospel presentation. It is meant to be comprehensive, aimed at helping churches, mission agencies, and field strategists reflect on the strengths and weaknesses of any present or potential resources they might use. Second, I give a single example of a gospel tract that I developed, which is consistent with the material in the book. Third, I list every verse in the Bible that explicitly uses the Greek or Hebrew words for "gospel" or "to evangelize." Accordingly, readers can more easily examine many key passages that support the conclusions made in this book.

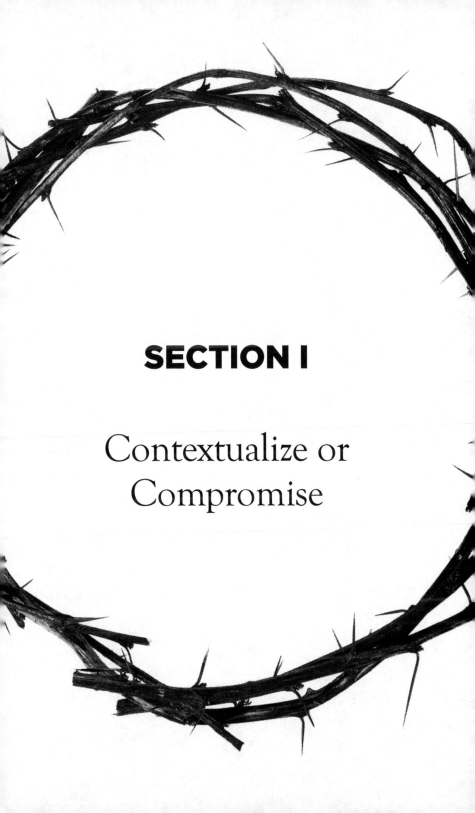

SECTION I

Contextualize or
Compromise

1

Context Is King: A New Perspective on Contextualization

I once heard New Testament scholar N. T. Wright retell a conversation he had with his wife upon finding out that he was writing his book called *Simply Jesus*. At that point, he had already written a few books about Jesus. Wright explains more fully:

> When my wife knew I was writing this book, she said, "But you've written two or three books on Jesus already."
> And I said, "Well yes, that was a little while ago."
> She said, "Well, has Jesus changed during that time?"
> I thought for a minute; I said, "Well no, but *I* have."[3]

Wright stumbles onto a truth few have grasped, much less applied: the Bible's original meaning does not change, *but we do*. As result, we will notice new things as we mature or our personal circumstances change. It also means that we naturally either overlook or underemphasize certain aspects of the text that lie outside our common experience. The situation is further complicated when we imagine the many legitimate perspectives that other people might bring to the text.

Perhaps someone might complain by saying it doesn't matter what any person thinks; instead, we just need to start with Scripture. We should ask, "What does the Bible mean?" In fact, even this question is less straightforward than it seems. In using that question, a person could be asking, "What is the author's *meaning* in his original context?" On the other hand, a person might intend to ask, "What is the *significance* of the passage for us today?"

These two questions are different. The first one concerns interpretation; the second has to do with implications for the reader. There is a difference between an interpretation and its implications. Many people normally think about contextualization as nothing more than the latter. Once we have a right interpretation, we can get on with the business of contextualization—figuring out the correct application or illustration to help people obey the gospel.

All this talk about the reader and application may overlook something more basic. It is not always so easy to figure out the author's original meaning. Just like any letter or book, there are levels of meaning to a given biblical text. Interpreting the Bible is not always about having the right or wrong answer; one also must discern varying shades of emphasis. These observations should serve as a warning. When talking about contextualization, we can quickly get ahead of ourselves.

We never want to make interpreting and applying the Bible more difficult than it really is; however, I do not think that is the issue we face here. Truthfully, we may suffer the opposite problem—we may actually underestimate the challenge before us. The idea that interpreting and applying the Bible could get any harder will make some readers want to close this book right away. I encourage you not to do that. Be assured that denying the problem doesn't make things any easier; it will only lead to more difficulties. The problem is not going away anytime soon.

This complex dynamic is exactly what contextualization is about. Contextualization is concerned with the truth in the concrete. Yet, it will take something of a counterintuitive approach to help ease the tension between text and contexts. Contextualization takes a big-picture view of a situation to get at the underlying dynamics at work. At first, contextualization appears too abstract, lacking much practical value. In reality, contextualization reflects the problem it tries to solve. Although it is full of complexity and nuance, contextualization involves finding practical solutions for specific problems and places. It brings about change by helping people see things from multiple angles. In every area of life, there are few things more practical than perspective. Greater perspective reveals to us more of the truth. As a result, we gain humility and wisdom to face reality.

For the moment, let's not get ahead of ourselves. Understanding the concept of contextualization is the first step and is a formidable task in itself. Learning to do contextualization can initially feel overwhelming. It's like trying to discern the story being told by a piece of symphony music while your child whispers questions in your right ear and your boss continues to send text messages to the phone in your left hand about the big meeting you have the next day. This chapter (and the book) takes a serious and practical look at contextualization. When possible, it's best to keep things simple. So we begin with the question, "What is contextualization?"

What Is Contextualization?

The word "contextualization" inspires two opposite kinds of responses. On the one hand, many people seem to agree that contextualization is important. One increasingly hears people even say that contextualization is essential and necessary. On the other hand, there are others who are less enthusiastic about the whole idea. The reasons vary. A biblical scholar once asked me why the fuss over contextualization, "Why can't we just go right from the text to application?" Of course some missionary practitioners scratch their heads, readily admitting that they are not quite sure what contextualization even means.

It is understandable that most definitions of "contextualization" are rather general. To some degree or another, contextualization involves multiple cultural and historical contexts as well as a plethora of academic disciplines. The sheer variety within the topic makes defining contextualization a feat in itself. Nevertheless we can hardly apply an idea when we only have a vague notion of it in our heads.

This chapter attempts to bring some needed clarity to the conversation. It lays the foundation for doing contextualization by both explaining its meaning and its significance. Without rehashing the various books and articles that have been written on contextualization, this chapter identifies a number of points about which evangelicals can agree. In addition, I hope to advance the discussion by identifying some areas that have not received adequate attention. In so doing, readers can see clearly why contextualization concerns more than simply cultural "relevance." Contextualization is not merely an important additive to mission theory; it is inevitable. In the same way architectural plans determine the design for a building, so also contextualization is an essential element of mission strategy.

Evangelical Views on Contextualization[4]

How have evangelicals defined "contextualization"? David Hesselgrave and Edward Rommen's *Contextualization* is a standard evangelical book on the subject. Their definition echoes the view of many others. They write,

> Christian contextualization can be thought of as the attempt to communicate the message of the person, works, Word, and will of God in a way that is faithful to God's revelation, especially as it is put forth in the teachings of Holy Scripture, and that is meaningful to respondents in their respective cultural and existential contexts.[5]

They further emphasize the point that the gospel does not change; rather, contextualization is concerned with discerning its implications for a given culture. In particular, contextualization seeks ways to communicate and apply the biblical text.[6]

When we look at other writers, certain patterns emerge. First of all, they consistently attempt to define the relationship between the Bible and culture. As one person succinctly put it, "We understand contextualization as the various processes by which a local church integrates the Gospel message (the 'text') with its local culture (the 'context')."[7] Kevin Greeson says contextualization tries "to adapt the style, form and language of the Christian faith and message to the culture of the people one is seeking to reach."[8] Scott Moreau summarizes the most common approach among evangelicals, "There is a core message of universal truth which must be translated into each new cultural setting in a way that remains faithful to the core. Because the content of that message is absolute and authoritative, the contextualizer's task is to change the form of the message."[9] In short, the message in Scripture is constant; however, its presentation depends on the culture. Somehow, unchanging truth is conveyed through any number of flexible forms.

Second, authors repeatedly narrow their focus on communication or application. David Sills plainly states, "Contextualization is simply the process of making the gospel understood."[10] Moreau's summary reflects the opinion of many others when he says, "Contextualization is the process whereby Christians adapt the forms, content, and praxis of the Christian faith so as to communicate it to the minds and hearts of people with other cultural backgrounds."[11] For many, this understanding of contextualization follows naturally from an evangelical view of Scripture. If God's self-revelation is without error and transcends culture, then contextualization should not change the meaning of the Bible itself. Accordingly, many attempts to contextualize the gospel center on communication "bridges" and "redemptive analogies."[12] Thus, evangelicals typically regard contextualization primarily as a task concerning the communication and application of timeless truths.

Do We Need a New Perspective?

So what is the problem? Why do we need a new perspective on contextualization?

A growing number of thinkers have challenged the typical way of looking at contextualization, especially the relationship between theology and culture. Lesslie Newbigin highlights a fundamental problem in the way people often separate gospel and culture. Accordingly he asserts, "We must start with the basic fact that there is no such thing as a pure gospel if by that is meant something which is not embodied in a culture."[13] More recently, Baker and Dean Flemming distinguish contextualization from mere communication, arguing that contextualization "touches on *how we do theology*,"[14] such that one's cultural context actually shapes the message.[15]

As radical as these comments may sound at first to some, they are not isolated objections. Rather, they reflect the growing concerns of many Christian theologians and missionaries. In essence, some worry that we inadvertently compromise the gospel by abstracting it from culture. Consequently, we settle for a simple "kernel" of truth.[16] By comparison, consider Christ's incarnation. We see the divine and human united in Christ's nature. Although Christ in deity transcends culture, he revealed himself in a specific historical and cultural setting. Without compromise, Jesus' humanity expressed his deity. This is how we know Christ—concretely, not merely as an abstraction. Even in resurrection, he is known as Christ in bodily form. In the same way, we understand God's revelation in Scripture through a particular cultural lens.

Reinterpreting Contextualization

Without a new perspective, we cannot put our principles of contextualization *into practice.* Why? I have explained the answer elsewhere in more detail.[17] I will summarize by listing two reasons evangelicals struggle to do contextualization.

First, they tend to "assume the gospel." Of course such a claim might sound counterintuitive, perhaps even provocative. Yet it is all too easy to assume a certain cultural expression of the gospel message as though it were in fact that of Paul, John, or any of the other biblical writers. In effect, evangelicals tend to have a rather fixed framework for understanding the gospel. Traditional categories and images are often prioritized that do not necessarily reflect the entire biblical context nor the ancient cultures represented in Scripture. By "assuming the gospel," we "beg the question," a logical fallacy in which one assumes a certain conclusion within his or her premises. Subtly Christians may

> commit a similar error when they assume the gospel yet without having decided what counts as a genuine contextualization. Contextualization inevitably turns into a task of communication, application, and bridge building. One then measures biblical faithfulness by the degree to which the "contextualized" theology conveys the narrower guilt/law based message prevalent in Western theology.[18]

Consequently it is possible to unwittingly "Judaize" (i.e., "Westernize") our listeners.

This first problem may result from a second, more fundamental oversight. Everyone who contextualizes the gospel must first know what the Bible says, yet one can quickly forget that we all interpret the Bible through a cultural lens. Our worldview has great influence on our interpretation. It can be no other way. Our cultural perspective can either open up the text, giving fresh insight, or it might hide certain facets of a passage that are unfamiliar to our own experience.

Contextualization begins at the point of *interpretation.* The way we interpret the Bible will and ought to determine how we communicate and apply it. Therefore, we must guard against any tendency to separate interpretation from the contextualization process. We have started the process of contextualization even before we try to communicate or apply the gospel.

There are practical implications when we recognize the true starting point of contextualization. There is no simplistic way to go about this process. When one tries to think through all that is involved in contextualization, it is not surprising that people would feel a sense of despair or frustration. How practically are we to integrate and apply the complex array of relevant information, whether from anthropology, theology, sociology, or biblical studies?

This book is written to answer exactly this sort of question. It proposes a way forward. In the coming chapters I will develop a model that builds on the perspective that contextualization begins with interpretation. By using this approach, Christians throughout the world will be better equipped actually to contextualize the gospel in any culture.

Contextualization Is Humbling

It is critical to distinguish biblical interpretation from theology. Theology is the result of biblical interpretation. Theology should be based on sound interpretation methods. For many, the two can easily get confused. After all, much teaching in churches and books emphasizes systematic theology and rightly ordering our doctrine. Such teaching is no doubt important, but it must not come at the neglect of Christians learning the process by which they can make these conclusions for themselves.

If we ignore the distinction between interpretation and theology, we open ourselves to various dangers. For instance, authority subtly shifts from the Bible to the Bible teacher. If readers do not have a good grasp of the interpretation process, they must simply take the pastor or teacher at his word. This eventually creates bad habits. Students and congregants have a difficult time checking whether the teaching is completely correct or even whether certain emphases are being put in the right place. Over time, readers begin assuming the meaning of a biblical passage without giving it the careful attention it deserves. People begin using Bible verses as mere "proof texts," trying to justify conclusions they assume in advance to be true. Even worse, some may commit "eisegesis," whereby they subtly force their own assumptions into the text and thus change the meaning without ever realizing it.

Contextualization is not something that flows in one direction—from the West to the rest of the world. Contextualization is a community effort. The church spans the globe and extends many years back into history. In order to do contextualization well, we need to consciously engage in conversation with those from around the world, people from other academic backgrounds, as well as those in our history books. Vanhoozer issues a helpful warning:

> Western theologians must be aware of the cultural beams in their own eyes before attempting to remove specks from non-Western eyes. It is ultimately for the sake of better biblical interpretation that Western theologians need to pay attention to how the Bible is being read and practiced in the non-Western world.[19]

We should nurture a healthy skepticism concerning our personal theology. Certainly it is incomplete in places. Perhaps we at times confuse major and minor points of a doctrine. In other words, contextualizing the gospel requires us to listen with humility to the perspectives and experiences of others.

Contextualization cannot be defined merely in terms of communication or application. I suggest that contextualization refers to the process wherein people interpret, communicate, and apply the Bible within a particular cultural context. Exactly what this looks like will be unpacked throughout the rest of the book. Good contextualization seeks to be faithful to Scripture and meaningful to a given culture. It prioritizes biblical theology and interpretation. Those who contextualize the gospel strive to grasp internally the longings, habits, and ways of thinking of those around them. The process tests both our character and our minds. Contextualization necessitates humility and a passionate commitment to persevere in rigorous reflection and mutual collaboration.

Contextualization Is Inevitable

We should communicate and apply Scripture in a way that is faithful to the original meaning of the text. *If only it were that simple.* This point is uncontroversial; however, actually doing it is more of a challenge. No modern reader lives in the same cultural world as the biblical authors. We all read the Bible through a sort of prism that refracts the light of our understanding across a number of historical and cultural mirrors. We don't simply live in megacultures like America, China, Europe, or India. The way we see the world and thus read Scripture is influenced to some degree by countless subcultures—including our family, our school, our denomination, our church, etc. We can also add an additional layer—history. We don't interpret the Bible in a vacuum. Two thousand years of church history shape our assumptions about the Bible and even the questions we ask of certain passages.

We might try to solve the tension by quickly appealing to the Holy Spirit, but we can't simply claim that the Spirit guards us from cultural influences by illuminating the meaning of a passage to us. First of all, we have to remember that the Holy Spirit guided the biblical writers, who wrote using words, metaphors, and symbols rooted in specific cultures (cf. 2 Pet 1:20,21). Second, whose illumination do we trust? For example, one person might say the Spirit gave him illumination that only affirms believer baptism; another might argue that the Spirit revealed that infants could be baptized. The Spirit only teaches finite, culturally bound people with limited perspectives. We mustn't try to apply the doctrine of illumination abstracted from the facts of history.

Returning to the point, we must recognize that there will always be some difference between our theology and what is the actual, original meaning of the text. Of course we can have truly biblical theology; however, our theology will inevitably reflect something of our own backgrounds. Bruce Nicholls comments, "It is now widely accepted that all theology, including biblical theology, is culturally conditioned and therefore in some sense relative. Theologizing is understood as a human fallible process, so that no theology is perfect or absolute."[20] In other words, our theology even at its best will be genuine truth from a certain cultural and historical perspective. Even from our limited vantage points, we can see truth. We needn't despair.

Let me be quick to say, *this is not relativism.*[21] Rather, we simply want to be honest with the facts. As David Clark puts it, "All interpretation begins with the assumptions, values, beliefs, and experiences that a reader brings to the text."[22] Thus, he adds, "The idea that one can achieve an acultural theology [is a] 'fundamental fallacy.'"[23] Even biblical truth is expressed from one perspective and not another. An example from daily life illustrates the point. Ask yourself, "*Who* is the oldest woman in your house now?" Depending on your perspective, your answers might be "Mom," "my wife," or maybe "my daughter." Each of these could be absolutely true statements but from a relative and distinct viewpoint. Vanhoozer concludes, "We don't simply read cultural texts but we read through them. In short: the cultural texts we love best come to serve as the lens through which we view everything else and as the compass that orients us towards the goal."[24]

All theology is contextualized theology.[25] Accordingly, we do not have a choice whether we will or will not contextualize. It is inevitable. However, what we do control is the way we do it. We can and should be very intentional about our process. Otherwise we take an ill-fated risk by unwittingly surrendering ministry to numerous unchecked assumptions that may obscure the truth and hinder fruitfulness.

Contextualization Is Essential

Contextualization is a gospel issue; it is not simply an optional strategy among others for doing ministry. Precisely because contextualization is inevitable, it is essential. For some people, contextualization may sound like an intimidating concept. Others may too quickly assume they "get" contextualization and thus do not give it the thought it deserves. Both extremes tend to neglect taking contextualization seriously.

There are numerous risks to not (intentionally) contextualizing the gospel. David Sills drives home the point clearly when he says, "If one does not contextualize, he is doing just that—changing the gospel. He becomes a modern-day Judaizer. He is in effect telling his hearers that they must become like him to be saved."[26] I venture to say few missionaries would do this intentionally. However, the implicit message is heard clearly.[27]

There is a subtle danger in repeating an error similarly committed by Paul's opponents. For them, the Old Testament and its symbols (like circumcision) manifestly were gifts to the Jews, not Gentiles. That is, Gentiles had to become Jewish in order to be counted as God's people. It is possible for us to do that with our theology. If we assume that Western theology is the primary or fundamental way to formulate doctrine, we inevitably force non-Western people to conform their basic categories of thinking to those found in the traditional Western culture.

For example, what if a non-Westerner does not struggle with "doing good works to earn salvation" as is often stressed in the West when talking about justification? What if the bigger problem is ethnocentrism and competing for "face" or honor? People should know that justification speaks directly to those issues (if not more) as to one's effort to earn God's favor.[28]

Dean Flemming highlights a second danger—syncretism. Syncretism emerges whenever the biblical message is made to harmonize so closely with a given culture (or subculture) that the biblical truth is compromised.

Syncretistic theology and practices reflect the culture more so than the biblical text. His comments remain among the most important I've read on this topic.

> But could it be that *refusing* to contextualize the gospel poses an even greater risk of syncretism? Consider the situation today—not unlike that of Colossians—when the gospel meets worldviews that are burdened with fear of unseen powers thought to control practical realities such a crops, health, and family relations. In many cases, the Christian message that has been imported to these contexts from the West has failed to address such issues. As a result, people can easily assume that Jesus is powerless to overcome the forces that influence their daily lives. Like the Colossian syncretists, converts may look for supplements—shamans, amulets, rituals, or occult practices—to protect them from hostile spirits. Ironically, a gospel that neglects such worldview issues may unwittingly end up promoting syncretism instead of preventing it.[29]

Flemming's poignant insight is a sober reminder. We must not fear contextualization, nor should we assume that good contextualization happens without intentional reflection.

Similarly, local Christians in less Christianized settings may wrongly interpret the gospel because they use cultural lenses that distort the Bible's original meaning. In this case, gospel presentations suffer *cultural* syncretism. The cultural context acts as the authority over the biblical text. People confuse Scripture and culture.

Christians around the world run the risk of a second type of syncretism, which is often overlooked. Without some method to guide the process, gospel presentations can suffer from *theological syncretism*. How does this happen? This might emerge when missionaries communicate the gospel using familiar expressions from their home culture. For example, a missionary from America might uncritically translate a presentation like the "Four Spiritual Laws" or the "Romans Road" without consideration as to whether categories like "law" and "guilt" convey the same thing in a place like East Asia as they do in the American "Bible belt." In this kind of syncretism, theological presuppositions limit the scope of biblical passages one uses to share the gospel (e.g., Romans, Galatians). People confuse the gospel with their own theological tradition.

Without intentional contextualization, we run a third risk—undermining a right doctrine of Scripture. John Walton's comments about the Old Testament also apply to the entire Bible, "[It] *does* communicate to us and it was written for us, and for all humankind. But it was not written *to* us."[30] Once again, we must not confuse the Bible and our own theology. In Scripture, God revealed himself across many cultures. He is not the God of any one single culture. The one true God revealed himself so that people from every time and place could understand the Bible's message; this does not deny difficult passages. The point is that the Bible communicates in every *cultural* language (regardless of whether a culture emphasizes honor/shame, law, collectivism, filial piety, animism, etc.). If we do not take intentional steps to contextualize the gospel, we will default to the formulations that appeal to our home church or culture. Perhaps this is one small reason why Western missionaries (in China at least) hear people say that the Bible is a "Western book." Missionary explanations of the Bible often *sound* Western.

We can turn these risks into positive statements that highlight the opportunity that contextualization provides. First of all, good contextualization conveys to listeners that God sent Jesus to save all nations; becoming Christian does not mean rejecting non-Western culture. Second, contextualization protects us against syncretism. In this way our theology and practice will be faithful to Scripture. Third, contextualization shows people that the Bible speaks to their own culture. It has meaning for anyone from any local culture.

Distinguishing Two Kinds of Contextualization

The key point of tension in contextualization debates is how to relate the Bible and culture. In principle, evangelicals affirm the authority of Scripture over culture. Yet what does this practically mean for culture? It would seem that a one-way exchange from Scripture to culture naturally leads to some of the problems discussed above. What is culture's role in shaping theology? And can it influence contextualization without usurping Scripture? If we are to make progress in addressing these questions, we will need some new categories and ways of looking at the problem.

In order to develop a practical model for doing contextualization, we need to distinguish two kinds of contextualization. I am not talking about the various expressions of contextualization—interpretation, communication, and application. These two kinds of contextualization help us to clarify the interrelationship between the Scripture and culture. Contextualizing begins whenever we read the Bible from the perspective of a given context. Contextualization is not primarily something we *do to* the gospel. Broadly stated, it is the mind's perception of and response to the gospel. In actual fact, contextualization further subdivides into two types. The first is *exegetical* contextualization; the second is *cultural* contextualization.

Exegetical contextualization refers to one's interpretation of Scripture from a cultural perspective. It means locating the cultural context within the biblical text. Accordingly, someone with an East Asian worldview will more naturally see a number of concepts within the Bible that reflect the distinctives of his or her culture (e.g., honor, shame, and collective identity). This contextualization means seeing what is true of our cultural context within the Bible itself. This is not eisegesis, whereby one forces foreign ideas into Scripture. In exegetical contextualization, one sees what actually is in the text already. In short, we interpret Scripture using a cultural lens, regardless whether one knows it or not.[31]

What might this look like in practice? In an East Asian context, an exegetically contextualized theology would take seriously the frequently used language about God's people not being "put to shame." Also, one could highlight instances of collectivism in both the Testaments, such as when individuals represent entire groups. Stephen's sermon in Acts 7 recounts Israel's history in view of the stubborn refusal of his contemporaries to accept Christ. Context shapes the content of one's presentation. For instance, Abraham's justification is interpreted in two contrary but not contradictory ways due to Paul and James writing from two different settings (cf. Rom 4; Gal 2:16; Jas 2:21–23). Likewise in Hebrews 11, situational needs produced the biblical theology thematically oriented on faith.

Cultural contextualization refers to the interpretation of culture using a scriptural perspective. It nestles the biblical text within a contemporary cultural context. Hence, one looks at a culture and identifies various concepts that already exist in the Bible. When examining a culture like China, the contextualizer might notice how well the Chinese understand the family motif. An "underground" church is actually called a "family" church (家庭教会). Likewise, one may observe common features within the histories of China and Israel. Both nations suffered from imperialism and have demonstrated strong degrees of ethnocentric/nationalistic prejudice against outsiders. Cultural contextualization means seeing what is true about a culture as a result of one's having a biblical lens. The Bible provides a fresh assessment of the culture

Practically speaking, what does cultural contextualization look like? One could point to rampant consumerism and the fear people have of losing face. In light of Romans 6, we might say people have become slaves to their homes, cars, or even to their own families. Only Christ sets them free. Exodus language is also brought forward to Paul's contemporary context in 1 Corinthians 5:7, "Cleanse out the old leaven that you may be a new lump, as you really are unleavened. For Christ, our Passover lamb, has been sacrificed."

Concluding Thoughts

We need a new perspective on contextualization. In reality, we need multiple perspectives. This should not surprise us. In Scripture, the one true God revealed himself through history to many cultures. He promised to bless all nations through the offspring of one man, Abraham. This God raised Christ from the dead to reign as the one rightful king and mediator for the world. In other words, we are in constant need of a bigger view of God, the gospel, and the church's mission.

In the introduction, I called to mind a fundamental dictum of interpretation, "Context is king." We interpret the meaning of words and ideas within their surrounding context. The question now appears to be, "*Which* context is king?" We seem to have multiple contexts in conflict with one another. We are caught in the middle. Contextualization, if done well, keeps in perspective for us the fact that Jesus is King of every context.

In Isaiah 40:8,9 the prophet announces the gospel, twice even using the standard Hebrew word בשׂר. He proclaims,

> The grass withers, the flower fades, but the word of our God will stand forever. Go on up to a high mountain, O Zion, herald of [the gospel]; lift up your voice with strength, O Jerusalem, herald of [the gospel]; lift it up, fear not; say to the cities of Judah, "Behold your God!"

We live in a world of individuals and cultures that fade away like the grass and flowers. In the coming sections we will explore the path up that high mountain where we will have the perspective to see the world a little more like God sees it. From there the gospel message will carry further to the surrounding nations. Perhaps our model of contextualization proposed in the next section two will serve as one map among others to guide our path up the hill.

KEY POINTS

- Evangelicals have often viewed contextualization as communication and application.
- Contextualization concerns the relationship between the biblical text and cultural context.
- Contextualization begins with interpretation.
- We should not confuse biblical truth and our own theology.
- Culture inevitably influences the way we interpret the Bible and thus our theology.
- All theology is contextualized.
- Contextualization helps us avoid a number of dangers.
- We should distinguish two kinds of contextualization.
- Exegetical contextualization refers to one's interpretation of Scripture from a cultural perspective.
- Cultural contextualization refers to the interpretation of culture using a scriptural perspective.

2

A Common Problem: Compromising the Gospel by Settling for Truth

"Why did you marry your wife?" The man confidently answered the question, "That's easy—because she's a woman." It is hard to dispute the point that this man's reply is correct. At some level, even if only a technicality, his wife's gender is a reason why he married his *wife*. Though the conversation is fictional, it aptly illustrates two points.

First, the question "why" can have multiple answers. Recently I heard a small group leader ask some other Christians, "Why did you become a Christian?" One woman answered, "Because my grandmother believed in Jesus and shared with me." However, this was not the group leader's meaning. He was not inquiring about the circumstances on their conversion; he was asking about their heart and motives.

Second, one sees how an answer may be completely true yet thoroughly miss the point at hand. Among the various true words that could be said, not all are relevant to a given context. Many people have had a similar experience when studying the Bible. Someone asks about the "meaning" of a text, at which time some people immediately talk about the *application* of a scripture passage, skipping over the intended message of the author in its original context.

Much damage is done to the gospel and thus to missions when we settle for what is merely true. On the one hand, countless church divisions arise from false dichotomies that may amount to barely more than questions of emphasis. On the other hand, Christians may preach a "true" gospel yet be written off as irrelevant and foreign. To make things worse, missionaries may entrench themselves even more in their theological positions, claiming that the gospel is "foolishness" to their hearers, who are simply "blind" to the truth. We must consider the possibility that missionaries (as well as any other Christian) may in fact compromise the gospel even while affirming "right" interpretations. As a result, contextualization becomes excessively complicated and our theologies contorted.

One does not have to surrender his or her conviction of absolute truth to recognize the relative nature of biblical truth statements. For instance, many would be inclined to fire a pastor who emphasizes that "a person is justified by works and not by faith alone," despite the fact that this is a direct quotation of James 2:24 (cf. Rom 2:6,7, which echoes Job 34:11; Ps 62:12; Prov 24:12; Jer 17:10; and even Jesus in Matt 16:17). Conversely, few would quibble with the person who similarly exhorted, "one is justified by faith apart from works of the law" (Rom 3:28). The statements by James and Paul are both true—*from a certain perspective.*

Similarly, Chinese evangelists inquire with perplexity how it is that "God cannot be tempted with evil" (Jas 1:13) if Jesus is divine yet was tempted by Satan in the desert. Obviously, having an "either-or" perspective is not always helpful when interpreting the Bible. Often one needs to seek a "both-and" solution in order to preserve the whole body of truth.

If this point is not heeded, then a person can defend a "right" interpretation but wrongly sever it from the original text and thus undermine its significance for a particular context. At the worst, "right" statements can so distort the truth that they undermine the gospel entirely. For example, Paul's Jewish readers would have been quite right to say that Israel had been chosen as God's people to be blessed; however, this misses the bigger point of the Abrahamic covenant. Israel was blessed *in order to* be a blessing to the nations![32]

"It's Not Wrong" and Other Ways We Miss the Point

Given that interpretation should determine application, it is a mere issue of nuance how one decides on a range of biblical and theological controversies. The way we read a certain phrase or the weight given to one motif over another sets the trajectory for the theological conclusions and missiological applications that follow. Potential problems are compounded when missionaries lack either theological training or the humility to see the weakness in their views. When debates are settled by "commentary wars" (in which people assert the comments in their study Bibles), then a stalemate is reached when someone finally exclaims about his or her own view, "It's not wrong!"

In what follows, we survey a number of highly controversial topics where we have to examine whether or not people are "right" in what they affirm but "wrong" in what they deny. When this happens, contextualization is stunted by partial readings or by confusing the main point of a text with its implications. Given the volumes that are written on each of the topics to be mentioned, this chapter cannot attempt to elaborate upon nuances and defend the competing perspectives. Furthermore, it would be shocking if most readers did not disagree with or at least have great reservations about some of the proposals I suggest below.

Even if people disagree with what is said, humility requires that interpreters at least consider the implications of such "both-and" interpretations. What if they are true and we have confused the primary point with its implications? In that case, one is not fighting against some heterodox or dangerous interpretation. Rather, one would be pitting scripture against scripture. The problem of conservative readings then may resemble that of so-called liberals, since the meaning of the text may still be distorted via selective focus and emphasis. For disclosure's sake, my background and close friends vouch for the fact that I am an evangelical with conservative leanings. Yet, I have found that whenever one takes seriously the possibility of "both-and" interpretations, many people will be ready to accuse him or her of being a closet liberal.

Emphasis is part of the original meaning of an author. For those who hold the Bible to be authoritative for Christian life and ministry, it is not enough to settle for mere truth. No doubt many fear that relinquishing a traditional interpretation is a step down the slippery slope of compromise. Of course any Protestant can easily recognize an equal danger at this point—holding too tightly to tradition at the cost of Scripture. It can allay fear simply to admit the possibility that we may not be fighting about what is true and false but instead what is primary and secondary.

Distinguishing True-false and Primary-secondary

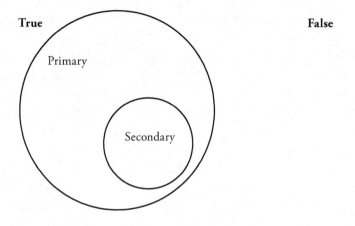

Figure 1: Distinguishing True-false and Primary-secondary

C. S. Lewis puts it succinctly, "Put first things first and we get second things thrown in; put second things first and we lose both the first and second things."[33] His principle is not only relevant and encouraging but also sobering. Reflect again on the opening conversation about a wife being a woman. Being a wife implies being a woman; being a woman does not necessarily mean being a wife. Though the logic is basic and obvious in this instance, one could miss such implications when talking about complex theological and missiological ideas.

If we do in fact emphasize true but secondary points in Scripture, then what many things might we be overlooking, which God has revealed and may greatly impact missionary practice around the world? It is critical not to confuse questions of truth and matters of emphasis. Wright summarizes the point more sharply: "By what right do we take scripture and find ways of making it talk about things we want it to talk about?"[34]

"It's Completely True and Wonderful, But . . ."

What are some biblical truths that are commonly taught within the church but miss the main idea of the text? Let's start with some ideas that most people could agree with. The David-and-Goliath story is typically presented as teaching that God takes care of the little guy. Though this is a true point to draw from the passage, it should not be missed that God is using David so "that all the earth may know that there is a God in Israel" (1 Sam 17:46). God is center, not the individual.

Pastors often suggest that being made in the image of God means we are rational, moral beings. True enough, but this is almost trivially true since being made in the image of God primarily points to how we are to honor God via our vocation to be fruitful and exercise authority over the earth as God's "under-kings" (Gen 1:26–28; cf. 1 Cor 11:7's emphasis on honor). One can survey a litany of gospel tracts that emphasize *eternal* life; that is, the length of time is given prominence. Yet Jesus reorients our Western fixation with time when he says, "And this is eternal life, that they may know you the only true God, and Jesus Christ whom you have sent" (John 17:3).

Why did Jesus die? John Piper rightly puts first things first when he highlights, from Romans 3, that Christ died for God in order to show God's righteousness.[35] If the church merely assumes the importance of God's glory such that it has no practical effect upon one's regular reading of Scripture, it will not be long before it is forgotten altogether. In addition, Wright makes an observation about Paul's answer to the question why Jesus became a curse. It is not simply because Jesus loves us (though true). More precisely, it is "so that in Christ Jesus the blessing of Abraham might come to the Gentiles" (Gal 3:14).[36]

More controversial are questions about the gospel. In these debates, one side tends to accuse the other of being "reductionistic" and creating false separations. For instance, Scot McKnight's *The King Jesus Gospel* (Zondervan, 2011) drew much concern from those who feared he was dichotomizing "salvation" and "story," or salvation from Christ's kingship (even though McKnight repeatedly says otherwise). However, *what if* McKnight is right (and, thus far, I have found no one who challenged his *exegesis* itself)?

There is great consensus that historically and biblically speaking the concept "gospel" refers to an announcement on kingship or to a king's victory.[37] If the gospel announces Christ's lordship over the world (cf. Rom 1:1–4;

1 Cor 15:4–8,20–28), and salvation is the wonderful implication of that gospel, then how would it radically reshape the way we evangelize to give priority to Christ's identity and work *then* making clear the hope of (individual) salvation? The "then" implies "and." There is no true separation. *Because* Jesus is Christ (i.e., King) and has defeated death, *therefore* people can be saved.

Likewise, what happens when one preaches that salvation is "going to heaven"? This "true" comment may obscure ideas that are more central to the biblical hope, such as resurrected bodies and new creation. In addition, it is true that the gospel magnifies the death of Christ, but Paul says Jesus' death means nothing if he did not resurrect (1 Cor 15:14–19). For Paul and the sermons in Acts, *the resurrection* is prioritized. Sadly, too many gospel tracts and confessions barely mention and even omit the resurrection.[38] Yes, Jesus died on a cross. While this is glorious and true, there is an even bigger point to be made—he rose!

One of the most important debates among theologians over the past few decades concerns the "New Perspective on Paul," which examines the meaning of justification. Is justification about ecclesiology or soteriology? Although the "old" and "new" perspectives would admit that justification affects both, few show *how* Paul integrates both into his doctrine. In particular, some says that the "Law" refers to the Mosaic Law and is an ethnic badge signifying Jewish identity. Traditionalists affirm that "law" in Romans and Galatians refers to a general moral law and that Paul opposes legalism or works-righteousness, not ethnocentrism.

Is the law primarily an *ethical* or an *ethnic* category? How missionaries answer that question will greatly affect the message they preach. For example, what is one to do with the typical Chinese or atheist who in no way tries to gain God's salvation via works-legalism but instead goes about his life seeking to gain face from family and peers? What are we to do about the fact that "law" is not a major cultural motif in Chinese thinking, but rather honor/shame is the foremost concern? Is one forced to first change his worldview to a more legal orientation so that he can understand the Westernized gospel presentation? Once he becomes sufficiently Western, then he can become a Christian? Consider the Chinese word for "sin," translated *zui*, which means "crime." By choosing a legal motif, missionaries often confuse Chinese people, who are immediately confused to hear that they are "criminals."

However, we should observe that not even Paul absolutely prioritized the legal motif when describing sin. Romans 2:23,24 says, "You who boast in the law *dishonor God* by breaking the law. For, as it is written, 'The name of God is blasphemed among the Gentiles because of you.'" In Greek the verb of verse 23 is "to dishonor." "Breaking the law" is simply the *means* by which these Jews dishonored God. Breaking the law is sin, but sin most basically is the dishonoring of God (cf. Rom 3:23). Furthermore, Paul's extended condemnation of the unrighteous person in Romans 1 never once mentions the "law" motif.

One can rightly affirm the points that justification has a legal dimension and that "law" is a moral, God-oriented category; nevertheless, consider the implications if Paul actually reverses what people traditionally think to be first and second. What if Paul is fighting against an ethnocentrism that supposes being Jewish is the most basic precondition to being justified as one of God's people? What if the Jews regarded works of the law as a means of "ascribed" honor, not simply "achieved" honor?[39] From an honor perspective, legalism in not the only reason one might boast. The Mosaic Law is ethnic inasmuch as it distinguished Jews from Gentiles; it is ethical in that the Law issues forth God's own commands to his people.

Yet Paul is not rebutting the moralistic Gentile who thinks circumcising himself will save him apart from his becoming a Jew. The Mosaic Law's ethical force was felt within an ethnic context. However, if we emphasize a right doctrine—that God's Law is authoritative and shows people to be sinners—we can easily miss how Paul is overtly confronting ethnocentrism *as a soteriological problem*, not merely a sociological issue. By putting first things first, we see how Paul addressed the same sort of problem evident around the world in our day—ethnic and group pride—without losing the legitimate *application* that we are not saved by slavish conformity to God's decrees.

Consider whether it is right to say the following: "God is love but he is also righteous; therefore, he must punish sin." No doubt, someone can affirm this as true. On the other hand, this is not the *typical* way that the Bible talks about God's righteousness. Certainly, punishing sin is right, and various texts link God's righteousness and punishment; yet these punishment verses typically come in a context in which God is *saving his people*.[40]

To look at it from another angle, assess which of the following sentences is correct: "*Although* God is righteousness (and must punish sin), *yet* he saves sinners," or "*Because* God is righteous, *therefore* he saves sinners." The first sentence makes God's righteousness an obstacle to salvation; the latter treats God's righteousness as the reason for salvation. The first sentence is a rather standard way of speaking within evangelical circles.[41] Although true enough, it obscures the Bible's main point when using this sort of language.

Among many passages that could be cited, Psalm 143:1,11 illustrate the Bible's own way of talking about God's righteousness. The psalmist prays, "Hear my prayer, O LORD; give ear to my pleas for mercy! In your faithfulness answer me, *in your righteousness!* ... For your name's sake, O LORD, preserve my life! *In your righteousness* bring my soul out of trouble!" Likewise, Psalm 51:14 says, "Deliver me from bloodguiltiness, O God, O God of my salvation, and my tongue will sing aloud of your righteousness." The verse makes no sense if David refers to God's righteousness as God's punishing David's sin. We should not set God's "saving" righteousness against his "penal" righteousness. After all, *God saves his people by judging their enemies.* Wrath is the means by which God remains faithful to his promises. It is true that God's righteousness most broadly points to God's doing right. However, we do not want to function-ally edit out the Bible's primary connotation of God's righteousness because theologians have traditionally highlighted what is merely a true implication.

Other topics suffer a similar fate whereby the main idea is sacrificed because some other idea "is not wrong." Yes, the resurrection has apologetic value, but the Bible stresses its theological importance. Yes, we are all sinners subject to death because of Adam, but this statement may not account for the function Adam serves within Paul's theology; within Acts, no one begins with Adam as a proof text for the fact we are all sinners.

Yes, Jesus is both divine and human, yet what is sacrificed when missionaries miss the primary meaning of the terms "Son of God" (i.e., Israel's King; cf. 2 Sam 7:14; John 1:49; et al.) and "Son of Man" (cf. Dan 7:13)? How would it affect missiological labor to use titles as Nathanael used them, "Rabbi, you are the Son of God! You are the King of Israel!" (John 1:49)?

Yes, it is true Genesis 1 teaches that God created the world, but this ought not cause us to focus on secondary concerns of the text itself. Rather, like the psalmist who interprets Genesis 1, so also we should give our foremost attention to the fact that *this one true Creator God* is glorious, sovereign, and worthy of praise (see Ps 104). Theism and monotheism are true enough (even the demons believe this and shudder, Jas 2:19), yet overemphasizing these and other "right" interpretations can lead to innumerable "wrong" approaches to contextualize our message and strategy.

Conclusion

Are missionaries teaching "the right doctrine from the wrong texts"?[42] If so, we may overlook many ideas that God has revealed and what the original authors intended to convey. The point of this chapter is not to offer a defense for each of the various points of debate. Instead it argues that we risk compromising the biblical message when we settle for truth—what is merely true but not the main point of a text. In the process, one sees the fundamental importance of hermeneutics (not just theology) in missions and the global church. Missionary training must emphasize biblical theology, not simply systematic theology. In so doing, the Bible will not merely answer *our* questions; furthermore, it will pose many unexpected questions of its own, which should shape one's theology and missiology.

Missionaries might assume that what they learned in their home culture will have equal relevance to the cultures in which they serve. Certainly they may hold to many right doctrines and sound applications. However, one should not confuse right doctrines in general and right interpretations of particular passages. What is taught in Galatians may not be what is taught in John's Gospel. Two passages may make different points.

Why is this relevant for missions and specifically contextualization? Contextualization suffers when we settle for what is merely true. If we prematurely assume a particular doctrine or emphasis when reading a biblical text, we may miss key ideas that are especially relevant to the cultural contexts in which we preach the gospel. We may quickly read past important concepts that help people better understand the gospel. In addition, we could subtly present the message in a way that both veers from the original meaning of the text and also sounds foreign to our listeners. Without knowing it, one might unwittingly present truth in an untrue way. Accordingly, these so-called contextualizations are neither faithful to Scripture nor meaningful to local cultures.

In short, this chapter highlights a simple but easily missed point: one may have a "right" answer but still be wrong. From one perspective, the logic of our conclusions may be sound. However, when interpreting the Bible, we might ignore the main point of a text or simply be ignorant to the ways our own context influences our reading. Consequently the church will be hindered in its application of Scripture.

People who minister cross-culturally need to be especially conscious of this fact: they too have blind spots that could unknowingly affect their teaching and practice. Ironically, local Christians may inherit the missionaries' cultural blind spots (when it comes to their faith), even though that area of weaknesses is not inherent to the local culture. For example, a Chinese Christian may understand the importance of group identification *as a Chinese person*, yet be quite individualistic in his or her involvement with the church. We compromise the gospel when we settle for what is merely true, because many "right" answers can lead to applications that are not appropriate to the text or the local context. These so-called "contextualizations" may lead to an unexpected sort of syncretism. This is a syncretism oriented to a denomination, theological tradition, or the missionary's home culture.

KEY POINTS

- Contextualization suffers when we settle for what is merely true.
- We compromise the gospel when we settle for truth.
- Right doctrines are not necessarily the right interpretations for certain biblical texts.
- What is "true or false" should not be confused with what is "primary and secondary."
- Biblical passages may speak to the needs of a local culture; however, missionaries might miss the point when they only talk about applications more relevant to their home culture.
- Without knowing it, we might unwittingly present truth in untrue ways. It is possible for contextualizations to teach truth yet not be good.

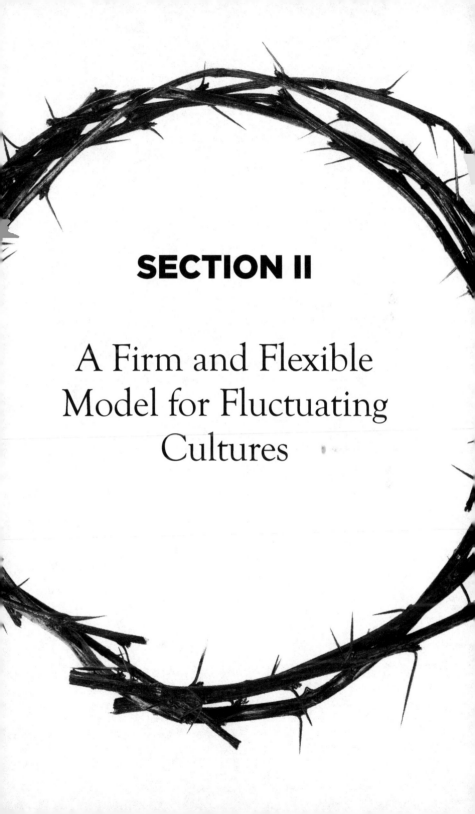

SECTION II

A Firm and Flexible
Model for Fluctuating
Cultures

3

Pattern:
How Does the Bible Frame
the Gospel?

We can all agree on at least one thing—there is only one gospel (Gal 1:6–8). Ironically, evangelicals hardly agree about the answer to the question, "What is the gospel?" There seems to be even less consensus about how to contextualize it.

Many people agree that Scripture must be central and decisive in contextualization. Unfortunately it has proven more difficult to move beyond this basic principle. Hundreds of books, articles, essays, and blog posts mull over the relationship between the Bible and culture. Despite such labor, evangelicals struggle to develop methods of contextualization that both recognize the Bible as supremely authoritative and reveal God's truth in a culturally meaningful way. Gospel presentations should make sense in diverse settings yet without importing unnecessarily foreign elements.

In this chapter I begin to lay out a model whereby people can contextualize the gospel in any culture of the world. First, we will consider recent debates concerning "What is the gospel?" One's understanding of the gospel inevitably influences his or her view on contextualization. If people cannot agree on the gospel, how can they agree on contextualization? Our understanding of the gospel needs to be rooted in biblical theology, not simply systematic theology. By keeping in mind the grand narrative of Scripture, we can better discern and balance the various themes that belong to a more fully biblical gospel. In addition, it will become quickly evident that this broader perspective on the gospel better enables us to share the message.

Second, the chapter makes a key observation about the gospel that will help people to contextualize it more easily. Specifically, we note how the Bible consistently *frames* the gospel. Although the gospel has a firm framework, there remains a fair degree of flexibility in the way one can present it. It is critical for contextualization that we distinguish two aspects of a gospel presentation—its firmness and its flexibility. In so doing, we begin developing a model for contextualization that is both firm and flexible.

How Do We Agree on Contextualization If We Disagree about the Gospel?

How do we contextualize the gospel when people have difficulty agreeing on what exactly it is? In recent years countless books, articles, and blogs have debated the question, "What is the gospel?"[43] Trevin Wax has compiled an extensive collection of "gospel definitions" as articulated by various Christians throughout history.[44] There seems to be as much diversity as there is agreement when defining what exactly is the gospel. He broadly summarizes that Christian gospel presentations often recount the story of the individual believer, Jesus, and of creation.[45]

Even if people admit that the gospel at some level contains these elements, many either tend to emphasize one aspect of the gospel over against another, or perhaps they deny altogether that other parts are included in the "gospel." For example, Matt Chandler says, "The Bible establishes two frames of reference for the same gospel."[46] Specifically, the "gospel on the ground" refers to the call upon individuals to repent and be forgiven of sin because of Christ's death. The "gospel in the air" links "human salvation to cosmic restoration" as told in the "meta-narrative of the Bible's story of redemption."[47]

In slight contrast, Greg Gilbert offers a narrower view of the gospel. He challenges what he calls "three substitute gospels." He claims, "'Jesus is Lord' is not the gospel," the paradigm "'creation-fall-redemption-consummation' is not the gospel," and "cultural transformation is not the gospel."[48] He adds, "It should be obvious by now that to say simply that 'Jesus is Lord' is really not good news at all if we don't explain how Jesus is not just Lord but also Savior."[49] Problematically, he presumes that those who preach the gospel as Jesus' kingship separate his being Lord from his being Savior, perhaps even "mak[ing] their center something other than the cross."[50] As a result, Gilbert denies other emphases in order to isolate one strand of thought—the individual sinner in need of forgiveness by the God who judges in wrath.

For many people, the "gospel" is virtually synonymous with justification. In the Gospel Coalition's book *The Gospel as Center*,[51] contributors use words like "justification" and "righteous(ness)" at least 385 times. More specifically, a search of the book shows approximately 185 instances of the words "justify," "justified," and "justification."[52] "Righteous(ness)" is used no less than 200 times. Also, the terms "impute(d)" and "imputation" appear about 27 times. Not surprisingly, Romans 3 alone is cited 25 times.

In *The King Jesus Gospel*, Scot McKnight contrasts yet complements the views already mentioned. He calls such presentations *soterian* in that they reduce the gospel to a message about how individuals get saved.[53] While not denying the importance of individual salvation, McKnight responds, "Who wants an irreducible minimum gospel? . . . I want the full, biblical gospel."[54] He suggests that traditional evangelicals "skip from Genesis 3 to Romans 3" when trying to understand and communicate the gospel.[55]

McKnight argues that salvation is the result of the gospel, which is the story of how Jesus brings about "the resolution and fulfillment of Israel's Story and promises," culminating in the kingship of Christ over Israel and the world.[56] Wax finds no problems with McKnight's exegesis but worries that "sharp distinctions can sometimes lead to subtle distortions."[57] Rather than dichotomizing "gospel" from "salvation," McKnight sees individual salvation as *one important aspect* of the gospel. He rejects formulations that separate Jesus as Christ/Lord and Jesus as Savior.[58] McKnight attempts to help readers "relearn how to frame the gospel as the apostles did."[59] Accordingly, he says the apostles frame their gospel presentation not around an atonement theory but more precisely by "the story of Israel."[60]

We can easily see some truth in each of the perspectives mentioned above. It is more difficult to see where exactly the problem lies within the gospel debate. It is not so much *what is affirmed* that is mistaken. Instead the tension seems to be found in what particular views *omit* or *deemphasize*. It is very difficult to debate points of emphasis or to compare one metaphor against another. This is especially true when one camp does not overtly deny another's view.

Contextualization that Saves the Gospel

Sadly, in this kind of debate, the first casualty might be the gospel itself. Someone could get the sense that Christians are preaching different messages.

In fact, the differences concern points of emphasis. No one wants to preach a "reductionistic" gospel. In other words, we never want to choose one aspect of the gospel at the expense of another. This is exactly what can happen when we oversimplify the message by forgetting the narrative biblical context from which it comes. How can we present a gospel that is robust and not reduced?

Theologians and missionaries must constantly make decisions about what themes should be highlighted and how to relate main ideas to their contexts. Westerners are generally prone towards either-or thinking.[61] When this enters the church, people easily confuse what is true/false with what is primary/secondary. We need an approach to contextualization that takes a *both-and* approach. Such an approach would relate the assorted building blocks of truth, whether they are white, yellow, black, or brown.

An analogy illustrates the problem we face. Suppose someone asks, "Tell me about your body." In reply, one might say, "Well, it has four chambers that are full of blood. One half pumps blood through veins. The other half uses arteries." That would be accurate in a strict though peculiar sense. Depending on one's perspective, the heart *both* is *and* is not the body. That is, the heart is an essential part of the body, yet it in no way constitutes the whole of what is referred to when one speaks of a body. Still, such a reply does not really answer what presumably is really being asked. One should describe the body from a broader perspective rather than just one part of it, regardless of how crucial that individual part is to the whole.

Similarly, we can ask, "Is the 'Plan of Salvation' the gospel?"[62] To say whether the Plan of Salvation is or is not the gospel—either way—requires a bit of unavoidable linguistic gymnastics. Just as the heart "is" the body, so too is the Plan of Salvation. Yet it is *not* the gospel in the same way that the heart is not equivalent to the body. Most people would not talk as if the heart itself were the whole of the body.

Perhaps it is best simply to say the Plan of Salvation is not the *whole* gospel. If people only explain "how one is saved," they do not proclaim the full gospel as the disciples preached it. "How" one gets saved can easily reduce the gospel to issues of mechanics. One can lose the whole in view of the parts, forsaking the proverbial forest for the tree. The gospel also answers other questions besides "how" an individual gets saved. The gospel mainly says something about God himself. It is an announcement about who God is and what he does in history.

That said, if we do not highlight salvation, which is the significance of the announcement, then we also have not preached the gospel. After all, saying that "Jesus is King" to someone who knows neither who Jesus is nor the role of a king would hardly be speaking "good news." It would be akin to claiming "Fred 当老师" to someone who only speaks English. This statement is simply garbled news, being neither good nor bad.

Implicit within any such announcement is that the listener understands the significance. Problems come when we only talk about a single aspect of significance (e.g., human salvation), skipping the fundamental announcement of *who* Jesus is and the fact that God's glory will permeate his new creation. Otherwise we *de facto* make the gospel centered on humans. Along this line of thinking, once one gets "saved," there is not much left to say that compares in importance. Naturally this will not bode well for discipleship; that is, the rest of the Christian life after conversion.

A hypothetical scenario may explain why it matters whether one skips the announcement and goes directly to salvation. Perhaps someone might say, "That couple just married. They slept together and now she is pregnant!" What happens if we overlook the first part? We are left hearing only about a function or activity robbed of its proper relational context that gives significance to the benefits/results. Announcing the pregnancy apart from the first part may even sound unbelievable or scandalous, depending on one's context (e.g., Mary's pregnancy with Jesus). While intimacy and children are wonderful blessings of the marriage, they still do not make up the whole of what it means to be married.

Finding the Whole Gospel in the Whole Bible

In order to agree on how to share the gospel, we must find common ground as to the content of the gospel. People should be able to agree on the big ideas that shape the biblical gospel, even if there is disagreement about smaller points of emphasis and verbiage. However, a fundamental problem plagues the "What is the gospel?" debate. Authors cannot seem to agree on which Scripture passages to use when defining the gospel. Not surprisingly, the texts one chooses will determine the major themes and scope of one's gospel presentation.

Greg Gilbert, for example, says we should not limit our understanding of the gospel to a word study on the word "gospel" since there are many passages that do not use the word but surely convey the message. Instead he suggests using Romans 1–4 to find a "shared framework of truths around which the apostles and early Christians structured their presentation of the good news of Jesus."[63] Gilbert is correct that people should not limit their understanding of the gospel to places that explicitly reference a word. Nevertheless his argument is problematic.

Passages that *overtly* articulate the gospel are essential for defining the explicit contours of the message. Such texts are critical for making sure we are not overly selective in emphasizing one aspect of the gospel over another. We should be wary of defining the gospel in a way that does not echo the usage of the word "gospel" in the most explicit contexts. When Gilbert examines Romans 1–4, he skips over Paul's single most explicit summary of the gospel in the letter. In Romans 1:1–4, Paul writes that he is

> set apart for the gospel of God, which he promised beforehand through his prophets in the holy Scriptures, concerning his Son, who was descended from David according to the flesh and was declared to be the Son of God in power according to the Spirit of holiness by his resurrection from the dead, Jesus Christ our Lord.

Unfortunately Gilbert calls Romans 1:1–7 merely Paul's "*introductory remarks* [after which] Paul *begins* his presentation of the gospel by declaring that 'the wrath of God is revealed from heaven,' (v. 18)."[64] Gilbert overlooks the message that Paul explicitly calls the "gospel." This is because Gilbert presupposes a certain (traditional) understanding of the gospel. Intriguingly, he mainly focuses on a section of Romans (1:18–3:26) that only one time uses the word "gospel" (2:16) and does so to highlight judgment not salvation.

Other popular evangelical books do not focus on biblical passages that directly use "gospel" language.[65] In *The Gospel as Center*,[66] Paul's summaries in Galatians 3:8 and 2 Timothy 2:8, Luke's accounts of Paul in Acts 13:32 and 14:15, and OT texts like Isaiah 40:9 and 52:7 are never discussed. Also, 1 Corinthians 15:1–8 is mentioned very briefly in only two places.[67] Romans 1:1–4 is cited just once.[68] Neither Romans 1:1–4 nor 1 Corinthians 15:1–8 are used in the chapter "What Is the Gospel?"[69] In *The Explicit Gospel*, Matt Chandler acknowledges the importance of perspective and of using the whole Bible in order to perceive the whole gospel.[70] His usage of 1 Corinthians does go beyond that found in *The Gospel as Center*.[71] Yet *explicit* gospel summaries such as Romans 1:2–4; Galatians 3:8; 2 Timothy 2:8; and others are entirely left out of the book.[72]

Paul's sermons in Lystra and Athens (Acts 14; 17) further complicate questions about what is the gospel and how to contextualize it. His message in overwhelmingly Gentile contexts seems to contrast sharply with his presentations elsewhere among more Jewish audiences.[73] Rather than overtly citing Jewish Scripture, Paul is more philosophical, pointing to nature in order to identify the one true God.[74] Whatever his initial presentation, it is informative that "Jewish elements" of the gospel are pervasive in Paul's letters to Gentile Christians, such as in Romans, 1 Corinthians, and Ephesians. How is one to grasp Paul's view of the gospel and contextualization given such contrasting evidence? Even though Paul does not explicitly cite Old Testament texts, does he have a framework by which he presents the gospel in Lystra and Athens?

A *Biblical* Contextualization Requires a Biblical Theology

We should now examine a range of texts throughout the canon that directly speak about the gospel. In so doing, we will observe a pattern whenever biblical writers discuss the gospel. Accordingly, we will better discern how to relate the complementary answers given to the question, "What is the gospel?" In addition, it will become more apparent how one might balance these competing perspectives discussed above.

There are advantages to seeking common ground between the various "gospel" texts found throughout the entire Bible. First of all, because we do not restrict ourselves to a "canon within a canon," we increase the possible number of outcomes to be gained in the contextualization process. After all, one is not limited to a particular theme prominent within a narrow set of texts. As a result, we can draw from a rich array of images and interweaving motifs that span the canon. Second, people guard themselves from provincialism and rancorous debate when they acknowledge that other views have legitimate biblical support. One need not pose false either-or scenarios wherein the different theological camps feel their position is being threatened.

Third, this canonical approach not only makes one's contextualization methodology less arbitrary; it even gains credibility in that it begins with the entire biblical text in view. The resultant gospel contextualization can claim a fair degree of balance and comprehensiveness because it accounts for the diverse biblical answers to the question, "What is the gospel?"

Finally, this approach does not presuppose that non-Western Christians will develop theologies that equally emphasize those themes that Luther, Calvin, or Edwards stressed. Majority World theologians and pastors can remain firmly biblical without denying the insights of history. By analogy, one could compare the books of Genesis, Ecclesiastes, Ezekiel, Luke, Galatians, and 1 Peter. Their message, themes, tone, and style vary drastically. Their theologies are different but without contradiction.

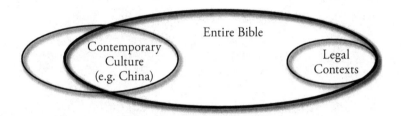

Figure 2: Overlapping Contexts

The above diagram illustrates the importance of using the full biblical context—the entire canon—in order to do contextualization.[75] Contextualization is more than bridging particular biblical ideas to a culture. It requires us to find where the major themes *throughout* Scripture overlap with a contemporary culture. If people only use a narrow set of verses and themes to evangelize, then a few consequences naturally follow. First, contextualization is reduced to finding communication "bridges" from a particular motif. Second, depending on where people are from, non-Christian listeners may have to convert culturally in order to accept the gospel presentation being conveyed.

How Cultural Context Shapes Our Biblical Theology

Take China as an example. If Chinese listeners hear a traditional law-oriented gospel presentation, they must use categories of thought typically not native to Chinese thinking. Instead of thinking in terms of face, relationship, and collective identity, the traditional Western gospel message focuses on legal guilt and is individualistic. On the other hand, when one draws from a fuller biblical theology (not merely systematic theology), then contextualization is not only more holistic but also more biblically faithful and culturally meaningful.

Figure 3 depicts the way Christians perceive the gospel. All people see the gospel through a cultural lens. Additionally, one's theological or denominational background shapes how the gospel is understood. Each perspective has limitations. The entire Bible provides a framework through which to balance these two lenses. If one is not careful, he or she will use a monocle, seeing the gospel through the lone narrow lens of his or her culture or theological camp.

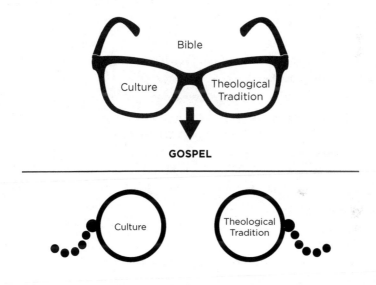

Figure 3: Lenses for Reading Scripture

It is biblical in only a narrow sense to limit the gospel to one single idea, namely individuals being saved from the wrath of God through Christ's death. Although a gloriously wonderful truth, it must not be separated from the totality of what Christ accomplishes. Focusing on this solitary achievement is like one seeing the sun's light refracted from a tin roof in contrast to one being blinded by the sun when looking directly at it. For all practical purposes, Gilbert refracts the glory of the gospel when he claims that both "Jesus is Lord" and "creation-fall-redemption-consummation" are *not* the gospel.[76]

We must not fragment the gospel with false dichotomies. He presumes that other perspectives "marginalize" the cross.[77] The assumption is unfounded. In fact, he may give a straw-man argument. He explicitly addresses "evangelical Christians," yet does not cite anyone who actually minimizes the cross in the way he accuses.[78]

We therefore see other reasons why it matters that we root contextualization in biblical theology, not merely traditional systematic theology. By limiting the gospel to those texts that teach justification by faith, one threatens to divide the church into needless controversy. In addition, missionaries defend a single expression of the gospel as if that expression was the totality of the gospel. Consequently, the work of missions is greatly hindered. David Sills aptly puts it this way:

> Because most missionaries and preachers want to avoid anything that would alter the gospel message, they shrink back from the hard work of contextualization. However, if one does not contextualize, he is doing just that—changing the gospel. He becomes a modern-day Judaizer. He is in effect telling his hearers that they must become like him to be saved.[79]

If we are not careful, we unintentionally distort the truth. Consider the repeated argument made by Gilbert:

> It should be obvious by now that to say simply that "Jesus is Lord" is really not good news at all if we don't explain how Jesus is not just Lord but also Savior. Lordship implies the right to judge, and we've already seen that God intends to judge evil. Therefore, to a sinner in rebellion against God and against his Messiah, the proclamation that Jesus has become Lord is terrible news. It means that your enemy has won the throne and is now about to judge you for your rebellion against him. . . . Just like the proclamation that "Jesus is Lord" is not good news unless there is a way to be forgiven of your rebellion against him, so the fact that God is remaking the world is not good news unless you can be included in that.[80]

At surface level, there is no problem in what Gilbert says. However, using biblical language in this way obscures, if not unwittingly undermines, what the Bible says. No doubt, it is a matter of perspective whether one calls this "good" news. Nevertheless in Scripture the gospel remains "good news" no matter who are its hearers. In other words, the gospel is good news not only when spoken to Christians but also when we preach it to non-Christians.

For example, when directly speaking to nonbelievers, Paul in Acts 13:32 and 14:15 explicitly tells his hearers that he is preaching the "gospel" (cf. Mark 1:15). The gospel is good regardless of what God's enemies think. The gospel is no less good simply because someone denies God's existence (i.e., atheists) or hates the biblical God (i.e., Hitler). Unfortunately, by limiting Christ's "lordship" merely to "judging evil," Gilbert's message makes it more difficult to understand passages where Paul overtly equates Jesus' lordship and the gospel. Paul says,

> If you confess with your mouth that *Jesus is Lord* and believe in your heart that God raised him from the dead, you will be saved. . . . For the Scripture says, "Everyone who believes in him will not be put to shame." For there is no distinction between Jew and Greek; for the same *Lord is Lord* of all, bestowing his riches on all who call on him. For "everyone who calls on the name of the *Lord* will be saved."

> How then will they call on him in whom they have not believed? And how are they to believe in him of whom they have never heard? And how are they to hear without someone preaching? And how are they to preach unless they are sent? As it is written, "How beautiful are the feet of those who preach the *good news!*" But they have not all obeyed the *gospel.* For Isaiah says, "Lord, who has believed what he has heard from us?" So faith comes from hearing, and hearing through the word of Christ. (Rom 10:9–17)

According to Gilbert's logic, Paul essentially says that people are saved by confessing Jesus as judge. Further, Romans 10:12 becomes difficult to understand since, according to his logic, our "enemy" (Gilbert's term) bestows his riches on us sinners.

In other words, if we get contextualization wrong, we mistake the gospel and bring harm to our listeners by setting up a fractured theological framework, making it hard for them to interpret Scripture after the initial presentation. Consequently, new believers naturally build upon the initial categories that are presented to them under the name of "gospel." For example, if evangelists only stress "law" and "judicial righteousness," new believers will constantly try to fit their theology and experience within these terms. If we limit lordship to judgment, then readers are not able to make sense of numerous passages that celebrate Christ's lordship. They will not see that "lordship" language more broadly connotes his kingship. Jesus is the King who frees us from the reign of sin and death (see Rom 5:17–6:23).

Similarly, many people, including Gilbert, restrict God's "righteousness" to refer to his holiness to judge evil.[81] Demarest's contextualization echoes Gilbert. Demarest goes even further, claiming that "the holy and righteous character of God" is an "obstacle" to salvation.[82] Again, this reductionistic contextualization directly contradicts biblical writers like David, who appeals to God's righteousness *in order that* God would save him (see Ps 51:4; 71:2; 143:1,11). In short, these contextualizations of the gospel mistakenly reduce the meaning of "Lord" and "righteousness" to that of "judge" and "angry against sin." These ways of speaking may be true *from a particular vantage point.* They may evoke a response from listeners.[83] However, these contextualizations do not represent a holistic biblical theology, and they ultimately stunt the growth of the believer.

How the Bible Frames the Gospel

The Bible consistently uses three particular themes to frame the gospel. These framework themes are creation, covenant, and kingdom.[84] Without exception, biblical writers always use one or more of these ideas in passages that explicitly reference the "gospel."

Again, we never want to limit our understanding to verses that explicitly say the word "gospel." However, these passages are essential for establishing a solid theological foundation. They provide a critical starting point for anyone who wants to share the gospel in a fully biblical manner. We should not assume certain passages communicate the gospel while overlooking places that explicitly outline a biblical view of the message. Therefore, if we define the gospel without reference to these passages, it is quite likely that we have a very limited or distorted perspective on the gospel.

How do these three themes relate to one another? I briefly want to preview the way each motif supports and explains the others. In short, because God is the Creator of the world, he is the King over all nations. However, humanity has acted as usurpers, creating idolatrous kingdoms to rival God's rule as the Creator-King. God therefore enacted a plan to rectify the world. Beginning with Abraham in Genesis 12, God established a covenant according to which he would bless all nations. Through a series of covenants that would follow (such as the covenants with Moses and David), God explains how he will set his creation right, overthrowing those who rebel against his reign. By understanding the Bible's inner logic, we can present the message in a more coherent and comprehensive fashion.

Kingdom: Our God Reigns

The gospel is first of all a message about God's kingdom.[85] This imagery is apparent even in the Old Testament. In Isaiah 52:7, which Paul quotes in Romans 10:15, one reads, "How beautiful upon the mountains are the feet of him who brings good news [מְבַשֵּׂר; εὐαγγελιζομένου, LXX], who publishes peace, who brings good news [מְבַשֵּׂר; εὐαγγελιζόμενος, LXX] of happiness, who publishes salvation, who says to Zion, 'Your God reigns.'" God is King. Isaiah 40:9 makes a similar announcement, "Go on up to a high mountain, O Zion, herald of good news [מְבַשֶּׂרֶת; εὐαγγελιζόμενος, LXX]; lift up your voice with strength, O Jerusalem, herald of good news [מְבַשֶּׂרֶת; εὐαγγελιζόμενος, LXX]; lift it up, fear not; say to the cities of Judah, 'Behold your God!'" In context, Isaiah proclaims that it is the "Lord God" [אֲדֹנָי יְהוִה] who reigns over the earth as the Creator-King, defeating "the rulers of the earth" (Isa 40:10–42:9). This meaning comes through even in contexts that are less overtly religious. For example, in Psalm 68:11–14, the women announce the defeat of enemy kings: "The Lord gives the word; the women who announce the news [הַמְבַשְּׂרוֹת; εὐαγγελιζομένοις, LXX] are a great host: 'The kings of the armies—they flee, they flee!' The women at home divide the spoil.... When the Almighty scatters kings there, let snow fall on Zalmon."

The New Testament is saturated with similar announcements of a kingdom-oriented gospel. In Mark 1:14,15 Jesus opens his ministry "*proclaiming the gospel* of God, and saying, 'The time is fulfilled, and *the kingdom of God is at hand*; repent and believe in the gospel.'" Likewise, Matthew 9:35 expounds, "And Jesus went throughout all the cities and villages, teaching in their synagogues and *proclaiming the gospel of the kingdom* and healing every disease and every affliction" (cf. Matt 3:2; 4:17; 10:7; 24:14).

Romans opens with one of the clearest summaries of the gospel in the New Testament. Paul calls himself an apostle,

> set apart for the gospel of God, which he promised beforehand through his prophets in the holy Scriptures, concerning his Son, who was descended from David according to the flesh and was declared to be the Son of God in power according to the Spirit of holiness by his resurrection from the dead, Jesus Christ our Lord. (Rom 1:1–4)

Some readers may easily miss the numerous kingdom references in this compact sentence. We should recall God's covenant with David: "I will raise up your offspring after you, who shall come from your body, and I will establish his kingdom. He shall build a house for my name, and I will establish the throne of his kingdom forever. I will be to him a father, and he shall be to me a son" (2 Sam 7:12–14; cf. 1 Chron 17:11–14). The royal offspring of David is called God's son.

This becomes a standard way of referring to Israel's King (e.g., Ps 2:2,6,7; 89:2,3,28,29,35,36; Heb 1:4). We can thus understand Nathanael's answer to Jesus, "Rabbi, you are the Son of God! You are the King of Israel!" (John 1:49; cf. 11:27). The surrounding verbiage in Romans 1:1–5 reinforces the message. Jesus is called "Lord" and "Christ," the title given to Israel's anointed King.

The gospel announces Israel's King, the Son of God, descended from David according to God's covenant promise. Second Timothy 2:8 may be the most concise synopsis of the gospel in the Bible, "Remember Jesus Christ, *risen from the dead*, the *offspring of David*, as preached in my gospel." What is most noteworthy here is the content Paul chooses to include in his summary. He is sure to highlight the fact that the gospel proclaims Jesus the Christ as the offspring of David. Paul simply repeats the constant emphasis found in the earliest sermons (cf. Acts 2–4). Paul's sermon in Acts 13 fully outlines all that has been said thus far. He exclaims, "And we bring you the good news [εὐαγγελιζόμεθα] that what God promised to the fathers, this he has fulfilled to us their children by raising Jesus" (13:32,33). The entire message focuses on the Davidic kingship of Christ.

Many people know that Paul recaps the gospel in 1 Corinthians 15:3–8, yet few note the explicit royal imagery that runs throughout the chapter. In the context that follows these opening verses, Paul explains the significance of the Christ's resurrection.[86] We cannot overlook 1 Corinthians 15:20–28, which states,

> But in fact Christ has been raised from the dead, the firstfruits of those who have fallen asleep. For as by a man came death, by a man has come also the resurrection of the dead. For as in Adam all die, so also in Christ shall all be made alive. But each in his own order: Christ the firstfruits, then at his coming those who belong to Christ. Then comes the end, when he delivers the *kingdom to God* the Father after destroying every *rule* and every authority and power. For he must *reign* until he has *put all his enemies under his feet.* The last enemy to be destroyed is death. For "God has put all things in *subjection* under his feet." But when it says, "all things are put in *subjection*," it is plain that he is excepted who put all things in *subjection* under him. When all things are subjected to him, then the Son himself will also be *subjected* to him who put all things *in subjection under him*, that God may be all in all.

The resurrection is the victory of Christ over God's enemies, particularly sin and death (see 1 Cor 15:54–56). Romans 1:4 and perhaps 2 Timothy 2:8 make a similar inference. This is how Jesus is crowned King.

Covenant: God Keeps His Promises

"Covenant" is a second major theme that consistently frames the gospel. We already see implicit references to covenant in the passages cited above. Romans 1:2 says that God promised the gospel "beforehand through his prophets *in the holy Scriptures.*" First Corinthians 15:3,4 twice states that the gospel is "in accordance with the Scriptures." Acts 13:17–41 makes repeated reference to God's covenant with David, as in verse 23, "Of [David's] offspring God has brought to Israel a Savior, Jesus, as he promised."

The gospel announces the fact that God keeps his covenant promises. The connection is obvious in Acts 13:32,33—"And we bring you *the good news that what God promised to the fathers, this he has fulfilled to us* their children by raising Jesus." In addition, Galatians 3:8 explicitly defines the gospel in terms of the Abrahamic covenant. Paul says, "And the Scripture, foreseeing that God would justify the Gentiles by faith, preached the gospel beforehand to Abraham, saying, 'In you shall all the nations be blessed.'" Notice that the Abrahamic covenant is not merely background for the gospel; rather, Paul directly equates the covenant with the gospel. Perhaps this also explains the reference to "all the nations" in Romans 1:5. Recall the entire context of Romans wherein Paul defends the gospel by explaining the implications of the Abrahamic covenant (see Rom 4).

In Ephesians 2–3, Paul richly expounds on the meaning of gospel. Ephesians 2:17 uses the verb εὐηγγελίσατο, whereas Ephesians 3:6,8 both use the noun εὐαγγέλιον. Notice the surrounding context. In Ephesians 2:12, Paul explains how the gospel saves the Gentiles, who were "alienated from the commonwealth of Israel and strangers to *the covenants of promise.*" Now "the Gentiles are fellow heirs, members of the same body, and partakers of the promise in Christ Jesus through the gospel" (Eph 3:6). Paul then elaborates upon God's purpose in his preaching. Paul aims

> to bring to light for everyone what is the plan of the mystery hidden for ages in God who created all things, so that through the church the manifold wisdom of God might now *be made known to the rulers and authorities in the heavenly places.* This was according to the eternal purpose that he has realized in Christ Jesus our Lord. (Eph 3:9–11)

This allusion is subtle but clearly connects back to the kingdom theme discussed above. The gospel proclaims to rulers and authorities that the Creator-King defeats evil and blesses all nations in keeping with his covenant promises.

Creation: There Is One God for All Nations

Finally, the biblical authors frequently frame the gospel using creation language. This theme establishes two key ideas: (1) the *sovereignty* of God and

(2) the *scope* of his kingdom. In other words, creation is the *realm* over which God *reigns*. All other authorities and powers must ultimately submit to him. Various passages convey the core message of Isaiah 43:15, which states, "I am the LORD, your Holy One, the Creator of Israel, your King." Isaiah 40–66 constantly emphasizes that God is the true Creator-King over against the false gods, whom idolaters worship. Thus, Isaiah 40:9,10 twice uses the Hebrew word for "gospel" (תְרֶשֶּׁבָמ) to describe the announcement made to Judah, "Behold your God!"

A number of passages that discuss the gospel also emphasize the *scope* of God's reign. For example, Colossians 1:5,23 speak of the "gospel," which "has been proclaimed in all creation under heaven." These two verses form something of a parenthesis around a densely worded reflection on Christ's work as "the firstborn of all creation" (1:15). The passage is not only full of creation imagery; it is also peppered with kingdom language (see 1:13,16). Paul's allusions are both subtle and overt.[87] God in Christ delights to "reconcile to himself all things, whether on earth or in heaven, making peace by the blood of his cross" (1:20).

Similarly, other gospel texts highlight the *reach* or *realm* over which God rules. Scot McKnight argues strongly that God's kingdom includes "a people governedd by a king," thus the "domain of 'church.'" (See *Kingdom Conspiracy*, 68–80.) According to Ephesians 2:11–3:13, a central idea of the gospel is that God has created from both Jews and Gentiles "one new man" [ἕνα καινὸν ἄνθρωπον] (2:15). Thus, the Gentiles are "fellow citizens" and "fellow heirs, members of the same body, and partakers of the promise in Christ Jesus through the gospel" (2:19; 3:6; cf. Gal 3:7–29). It is inherent to the gospel that it must be preached in "the whole world" (Matt 24:14; 26:13; Mark 14:9; 16:15). Because Jesus Christ is "Lord of all" (Acts 10:36), God commands us "to testify that he is the one appointed by God to be judge of the living and the dead" (Acts 10:42; cf. Rom 1:14–16).

Paul also employs the creation motif to preach the gospel. In Acts 14:15–17, Paul counters the idolatry in Lystra by proclaiming,

> Men, why are you doing these things? We also are men, of like nature with you, and we bring you good news [εὐαγγελιζόμενοι], that you should turn from these vain things to a living God, who made the heavens and the earth and the sea and all that is in them. In past

45

generations he allowed all the nations to walk in their own ways. Yet he did not leave himself without witness, for he did good by giving you rains from heaven and fruitful seasons, satisfying your hearts with food and gladness.

Besides the explicit verbiage in verse 15, the surrounding context makes clear that Paul indeed preaches the gospel (cf. Acts 14:7,21). Verse 22 subtly reinforces our previous theme by adding the phrase "the kingdom of God." In Acts 17:24–31, Paul famously uses creation imagery. He directly appeals to monotheism and preaches God as the Creator. Verse 18 reinforces the point that Paul proclaims the gospel, for "he was preaching Jesus and the resurrection." Once again, we find here the verb "to evangelize" (εὐηγγελίζετο).

Acts 17:31 illuminates another way Paul connects creation and kingdom language, stating that God "has fixed a day on which he will judge the world in righteousness by a man whom he has appointed; and of this he has given assurance to all by raising him from the dead." We must pay careful attention to Paul's verbiage. Besides Acts 17:31, the phrase "judge the world in righteousness" (κρίνειν τὴν οἰκουμένην ἐν δικαιοσύνη) used here occurs in the Bible only in Psalm 9:8; 96:10,13; 98:9.[88] Each context uses royal language about a king establishing a place of righteousness for his people. In fact, Psalm 96:2 says, "tell of his salvation from day to day," where the verb again is the typical word for "to proclaim the gospel [בַּשְּׂרוּ; εὐαγγελίζεσθε; Ps 95:2 LXX].

How Do Biblical Writers Use the Creation Theme?

When using the creation theme to frame the gospel, the main idea is not merely one's preaching monotheism. Of course monotheism is basic to the gospel and Christian theology. More to the point, God wants to make known his supremacy. Idols are false gods that challenge the one true God's kingship. The biblical writers are quite intentional in their use of creation imagery.

We now arrive at a key point in our discussion: *We cannot assume that we "frame" a gospel presentation in the same way the Bible does simply because we make sporadic allusions to the one true God who created the world.* Biblically speaking, framing the gospel according to the doctrine of creation has specific implications and functions. In what follows, I list ten ways that biblical writers use the creation motif. If we want to frame the gospel in a like manner, our presentations will make similar inferences.

Who Is the Creator?

First, our use of the creation theme ought to infer the fact that God is King. Hence Isaiah 43:15 states, "I am the LORD, your Holy One, the Creator of Israel, your King." Therefore, God deserves our allegiance. He has sovereign authority. He defeats all his enemies. Although the following passage never mentions the word "gospel," a thematic connection between the creation and kingship are clear in Psalm 74:12–17.

> Yet God my King is from of old, working salvation in the midst of the earth. You divided the sea by your might; you broke the heads of the sea monsters on the waters. You crushed the heads of Leviathan; you gave him as food for the creatures of the wilderness. You split open springs and brooks; you dried up ever-flowing streams. Yours is the day, yours also the night; you have established the heavenly lights and the sun. You have fixed all the boundaries of the earth; you have made summer and winter.

One cannot overstate this idea: monotheism in the Bible is not merely about the number of gods; it most fundamentally concerns authority and thus our loyalty.[89]

Second, this theme identifies the scope of God's kingdom. God is the God of the entire world. In Scripture, as with many contemporary groups, people believe that a certain god was tied to a particular location. Consider 1 Kings 20:19–30. The king of Israel defeats Ben-hadad king of Syria. In verse 23 we read, "And the servants of the king of Syria said to him, 'Their gods are gods of the hills, and so they were stronger than we. But let us fight against them in the plain, and surely we shall be stronger than they.'" The following spring, Israel is badly outnumbered by the Syrian forces. At that time, God's prophet tells the king of Israel, "Thus says the LORD, 'Because the Syrians have said, "The LORD is a god of the hills but he is not a god of the valleys," therefore I will give all this great multitude into your hand, and you shall know that I am the LORD'" (20:28). As a result, Israel's army routs their enemies

(vv. 29,30). God wants the world to know the whole earth is his kingdom. The gospel proclaims that the Creator is the one true God, thus countering the phenomenon whereby nations limit the scope of God's dominion.

What Has the Creator-King Done?

Third, the gospel makes known that the Creator is the Lord, the God of Israel. This God is specific. He is not abstract. *This God has acted in history.* We are not preaching a philosophy. God has revealed himself through Israel. Modern Christians could easily miss this point. One can mistakenly assume that monotheism and creation are issues concerning general revelation and thus have little to do with Israel. However, we do not want to settle for general revelation and proofs for the existence of "a god" who is like the Lord. The doctrine of creation distinguishes the Lord from a myriad of local gods. This should humble all nations.

Accordingly, when talking about God, we need to highlight his works in history in order to explain what God is like. We do not merely want to say he is omniscient, omnipotent, and omnipresent. This is how systematic theology describes God. Rather, we seek to emphasize *how* God demonstrates his character and attributes.

Consider a simple question—how does the Bible most often describe God? It does not use the categories of systematic theology. Instead God refers to his work in history. For example,

> God said to Moses, "I am who I am." And he said, "Say this to the people of Israel, 'I am has sent me to you.'" God also said to Moses, "Say this to the people of Israel, 'The Lord, the God of your fathers, the God of Abraham, the God of Isaac, and the God of Jacob, has sent me to you.' This is my name forever, and thus *I am to be remembered throughout all generations.*" (Ex 3:14,15; cf. Gen 50:24; Deut 9:5)

Similarly, various passages restate the idea of Leviticus 25:38, where God says, "I am the Lord your God, who brought you out of the land of Egypt to give you the land of Canaan, and to be your God" (cf. Deut 5:6,7). Likewise we see mention of creation in Isaiah: "Thus says God, the Lord, who created the heavens and stretched them out, who spread out the earth and what comes from it, who gives breath to the people on it and spirit to those who walk in it" (Isa 42:5). A number of passages repeat these ideas. Joshua 24:1–13 is especially rich in identifying the God of the gospel by way of his historical works. The present point is simply this: God does not want us to settle for people merely believing monotheism; even demons are monotheists (Jas 2:19). The Lord wants the nations to know what he is like and that he alone is God. He wants us to know what he has done in history.

Fourth, salvation depends on the one true God keeping his covenant; therefore, salvation is by grace. Galatians 3:15–20 makes a direct appeal to the one Creator God. Paul writes,

> To give a human example, brothers: even with a man-made covenant, no one annuls it or adds to it once it has been ratified. Now the promises were made to Abraham and to his offspring. It does not say, "And to offsprings," referring to many, but referring to one, "And to your offspring," who is Christ. This is what I mean: the law, which came 430 years afterward, does not annul a covenant previously ratified by God, so as to make the promise void. For if the inheritance comes by the law, it no longer comes by promise; but God gave it to Abraham by a promise.

> Why then the law? It was added because of transgressions, until the offspring should come to whom the promise had been made, and it was put in place through angels by an intermediary. Now an intermediary implies more than one, *but God is one.*

This passage is rather complex. At the moment I will only suggest a brief explanation, leaving it to the reader to study it for himself or herself.[90]

In verse 20 Paul mentions monotheism in order to deny the possibility that the law is able to bring about Abraham's promise (vv. 14,18). In verse 19 he reminds the reader that the law came through a mediator (i.e., *Moses*). However, Moses only represents one ethnic group—Israel; he does not represent Abraham's entire family. That is, Moses does not represent the one human family of God. God is one; therefore, his family consists of all nations. Accordingly, Moses' mediatorship is insufficient to make Abraham's blessing come to the Gentiles (see 3:16).

Notice Paul's train of thought in chapter 3. Verse 7 is Paul's thesis: "Know then that it is those of faith who are the sons of Abraham." Compare his concluding thoughts in verses 25–29. He says,

> But now that faith has come, we are no longer under a guardian, for in Christ Jesus you are all sons of God, through faith. For as many of you as were baptized into Christ have put on Christ. There is neither Jew nor Greek, there is neither slave nor free, there is no male and female, for you are all one in Christ Jesus. *And if you are Christ's, then you are Abraham's offspring, heirs according to promise.*

The final sentence—verse 29—summarizes the message of the entire chapter. In short, Galatians 3 reinforces our previous point: justification is through faith; anyone can be saved. In addition, *because there is one God, salvation comes from his keeping his promises. Salvation is by grace.*

Paul establishes the same point in Romans 4, a passage with striking parallels to Galatians 3. Keep in mind, Romans 4 stems from Romans 3:29,30, which also argued from monotheism. Romans 4:13–16 says,

> For the promise to Abraham and his offspring that he would be heir of the world did not come through the law but through the righteousness of faith. For if it is the adherents of the law who are to be the heirs, faith is null and the promise is void. For the law brings wrath, but where there is no law there is no transgression.

> That is why it depends on faith, in order that the promise may rest on grace and be guaranteed to all his offspring—not only to the adherent of the law but also to the one who shares the faith of Abraham, who is the father of us all.

The broader point of Romans 3:29,30 is stated more specifically in verse 16, "That is why it depends on faith, in order that promise *may rest on grace* and be guaranteed to all his offspring." As in Galatians 3, monotheism grounds justification *by grace.* The Creator keeps his covenant.

Why Is the Creator-King Important?

Fifth, a creation-framed gospel makes clear that all nations have a common origin. This message should humble every social group. Ethnicity, country, family, bloodline, culture, education, economic status, and gender do not give a person legitimate reason to feel a sense of superiority over others. Because God is one, we should not boast nor compare ourselves. No single culture in the world makes its people become essentially different from those in other cultures. Culture is a second-level distinctive. Fundamentally we are *human* first and foremost. We all have the same basic problem and need. Those from every culture are made in the image of the one true God. Humanity all comes under the authority of Christ.

Sixth, the kind of monotheism that frames a biblical gospel presentation will narrow the way by which one can be saved. Salvation only comes through the God of those ancient Jews. Jesus in John 4:22 says to the Samaritan woman, "You worship what you do not know; we worship what we know, for salvation is from the Jews." Therefore, *this* God defines what salvation is. Contra the various conceptions imagined by other religions, Jesus explains salvation according to biblical monotheism: "And this is eternal life, that they know you the only true God, and Jesus Christ whom you have sent" (John 17:3). This salvation accords to God's historical plan and purpose (Eph 1:9,10). He uses particular ways to reveal his righteousness, wisdom, and power.

Seventh, the Bible uses the creation theme, particularly monotheism, to instruct us that salvation comes only through Jesus Christ. More simply, the creation theme ultimately should lead directly to Jesus as Savior. Hence 1 Timothy 2:5 says, "For there is one God, and there is one mediator between God and men, the man Christ Jesus." Similarly, the entire argument in Galatians 3, which we looked at above, hinges on the fact that "God is one" in order to confirm that only those who are in Christ enjoy the blessing promised to Abraham. Accordingly, people should not wrongly think that certain local leaders, shamans, or historical prophets could represent us before God. Jesus alone is humanity's representative.

An eighth implication of the doctrine of creation is that anyone can be saved. People do not need to belong to a particular social group or class. In Romans 10, Paul again appeals to monotheism to explain that salvation is not limited to any one group of people. In Romans 10:12,13 Paul says,

"For there is no distinction between Jew and Greek; *for the same Lord is Lord of all*, bestowing his riches on all who call on him. For 'everyone who calls on the name of the Lord will be saved.'" Because "the same Lord is Lord of all," anyone can be saved.

How Do We Respond to the Creator-King?

Ninth, Paul uses monotheism in order to explain that justification only comes through faith. In Romans 3:28–30, Paul writes, "For we hold that one is justified by faith apart from works of the law. Or is God the God of Jews only? Is he not the God of Gentiles also? Yes, of Gentiles also, since God is one—who will justify the circumcised by faith and the uncircumcised through faith." Notice his logic. Verses 27,28 first contrast faith and works. In verse 29 Paul then introduces a rhetorical question wherein he seems suddenly to start talking about Jews and Gentiles. According to many traditional Protestant interpretations, this Jew-Gentile distinction seemingly comes out of thin air. However, it makes sense in the context of Romans (and the entire Bible). What is the big issue at stake in Romans 3:29? It is Christianity's most central doctrine—monotheism.

According to Paul's way of thinking, if the law justifies people, then God is only God of the Jews. However, God is also the Gentiles' God. Why? Paul gives a single reason: "God is one." In Paul's view, keeping the Mosaic Law meant being a Jew. After all, Gentiles do not have the law by birth (Rom 2:14,27; Gal 2:15).[91] The Mosaic Law demarcates those who are Jewish. Therefore, if one supposes that justification depends on keeping the Law, then we can infer from Romans 3:29 that God is "the God of Jews only." However, this error is blatant. Since the world only has one true God, then Israel's God is God both of the Jews and the Gentiles. The world does not have multiple gods. God is one. In short, Paul uses *monotheism* to defend justification by faith. This line of thinking should startle many of us. If our previous understanding of monotheism does not naturally seem to lead to a similar doctrine of justification, then we should reconsider our notions about monotheism.

Finally, the way the Creator saves humanity humbles every nation. People can no longer boast. The Jews have no special privilege with respect to salvation. People can no longer make comparisons. This is Paul's major point in Romans 11:11–32 (esp vv. 18–22,25–32). Teaching Israel's history is important.

One reason to preach the Old Testament is to remind people of God's grace. Thus, in Ephesians 2:11–12 Paul tells Gentiles (like most readers today):

> Therefore remember that at one time you Gentiles in the flesh, called "the uncircumcision" by what is called the circumcision, which is made in the flesh by hands—remember that you were at that time separated from Christ, alienated from the commonwealth of Israel and strangers to the covenants of promise, having no hope and without God in the world.

From the doctrine of creation, we further learn that God's way of saving people should make us humble.

All that I have just said simply illustrates how people in the Bible use the "creation" theme and so help us to preach the gospel more faithfully. "Creation" is not merely background for the gospel. It has a number of critical implications for ministry. Our contemporary presentations should likewise carry these specific creation implications.

Conclusion

In conclusion I draw together a few main ideas from the chapter. Without exception, the biblical writers use at least one of three motifs to frame their gospel presentations. These themes include creation, covenant, and kingdom.

What is the relationship between these three ideas? The one true God creates all things; thus, he is also the King of the world. Because his kingdom became corrupt, God established a series of covenants leading to the restoration of his creation. God covenants to bless the world through Abraham's offspring. In the Davidic covenant we find out that this promise is fulfilled in David's offspring, namely Jesus Christ. In this way, our Creator-King keeps covenant and establishes justice in the world.

Accordingly, this three-part framework ensures that we keep the gospel's core ideas at the center. Otherwise we will risk dividing the Bible into two parts—our favorite parts and everything else. Without this framework, we become disoriented and lose balance. Our gospel presentations quickly become too *narrow*. Whether through silence or de-emphasis, we *functionally* deny the entire Bible's value and authority. As we will continue to see in the coming chapters, these framework themes provide the context in which we can rightly interpret other important biblical motifs and doctrines. Accordingly, biblical theology should both ground and give shape to our gospel presentations.

KEY POINTS

- We need the entire biblical story to grasp the gospel.
- One must be careful not to limit the gospel to any one theme.
- Contextualizing the gospel foremost requires sound biblical theology, not merely systematic theology.
- In the Bible, people always use one or more of three themes to frame their gospel presentations. These themes include creation, covenant, and kingdom. Other motifs fit within this framework.
- If our gospel presentations are not framed by at least one of these three themes, then we are not preaching the gospel in the same way preached by believers in the Bible.
- Creation language conveys the *sovereignty* of God and the *scope* of his kingdom. The whole world is the *realm* over which God *reigns*.
- Biblical monotheism consistently carries royal connotations— God is King.
- Put concisely, the gospel tells how the Creator establishes his kingdom by blessing all nations (Abrahamic covenant) through David's promised royal offspring, Jesus Christ.

4

Priority:
What Questions Does the
Gospel Answer?

A FLEXIBLE WAY TO EXPLAIN THE MESSAGE

Gospel presentations in the Bible consistently answer four key questions. By identifying these questions, people can better understand and present the whole gospel from the whole Bible. This chapter surveys a range of passages in order to find out how the Bible answers these four questions. Among the many possible answers, Christians can find distinct ways to express the gospel across the world's cultures.

Christians need a contextualization method that has both flexibility and firmness. As was argued in the last chapter, the gospel has a firm framework. The gospel does not change. On the other hand, biblical writers clearly present the gospel in contrasting ways. Even within the Bible, there is no single prescribed way of preaching the gospel. In addition, the world's cultures are diverse and ever changing.

There is another reason to highlight the importance of having a flexible model of contextualization. Many people come from denominations and ministries with rigid traditions and ways of thinking. In keeping with one's background or tradition, a person might limit his or her view of the gospel to a particular book, passage, or doctrine. In so doing, he or she will veer towards theological syncretism, confusing the gospel with our theological tradition. However, Christians should not compromise the gospel by settling for mere truth. One does not need to pick one particular theological camp over against another simply because he or she does not know how to balance the complementary emphases and themes of the Bible.

Accordingly, we need a method of contextualization that is firm, flexible, and based on the entire biblical narrative. There is one gospel but many ways of expressing it. Different passages talk about the same topic and share common motifs. Within a single text, multiple images and concepts may be used, such that Peter can say Christ is a "cornerstone," and "whoever believes in him will not be put to shame," for Christians are a "chosen race, a royal priesthood, a holy nation," yet are "sojourners and exiles" in the world (1 Pet 2:6–11).

Naturally, many ideas in Scripture resonate with the values and thinking of people in contemporary cultures. There are people in the Bible as in modern times who uphold family honor and struggle to balance competing loyalties, whether they include the state, family, or friends. Likewise, others make offerings in temples, hide behind hypocrisy, or have ethnic/national prejudice. How do we utilize the similarities found between the ancient text and a modern context?

A few clarifying remarks are necessary in order to avoid confusion. First, resemblance between cultures does not imply some sort of equivalence. In different periods and places, what it means to "lose face" will vary. Second, one cannot expect to remain an effective communicator if he or she consistently uses abstract jargon. Therefore, it may not be helpful to always use anthropological terms like "honor/shame," "guilt-oriented," "collectivism," and "individualism." Instead, when preaching the gospel, we do better to use the symbols within a society that convey these concepts.

Take "honor and shame" for example. Reputation, name, job title, gender, as well as cars, clothing, and salary can indicate one's social status, thus a person's honor or shame. Likewise we could ask what things people deem valuable, what topics they like to talk about, or even what they fear or boast in. In China, while many idioms use the characters for "honor" (荣) and "shame" (辱), people more commonly convey these concepts using terms having to do with "face" (e.g., 面子, 脸) or someone's name (名字). Of course it would be helpful for people to consider nuances between words in a language. For example, *mianzi* and *lian* both mean "face" but can carry slightly different but important connotations.[92] By attending to these subtleties, one can more effectively express biblical truth.

Countless visual and verbal markers represent honor and shame across diverse cultures and subcultures. Consider Paul's complaint in Galatians 4:17 about those who trouble the Galatian church: "They make much of you, but for no good purpose. They want to shut you out, that you may make much of them." How do people around us today "make much of" one another? Maybe this entails sitting in particular seats at a banquet (cf. Luke 11:43). In China, one place of honor is the seat directly facing the door of the room. Or perhaps we curry favor with someone by pushing "like" on her Facebook page or mentioning her in a Twitter message. A person in America may not use words like gaining or losing "face," but they might talk about "people pleasing" or "trying to look good in front of others."

The Gospel Answers Four Key Questions

In debates about the gospel, a few distinctions are frequently made. On the one hand, people present the gospel in either a *propositional* or a *narrative* fashion. On the other hand, these gospel presentations may also be described as either *soterian* oriented (narrowly focused on individual salvation) or "kingdom" oriented (more broadly centered on God's rule over creation). Accordingly, conventional evangelism tools like the "Four Spiritual Laws" or the "Romans Road" represent a propositional, *soterian* approach. Perhaps "The Story" could be called a narrative, *soterian* presentation.[93] The gospel in McKnight's *The King Jesus Gospel* and N. T. Wright's *How God Became King* could be characterized as narrative and mainly oriented on God's kingdom.

These two sets of categories (propositional/narrative and *soterian*/kingdom) should not be confused. When contrasting propositional versus narrative presentations, I refer in part to the way in which a person constructs a gospel presentation. In particular, I highlight the scope of biblical passages one uses. Obviously the "Romans Road" narrowly selects a few verses from the book of Romans, which can be reviewed in a matter of minutes. They act as doctrinal statements demarcating what beliefs one must have to become a Christian. A narrative approach is typified by Chandler's "gospel from the air" (mentioned previously) and in works like Albert Wolter's *Creation Regained*[94] or *The Drama of Scripture: Finding Our Place in the Biblical Story* by Craig Bartholomew and Michael Goheen.[95] This approach emphasizes the richness and integrated nature of the biblical story.

By contrasting a *soterian-* and a kingdom-focused presentation, the main issue I have in mind is the breadth or scope of God's work and mission. When presenting the gospel, how much should we talk about what God achieves through Christ? Should the scope of our explanation be narrow, oriented around individual salvation? Or does the gospel necessarily include what God does in redemptive history for the entire cosmos? Throughout this book I suggest that a narrative, kingdom-oriented approach is preferable to a propositional, individual-centered presentation.

Consider the following sequence of statements. Which of these ideas is most basic or essential?

1. Christ is King.
2. [Why?] Christ defeated sin and death.
3. [Therefore] The world can be freed from bondage and receive blessing.
4. [Therefore] We must be loyal to him.

Which statement is the gospel? Are we to reduce the message to one discrete statement whereby the others are *not* the gospel message? Obviously they are inseparable. Each of them requires the others in order for them to have their intended significance.

Much of evangelicalism focuses on mechanics of theology (how a doctrine works) rather than purpose (why it is so).[96] Therefore, people reach an impasse as to what is most "fundamental" in theology debates (e.g., atonement theories, guilt vs. shame, etc.). One camp speaks about the parts (e.g., justification) that make the whole work. Another group might focus on the final goal (e.g., new creation). How does one define "fundamental"? By a thing's parts or by its purpose? From different perspectives, the answers could vary according to the context of the conversation.

To contextualize the gospel like Paul did, we must interpret the Bible the way Paul did.[97] People like Richard Hays (following J. C. Beker) highlight the point that Paul's gospel seems to have parts that are both constant and contingent.[98] "Constant" aspects of the gospel story include things like Jesus' death and resurrection. By "contingent," Hays highlights the elements of Paul's message that are shaped by the needs of Paul's context. How do we tie together both the constant and contingent? To say it another way, how do we present a "firm" *and* "flexible" gospel?

We are helped by the following observation: the gospel generally answers four key questions. These four questions help us organize the firm and flexible parts of the gospel. The exact wording of each question may be adjusted depending on the context.

1. *Who* is Christ?
2. *What* has Christ done?
3. *Why* is Christ important?
4. *How* should we respond?

One can speak about the gospel with reference either to God the Father or to Christ the Son. Thus, the first two questions could be rephrased from an Old Testament perspective. As we will see, Isaiah's "gospel" answers the question, "Who is God?" A second question can be stated, "What has God done?" which essentially asks, "What kind of a God is He?" We do not want to divide the Father and the Son. The point made here is simply that biblical writers at times interchange their language. They sometimes speak about what God has done while, at other times, about what Christ has done. Similarly, I will vary my own verbiage in the coming pages.

In what follows, I will first explain the rationale for each of these questions. Then we will see how Scripture answers them. Finally, I will offer a few broad suggestions for answering these questions in a modern context.

Who Is Christ?

The first question—*Who* is Christ?—is most fundamental. We could say both that Christ is "Savior" and that he is "Son of God." Likewise, God is Creator and King. This initial "who" question establishes the context and basis for the answers to the following question. Knowing who Christ is affects how one understands his actions (question 2), why he is significant (question 3), and thus how we should respond (question 4). Wherever one looks in Scripture, the gospel answers some or all of these questions: Who? What? Why? How?

Reflecting upon these four questions helps us to reconcile seemingly disparate answers to the question "What is the gospel?" The range of the questions ensures balance. The sequence also protects against the tendency to make the gospel human centered rather than God centered. Understanding and thus explaining the doctrine of salvation, which is especially stressed in question 3, depends on *who* Christ is and *what* he does. These initial two questions can be answered independent of any individual reader. They should naturally imply the answer to question 3 and so inspire worship (question 4).

The gospel centers on Christ. Thus, one's receiving salvation should ultimately result in his or her worship of Christ. *We preach soteriology for the sake of doxology.* At this point we see the weakness of *soterian* presentations, which can so heavily focus on personal salvation at the expense of Christology. Jesus can quickly be seen merely as a doctor of the soul who deserves our thanks rather than the King of kings who warrants our lifelong allegiance.

In order to understand the gospel at a heart level, we must first see God as worthy of all honor (see Gen 1).[99] He becomes the measure of all honor, the standard of morality, and the source of delight. It is only in this context—the presence of God—that we understand shame, thus the wretched wrongness of sin. Therefore, the real starting point of the gospel is recognizing *who* God is in Christ.

This opinion is not always accepted or emphasized by others. For instance, it is often said that we should talk long on judgment so that people might grasp the significance of God's grace.[100] However, this approach may undermine the underlying goal of the gospel. By depicting the gospel primarily as the escape from judgment, one can subtly focus listeners' attention on themselves and "what they get." As a result, they easily but mistakenly see Christ as little more than a fix to their problem. In this respect, such presentations run the danger of leading people to honor God only inasmuch as they see God willing to honor them.

The most basic content of the gospel answers the question "Who is Christ?" or "Who is God?" John Piper captures the point this way: "God is the gospel."[101] The goal of the gospel is to glorify God. It is sometimes called "the gospel of the glory of the blessed God" (1 Tim 1:11) and "the gospel of the glory of Christ" (2 Cor 4:4). Thus, the gospel above all aims to show the worth and greatness of God. Indeed this is the ultimate goal of God himself.[102] Many people would no doubt agree that God wants glory (even if they do not rank this as God's highest priority). One might say this is an obvious assumption. Yet there is a possible problem with assuming that God's glory is central. One tends to forget how much God's glory matters for theological thinking and practice. We become like fish that have little or no awe of the grandeur of the ocean, awakened only briefly by the realization that we might be removed from it.

Notice how Scripture talks about the human problem (i.e., what we mean when we say "sin"). Genesis, for example, does not start with human sin. Rather, Genesis 1–2 establishes a God-centered context by which we see God as Creator and King. Humans bear his image. Only then does the fall of humanity in Genesis 3 make sense. Paul likewise talks about the human condition. In Romans 1 he makes no mention of "law" or "sin." Rather, he describes human "unrighteousness" in this way: "They did not honor him as God or give thanks to him," they "exchanged the glory of the immortal God for images resembling mortal man.... They exchanged the truth about God for a lie and worshiped and served the creature rather than the Creator," and "They did not see fit to acknowledge God" (Rom 1:21,23,25,28). Notice that Paul defines the human problem *with reference to God's honor*. God's own glory is the measure of human shame (see Rom 1:24–28). Romans 3:23 is perhaps the most famous verse about sin in the Bible. It is easy to forget that Paul defines sin in terms of God's glory: "For all have sinned and fall short of the glory of God."

Furthermore, one should not overlook Romans 2:23,24—"You who boast in the law dishonor God by breaking the law. For, as it is written, 'The name of God is blasphemed among the Gentiles because of you.'" The main verb of the sentence is "dishonor" (ἀτιμάζεις), not "breaking the law," which actually is a prepositional phrase (διὰ τῆς παραβάσεως τοῦ νόμου). Most fundamental to sin is the dishonoring of God; breaking God's law is just one expression of sin.[103] In short, we should preach long on the glory of God; only then will people understand the meaning of sin and the significance of salvation.

For the sake of clarification, one final point is worth repeating. In making known the knowledge of God, one should not think merely in abstract terms—with reference to his omniscience, oneness, holiness, eternity, etc. This is the standard way that the doctrine of God is taught in systematic theology classes. Instead, a better approach is to talk about the ways God reveals himself in history. How does God describe himself? He is often spoken of as the one "who made heaven and earth" (Ps 115:15; 124:8), the "God of Abraham" (2 Chron 30:6; cf. Neh 9:7), and "the God of Israel" (Ex 5:1; Ezek 8:4). God is the God who works in history. By speaking in this way, we also protect against making sin and salvation abstract or otherworldly. Sin is relational and God's people long to be resurrected with Christ, living in a new heaven and new earth (see Acts 24:15; Rom 8:17–24; 1 Cor 15:20–58; Rev 21:1).

What Has Christ Done?

God's actions flow from who he is. They reveal his character. It is insufficient to say what he has done if we misunderstand *who* he is. The phrase "He saved me" can have significantly different connotations depending on whether "He" refers to a firefighter, a doctor, my king, or my clan's longtime enemy. Likewise, "He died instead of me" does not sound the same in every circumstance. Perhaps I am talking about a patsy, one who is unjustly blamed on my behalf. Or, "he" happened to be at the place I was supposed to be, except I ran late on that particular day. Consequently he took my seat on the bus when it crashed. We judge a person's action and character in light of who he or she is. Does such a person have the right to act that way? How do other people in a similar position behave? Do we find anything typical or extraordinary?

Furthermore, what someone has done in the past provides a basis for believing what he will do in the future.[104] This premise grounds Paul's point repeated in Romans 5:6–10.

> For while we were still weak, at the right time Christ died for the ungodly. For one will scarcely die for a righteous person—though perhaps for a good person one would dare even to die—but God shows his love for us in that while we were still sinners, Christ died for us. Since, therefore, we have now been justified by his blood, much more shall we be saved by him from the wrath of God. For if while we were enemies we were reconciled to God by the death of his Son, much more, now that we are reconciled, shall we be saved by his life.

In Hosea, God's actions reveal the kind of relationship he has with his people: "When Israel was a child, I loved him, and out of Egypt I called my son" (Hos 11:1). The Lord continues by recounting the way he has loved his people. The text makes clear who God is so that people can clearly see their own shame (Hos 11:1–12; 13:4,5; cf. Amos 2:9–11). If we want our listeners to glorify and love God, grasp the weight of sin and salvation, and so have faith in the promises of God, then our gospel presentations will recall the works of God in history. If people do not think God is trustworthy, then his promises will not sound like good news.

Why Is Christ Important?

Why does this message about Christ matter? This question needs little elaboration since theologians and pastors traditionally lay the greatest stress on this topic. In a word, the gospel is the message by which sinners are saved. Naturally, evangelism in its fullest sense requires we talk about sin in some form or fashion. This story is not complete without making clear God's reaction to sin.

God's response takes two forms. On the one hand, God will judge a sinful world. As Paul says, there will be a "day when, according to my gospel, God judges the secrets of men by Christ Jesus" (Rom 2:16). In Revelation 14:6,7, when the angel proclaims the gospel, he announces God's judgment:

Then I saw another angel flying directly overhead, with an eternal gospel to proclaim to those who dwell on earth, to every nation and tribe and language and people. And he said with a loud voice, "Fear God and give him glory, because the hour of his judgment has come, and worship him who made heaven and earth, the sea and the springs of water."

On the other hand, judgment has a positive side. In judging his enemies, God brings salvation to his people and righteousness to the earth. Accordingly, Isaiah writes,

Shower, O heavens, from above, and let the clouds rain down righteousness; let the earth open, that salvation and righteousness may bear fruit; let the earth cause them both to sprout; I the LORD have created it. Woe to him who strives with him who formed him, a pot among earthen pots! Does the clay say to him who forms it, "What are you making?" or "Your work has no handles"? (Isa 45:8,9)

In fact, the entire Bible reveals this pattern whereby God brings salvation through judgment.[105]

63

Although the gospel means "good news," it is not always evident to people why it is *good* news. One should recall that different things might sound good in one culture yet go unnoticed in another context. This fact does not make the gospel less "good." This dynamic prods us to consider how we can adjust our gospel presentations. We desire for people to see *all* that is good in the gospel. However, this takes time. Thus, we must take steps so that people can see, as much as is possible, what is good in this news. By drawing from the entire Bible, not simply our favorite texts, we gain a balanced perspective on salvation. By not developing a "canon within a canon," one identifies the major themes or motifs that God uses to explain salvation.

We do not want to confuse what is most central with what is a true but less emphasized blessing. For example, God will ultimately heal our broken bodies, yet laying stress on physical healings is not the most common way the biblical writers talk about salvation. By majoring on what is a minor theme, one can mislead people concerning the essence of salvation. A more prominent way of speaking about salvation is to speak about glory and shame. Christ is the "hope of glory" (Col 1:27). He will bring "many sons to glory" (Heb 2:10), for all who believe in him "will not be put to shame" (1 Pet 2:6,7; citing Isa 28:16). This language echoes the psalmist, "On God rests my salvation and my glory; my mighty rock, my refuge is God" (Ps 62:7).[106]

How Should We Respond?

The gospel is not mere information; it is a command. Evangelicals rightly emphasize the point that the gospel necessitates a response. This is one of the strength's of Gilbert's book. Paul proclaims in Lystra, "We also are men, of like nature with you, and we bring you good news, that you should turn from these vain things to a living God" (Acts 14:15). Jesus himself preached, "The time is fulfilled, and the kingdom of God is at hand; repent and believe in the gospel" (Mark 1:15). In some places we find that people should "obey the gospel" (Rom 10:16; 2 Thess 1:8; 1 Pet 4:17). Thus, a few expressions are used to convey humanity's appropriate response to the gospel. These include faith, repentance, and obedience.

One should not confuse the gospel and the response. Gilbert and DeYoung make a critical logical mistake when discussing Mark 1:15.

It is wrong to say that the gospel is the declaration that the kingdom of God has come. The gospel of the kingdom is the declaration of the kingdom of God *together with the means of entering it*. Remember, Jesus did not preach "the kingdom of God is at hand." He preached, "The kingdom of God is at hand; therefore repent and believe!"[107]

They misquote the end of the verse by omitting the last phrase in the verse. It should say, "repent and believe *the gospel*." One can see the point well enough. If they had included Jesus' final phrase "the gospel," their argument would clearly be shown mistaken. The *content* of the gospel and the *response* to the gospel are inherently separate ideas and should not be collapsed into one. Even if they are integrally related, the words and grammar prove the distinction.

Gilbert and DeYoung assert that the gospel itself *includes* the fact that we are saved if we respond with faith and repentance. However, this understanding makes no sense of the text. If this is Jesus' meaning, then he commands something like this: "repent and believe *that* you can repent and believe the truth *that* you can repent and believe. . . ."[108] The content of the gospel is distinct from our response to that content. If we must believe the gospel, yet that gospel is a conditional statement wherein we are to believe the gospel, we end up with a vicious cycle. More precisely, the "gospel," as the Bible uses the word, is not a "how-to" concept expressed in the form of a conditional sentence (i.e., "If . . . then . . ."); rather it is a declaration that implies a command.[109]

The Gospel in the Biblical Context

How does the Bible answer these four questions? This section summarizes and highlights the range of possible answers found within Scripture. An important point will be reinforced: these four questions are not arbitrary. They arise directly from texts that most explicitly discuss the "gospel." Given the breadth of texts and themes, a thorough exegesis of every relevant passage is impossible. Still, one should intentionally observe passages that use explicit gospel language. By necessity, we need to reexamine a number of verses already discussed in the last chapter. At first, readers may think I'm being redundant. However, this chapter looks at the same verses from a different perspective. Previously, we identified the themes that *frame* the gospel. We here have a more specific task in understanding the content that explains the gospel's significance.

We begin with a summary statement of the gospel. The gospel is the good news that God has accomplished his creation purposes by fulfilling his promises given through Israel. In particular, the gospel narrates how God reigns over all nations through Jesus Christ, who was crucified for human sin. Yet God raised Christ from the dead, thus defeating his enemies, the last being death. As a result, Jesus reconciles us to God the Father by redeeming us from slavery to sin, which is any idolatrous power that corrupts our desires and condemns us to everlasting shame. God will recreate the world in which the human family receives, reveals, and rejoices in God's glory. In response, God commands all nations to repent of their rebellion. Any who give their allegiance to Christ will not be put to shame.

The apostles did not have a set formula to suit every person in any circumstance. We share one gospel but use a variety of methods, stories, themes, and expressions. Among Jews and God-fearing Gentiles, Paul highlights the gospel's more explicit "Jewish" elements. These include the Abrahamic covenant and the promise that David would have a descendant rule forever over the nations. However, among those Gentiles who were not sympathetic to Judaism, Paul takes a different approach, yet without changing the basic elements of the gospel. The book of Acts explicitly tells us that Paul preached the gospel in Lystra, Athens, and elsewhere (see Acts 14:15,21; 17:18).

The Bible gives a number of complementary answers to each of the four key questions. One may use a variety of metaphors and stories to make the gospel clear for different listeners. Listed below is one biblically faithful way to answer these questions. They are also easy to remember.

1. God through Christ *reigns* over all nations.
2. God *resurrected* Christ, who died for human sin.
3. God through Christ *reconciles* humanity's relationship with God, with each other, and with the world.
4. All people from every nation are commanded to *repent* and give their loyalty to Christ as the supreme and saving King of the world.

The point must be reemphasized: these statements make up one brief outline of many possible answers. The person who shares the gospel must explain what these words mean. Listeners may not share the speaker's cultural, religious, or educational background. One cannot assume others understand the words and concepts being used.

By using a certain set of themes and verses, this does not imply that we deny the validity of other concepts or texts. One desires to be both faithful to the Bible and clear for our friends. There are other possible ways of explaining the gospel of salvation. For example, consider the question "Who is Christ?" At the heart of the question is the "who" that deserves our loyalty. The Bible gives a number of answers. God is Creator, King, Father, Shepherd, Master, Savior, and Husband to his people. The key idea highlighted here is God's supremacy. He is the highest authority, who sovereignly rules over all things with love, wisdom, and righteousness. God created the world to be a kingdom in which he manifests his own glory. Thus, humans, whom he created to reflect his rule over all things, will forever worship him.

Who Is Christ in Scripture?

What gospel texts answer the "who" question? We begin with Romans 1:1–5, which states that the

> gospel . . . concern[s] his Son, who was descended from David according to the flesh and was declared to be the Son of God in power according to the Spirit of holiness by his resurrection from the dead, Jesus Christ our Lord, through whom we have received grace and apostleship to bring about the obedience of faith for the sake of his name among all the nations.

It is not a side issue that Jesus is David's son, as evidenced by Paul's choice of emphasis when he succinctly recalls the gospel in 2 Timothy 2:8, "Remember Jesus Christ, risen from the dead, the offspring of David, as preached in my gospel." Michael Bird links the "who" and the "what" questions: "Yet, whereas 1 Corinthians 15:3–5 focuses on the *work* of Christ as the key ingredient of the gospel, Romans 1:3–5 centres on the *identity* of Jesus Christ as the content of the gospel."[110] Martin Luther similarly states the gospel in this way: "The gospel is a story about Christ, God's and David's Son, who dies and was raised and is established as Lord. This is the gospel in a nutshell."[111]

As previously observed, Paul later equates the statement "Jesus is Lord" with the gospel in Romans 10:9,14–17 (cf. Acts 10:36; 1 Cor 12:3; Phil 2:11). The apostles "did not cease teaching and preaching (εὐαγγελιζόμενοι) that the Christ is Jesus" (Acts 5:42). One sees a consistent pattern whereby an apostle's core message is summarized by the point, "Jesus is the Christ" (John 20:31; cf. Acts 3:20; 9:22; 17:3,7; 18:5,28). In 1 Corinthians 15, "the gospel [Paul] preached" explains that "Christ" is the "last Adam" who reigns as King over his enemies (1 Cor 15:1,3,20–28,45). Also, when Paul speaks of the "gospel [preached] beforehand to Abraham," he then proceeds to make the point that Jesus was the offspring through whom the Gentiles would be blessed (Gal 3:8,14,16). Put succinctly, the gospel announces that Jesus is the Christ, David's son, Israel's King, thus the Son of God (see John 1:49).

In the Old Testament we see a similar pattern where the words for "gospel" and "to announce the gospel" aim to highlight *who* God is. Isaiah 52:7 proclaims, "Your God reigns." God is King. Similarly Isaiah 40:9 declares concerning the Lord, "Behold your God!" In context, Isaiah proclaims that the "Lord GOD" (הֹוִהְי יָנָדְא) reigns over the earth as Creator because He defeats "the rulers of the earth" (Isa 40:10–42:9). The resounding echo throughout the rest of Isaiah (esp. chs. 40–52) is that the Creator God is King; earthly kings and their idols are nothing. One of the most striking passages comes in Isaiah 41. God first warns Israel not to fear, "for I am your God" (41:10), who is the "the LORD ... the King of Jacob" (41:21). After giving proof that he alone is God (41:22–24), we hear that he "shall trample on rulers as on mortar" (41:25). Finally, in Isaiah 41:26,27 the message being "declared" (ἀναγγελεῖ, LXX) is called "good news" (i.e., gospel; רֵשַּׂבְמ).

Jesus applies to himself Isaiah 61:1, which describes the actions of a victorious king:

> The Spirit of the Lord GOD is upon me, because the LORD has anointed me to bring good news [רֵשַּׂבְל; εὐαγγελίσασθαι, LXX] to the poor; he has sent me to bind up the brokenhearted, to proclaim liberty to the captives, and the opening of the prison to those who are bound." (cf. Isa 60:6; Luke 4:18)

Thus, Isaiah 43:15 summarizes Isaiah's gospel pronouncements: "I am the LORD, your Holy One, the Creator of Israel, your King."

In the New Testament, Paul preaches Isaiah's gospel. In Acts 14:15, Paul cries out, "Men, why are you doing these things? We also are men, of like nature with you, and we bring you good news [εὐαγγελιζόμενοι], that you should turn from these vain things to a living God, who made the heaven and the earth and the sea and all that is in them." Acts 14:7,21 make explicit that Paul is "preach[ing] the gospel" (εὐαγγελιζόμενοι) concerning the "kingdom of God" (Acts 14:22; βασιλείαν τοῦ θεοῦ). Similarly, in Acts 17:24–31, his gospel announces that the Creator "commands all people everywhere to repent, because he has fixed a day on which he will judge the world [κρίνειν τὴν οἰκουμένην] in righteousness by a man whom he has appointed; and of this he has given assurance to all by raising him from the dead" (vv. 30,31).[112] Finally, Paul speaks about the Thessalonians' reaction to the "gospel" (1 Thess 1:5; 2:2,4,8): they "turned to God from idols to serve the living and true God" (1:9). In short, the gospel of Isaiah and Paul proclaims the one true God as King above every idol that would seek to rival him.

What Has Christ Done in Scripture?

What has God done in Christ? A number of things could be mentioned by way of summary. He keeps his covenant promises to bless all nations. Likewise God through Christ defeats his enemies, including demons, disease, and death. The historical events of Christ's life, death, resurrection, and ascension are of critical importance. One must not overlook the repeated emphasis in the gospel that God keeps his promises. The "gospel [was] promised beforehand through his prophets in the holy Scriptures" (Rom 1:1,2; cf. 1 Cor 15:3,4). Acts 13:32–34 is quite explicit:

And we bring you the good news [εὐαγγελιζόμεθα] that what God promised [ἐπαγγελίαν] to the fathers, this he has fulfilled to us their children by raising Jesus, as also it is written in the second Psalm, "You are my Son, today I have begotten you." And as for the fact that he raised him from the dead, no more to return to corruption, he has spoken in this way, "I will give you the holy and sure blessings of David."

An intriguing passage is Hebrews 4:1–6, where the Creator (v. 4) gives people "the promise of entering his rest" [v. 1; ἐπαγγελίας εἰσελθεῖν εἰς τὴν

κατάπαυσιν αὐτοῦ], which is called the "good news" in verse 2 [εὐηγγελισμέ-
νοι] and verse 6 [εὐαγγελισθέντες]. In Galatians 3:8 Paul says "the Scripture,
foreseeing that God would justify the Gentiles by faith, preached the gospel
beforehand [προευηγγελίσατο] to Abraham, saying, 'In you shall all the nations
be blessed.'" Paul cites the promise made to Abraham in Genesis 12:3, which
shapes all of redemptive history to follow. Afterwards, this gospel is repeatedly
referred to as the "promise" (Gal 3:14,16–19,21,22,29).[113]

Perhaps the most unmistakable feature of the biblical "gospel" is Christ's
resurrection from the dead. I have already been mentioned numerous passages
such as Acts 13:30–37; Romans 1:4; 1 Corinthians 15; and 2 Timothy 2:8. The
clear message of 1 Corinthians 15:20–28,54–57 is that Jesus' resurrection
marks the victory of God over sin and death. In Paul's most concentrated
treatment on the resurrection, this stands out as the defining achievement of
Christ's resurrection. Other passages worth mentioning include Acts 5:30,42;
10:36–40; and Romans 10:9,14–16. A full resurrection theology will not be
developed here. The emphasis on the resurrection of Christ is so pervasive
throughout the New Testament, especially in the preaching of Acts, that one
wonders how people could emphasize the death of Jesus at the expense of his
resurrection.[114] It is the exception that Christ's resurrection is *not* mentioned.

Biblical Answers to the "Why" and "How" Questions

There are countless ways one could explain why the gospel is significant. We
have all sinned. This means we dishonor God by rebelling against him. God
saves people from the shame and condemnation of sin. Christ redeems us
from slavery and adopts us as children. We also could mention other possible
themes, like glorification, re-creation, purification, and justification. Nations
will be reconciled with one another.[115] Ultimately God will create a new heaven
and new earth. There will be no more sin and death since God will bring judgment upon the world's evil, putting to shame anyone who will not respond
to him in faith. There is no inherent tension between the so-called "King
Jesus gospel" and a *soterian* message. Michael Bird gives a balanced summary:

> But merely stating that Jesus is king is an insufficient representation
> of the gospel if we do not point out how he has shown his kingly
> power in giving himself up for our sins and being raised by God

for our acquittal. The gospel is a royal announcement that God has become king in Jesus Christ and has expressed his saving sovereignty through the death and resurrection of the Son, which atones, justifies and reconciles. There is no gospel without the heralding of the king, and there is no gospel without atonement and resurrection.[116]

Since so much as been written on these various themes, I will not belabor the point here.

Multiple verses in Scripture have already been given to demonstrate a right response to the gospel. In short, sinners turn from all idolatry to the one true God. "Repentance" refers to a changing of one's mind or heart such that one's sense of value, honor/shame, and identity are changed. In addition, we could talk about faith, which necessarily expresses itself in works (see the book of James). Faith not only entails trust, it especially has the idea of loyalty. Simply put, we must be united to Christ with our head, heart, and hands. People must so identify with Jesus Christ that he and his people share in one another's life and death, honor and shame.

Towards a Cultural Contextualization

In this section, we first return to the discussion that opened the chapter. My purpose is simple. I want to illustrate how we might present the gospel in a *flexible* way without compromising what is firm or unchanging. The four above questions help bridge the gap between the ancient biblical text and our modern context. No doubt, some readers will want a more concrete explanation, just to be clear about what I am saying. After all, genuine contextualization speaks to specific circumstances. It is more than a set of abstract principles. Therefore, in later chapters I answer these four questions in more detail from a Chinese cultural perspective. For the moment, however, I briefly preview a few possible answers that are both faithful to Scripture and meaningful for a Chinese context.

Contextualization begins in those areas where the biblical context overlaps with the contemporary cultural context (See figure 4 below). One often talks about certain parts of culture in abstract terms like "collectivism," "honor/shame," "patronage," or cyclical vs. linear views of time. After all, no one today existed in the time Scripture was written. That distance creates an unavoidable degree of abstraction. The critical point at this stage becomes finding how we move from abstract categories to their concrete modern expressions.

For example, what is the "cultural language" of honor/shame in places like France, India, and China? Each setting has different ways of expressing views about what is praiseworthy, embarrassing, or humiliating. In terms of spoken words, one does not commonly talk about "honor" and "shame" as much as one uses words like "face" (e.g., 脸, 面子). Actions also speak symbolically. For example, Kipnis describes a historical Chinese context: "*Ketou* and bows were one of the major components of peasant subculture. Residents who wished to construct themselves as nonpeasants tried to avoid situations that required bows and *ketou*."[117]

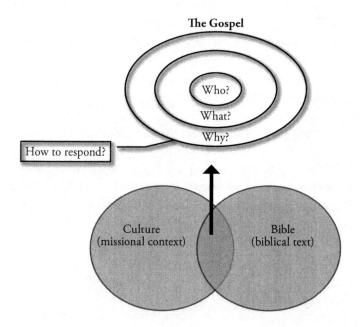

Figure 4: Gospel Presentations Answer Four Questions

We answer the four gospel questions by drawing from the areas where text overlaps context. Contextualizers use whatever cultural language best conveys the ideas needing to be expressed. Negatively, the four questions also provide a structure to explain the various "false gospels" that plague a local setting. Local cultures have functional gods and false ideologies that claim certain achievements and make promises. How are people supposed to respond to those idols in order to reap a benefit? Positively, these questions assist us in giving a holistic and meaningful gospel presentation.

I will very briefly highlight a few relevant ways of answering these questions in a Chinese context. How do we respond to the question, "Who is God?"? Who in Chinese culture receives people's highest praise and loyalty? We need to pay attention to these people as potential idols. In terms of position, such persons might include parents, teachers, politicians, and employers. Depending on the situation, we would positively affirm that God is a Father, King, and the Creator. Each of these answers naturally implies a particular range of metaphors, themes, and implications. One speaks differently within a familial setting than in a royal context. Various scholars have argued that the gospel, in the ancient world, would have been politically provocative.[118] Therefore, one might argue that in modern China a similar proclamation would be "Jesus is Chairman" (耶稣作主席).

What has God done through Christ? From a Chinese perspective, it is especially noteworthy that Jesus defeated death. The fear of death is so strong in China that people do not like to have phone numbers with the number four due to phonetics. The number four (四) sounds like the word for "death" (死). In defeating his enemies, Jesus retakes God's kingdom, which is occupied by human "imperialists." Jesus overcomes shame and is honored as King by his Father. Although God's children have made him lose face, nevertheless Jesus shows filial piety, ensuring that God will keep his promises. Accordingly, King Jesus vindicates the honor of his Father. The Creator's name will be perpetuated throughout the human family for all generations (cf. 传宗接代).

Why does this all matter? Jesus restores harmony to our fundamental relationships. God the Father is reconciled with the human family. Those who regard their ethnic group or nation to be at the center of human history (i.e., "middle kingdoms") will be humbled. Those who boast in their bloodline, traditions, or social status "will be put to shame." However, God honors all who give their allegiance to King Jesus just as the Father honors Christ (see John 17:22). As the head of the human family, Jesus endured human shame such that God's children now have a new hope—glorification.

How then are we to respond? We do not boast in self nor pursue our own face and fortune. In order to identify with Christ, we must share in his honor (before God) and shame (in the eyes of the world). It is only by forsaking other loyalties that one may come under the Father's name. We lose face in the eyes of others so that we may see and enjoy the glory of God's face. This implies practical obedience, which publicly manifests our honor for our King. Since God's children belong to one Father, they commit themselves to one another, seeking to faithfully represent his name in the world. Because humanity is a family, having the same origin, we cannot have any sense of cultural superiority or nationalism.

Conclusion

This chapter highlights a few critical elements within the contextualization process. First of all, we observed a range of ways the Bible talks about the gospel, being careful to interpret each passage according to its context. We need also to be aware of our own theological biases. Our individual traditions may give us correct answers to gospel questions. However, those explanations may not be the only nor even primary explanations in Scripture. Accordingly, it is important to slow oneself down when reading the Bible, starting with the most explicit texts before moving to less clear verses.

Throughout the Bible, gospel presentations typically answer four kinds of questions. One could give multiple answers to any one of these questions. They emerge from various texts and metaphors. Not surprisingly, different passages and cultures do not lay the same stress on every possible answer. A fruitful place to begin the contextualization process is the area of overlap between the biblical text and the cultural context. One steadily moves from the abstract to the concrete. In the end, we can express countless biblical ideas in any language by using a myriad of cultural images.

KEY POINTS

- To contextualize the gospel like Paul and others, we must interpret the Bible the way they did.
- The gospel presentations in the Bible tend to answer four key questions, in the following priority order:
  - Who is Christ?
  - What does Christ do?
  - Why is Christ important?
  - How should people respond?
- When preaching the gospel, Christians traditionally mainly tend to focus on the third question, concerning salvation.
- The content of the gospel is distinct from our response to it.
- Jesus *reigns*, having *resurrected* from death, and now *reconciles* people to God. Therefore, all nations should *repent* and believe.
- A key to contextualization is finding out where the biblical text overlaps with the cultural context.
- Thus, one seeks to find cultural language, symbols, and concepts that answer these four questions in biblically faithful ways.

5

Perspective:
What Is an "Implicit Gospel"?

This chapter makes a critical contribution to the overall contextualization model being developed in the book. Contextualization brings the Bible and culture together. The previous chapters draw from the grand story of Scripture, distinguishing two types of themes inherent to the gospel message. Some themes *frame* while others *explain* the gospel. Therefore, our presentations can be both firm and flexible. What about the culture? Individuals and the cultures in which they live are always changing. It is this constant fluctuation that makes contextualization so challenging. Therefore, this chapter explains how culture influences the way we understand, communicate, and apply the gospel.

In sharing the gospel, we inevitably pass along certain ideas and values without realizing it. Whatever our intentions, we all preach an "implicit gospel." This "gospel" refers to the implicit message that gets communicated (even unconsciously) to one's listeners. What do our gospel presentations imply, even if the ideas are not expressly stated? Despite our efforts to emphasize a particular point, we still convey many other implicit ideas. Our implicit gospel message comes from a variety of cultural assumptions. These assumptions subtly influence our thinking. It is quite possible that our implicit message has a greater effect on people than does our explicit message.

Organizing Principles

Everyone makes sense of the world according to a certain set of ideas and principles. These "organizing principles" are the basic categories of thought that help us get along in daily life. This section mentions a few of these principles. I will then explain how these organizing principles determine the content of our implicit gospel. Readers are encouraged to consider how these principles have already influenced their own understanding of the gospel. By making these principles explicit, we can be more intentional in our effort to do contextualization.

I will mention five principles or categories that shape a cultural worldview. This list is not meant to be exhaustive. Rather, it is only meant to illustrate how our cultural ways of thinking influence our view of the gospel. Worldviews are complex. Other themes could be added to those listed here. I highlight these cultural categories by asking five questions:

1. What is the fundamental *unit of society?*
2. What is the basic *nature of the world?*
3. What determines a person's *identity?*
4. Who is the highest *authority?*
5. How do we think about *morality?*

People from different cultures tend to answer these questions in diverse ways. For the sake of illustration, I will limit the number of possible answers to each question. Admittedly, many of the cultural descriptions I will use are broad, if not stereotypical. This oversimplification is necessary so that we do not lose sight of the larger goal of understanding how culture shapes our view of the gospel. Our present purpose is not to engage in a thorough analysis of human cultures.

What do we regard as the fundamental unit of society? In Western cultures, people stereotypically emphasize the individual above the group. Accordingly, Westerners often stress the importance of equality and individual rights. Thomas Jefferson famously captures the individualistic spirit. In the United States Declaration of Independence, he states, "We hold these truths to be self-evident, that all men are created equal, that they are endowed by their Creator with certain unalienable Rights." By contrast, other cultures highlight the group above the individual. For example, Eastern cultures are frequently described as being "collectivistic." The interests of a group are more fundamental than those of any one person. Likewise, people naturally divide the world into two groups—"us" and "them." The boundaries that distinguish one from another might include ethnicity, nationality, caste, family name, and language, among others.

We bring these patterns of thinking to our study of the Bible. Consider your assumptions about Scripture. Does the Bible (and the gospel) primarily address individuals or nations? Evangelistic tracts today tend to focus on the individual, whether in their graphics or in their language. For example, gospel tracts routinely use the singular "you" or "I." Furthermore, consider how contemporary gospel presentations explain human sin. Frequently, extended attention is frequently given to two individuals, Adam and Eve. At a theological level, this makes sense (see Rom 5:12–21; 1 Cor 15:40–49). From an evangelistic perspective, however, there is no precedent for this in the New Testament. No biblical writer or speaker ever opens his gospel presentation by explaining the fall of Adam.

Given this lack of precedent, then it would be just as legitimate to use the Tower of Babel story (Gen 11) to illustrate the problem of sin in the world. Genesis 11 focuses more on "nations" than individuals. Genesis 11:4 highlights the motive of the people, "Then they said, 'Come, let us build ourselves a city and a tower with its top in the heavens, and let us make a name for ourselves, lest we be dispersed over the face of the whole earth.'" Collectivistic societies also tend to be honor/shame cultures. The people who built the Tower of Babel wanted to "make a name" for themselves. By gaining honor for themselves, they would preserve the unity and security of their group.

Second, we could ask, "What is the basic nature of the world?" Specifically, do people in a certain culture see the world as a *unity*? Or do they emphasize its *diversity*? This is a question about how to relate the parts and the whole. Chinese culture, for example, lays greater stress on unity and harmony. This can be seen in many prominent cultural themes and values, including *guanxi* ("relationship" or "connections"), mutual dependence, nationalism, and tradition. People generally prefer to blend in so as to avoid drawing unwanted attention to oneself. In many Western countries, people tend to see the world much differently. In cultures that emphasize diversity, we can expect to see people place greater value on personal independence, ambition, creativity, and risk taking.

The Bible presents the world both in terms of its unity and diversity. Christians are united "in Christ," belonging to Abraham's one family. Church discipline is necessary for maintaining order among God's people, who are called "the body of Christ." The entire world belongs to the Creator-King, who is also Father over the human family. Nevertheless there is diversity within this unity. Christ's body has many "members," with particular gifts and callings. Difference is inherent to humanity itself because we are made "male and female." Additionally, countless theological ideas, including the gospel, utilize a variety of metaphors to talk about God and what he has done in the world.

Third, how do people in different cultures determine their identity? On what basis do people see themselves in one group but not in another? One can think of at least two possibilities. Stereotypically, Westerners tend to define themselves more in terms of their differences. People don't like being confined to a "label." Young adults often strive to "be their own person" and not do what everyone else is doing. They want to be unique; thus, they act in certain ways and wear clothing that will cause them to stand out. Sports competitions and reality television shows provide more examples of people who want to draw attention to themselves for one reason or another. By contrast, those in traditional cultures often appeal to their commonalities. For example, they might share an ethnicity or come from the same village. Likewise one may be lumped into a group according to family name or gender.

We see similar dynamics in the Bible. For instance, the Jewish leaders distinguished determined identity according to ancestry. In John 8:39 they brush off Jesus' comments by claiming, "Abraham is our father." Jesus' reply also appeals to "fatherhood" though redefined.

> If you were Abraham's children, you would be doing the works Abraham did, but now you seek to kill me, a man who has told you the truth that I heard from God. This is not what Abraham did. You are doing the works your father did. . . . If God were your Father, you would love me, for I came from God and I am here. . . . You are of your father the devil, and your will is to do your father's desires. (John 8:39–44)

In Matthew 12:48–50 Jesus similarly redefines identity after hearing that his mother and brothers were looking for him. He says, "'Who is my mother, and who are my brothers?' And stretching out his hand toward his disciples, he said, 'Here are my mother and my brothers! For whoever does the will of my Father in heaven is my brother and sister and mother.'" Elsewhere he categorizes people as either being "of this world" or "not of this world" (John 8:23; cf. John 17:14–16).

Paul follows a similar pattern of determining identity. He regards people as belonging to either one of two types—believers "in Christ" and unbelievers "in Adam" (see Rom 5:12–21). Why do those in the church share a common identity? Ephesians 4:4–6 explains, "There is one body and one Spirit—just as you were called to the one hope that belongs to your call—one Lord, one faith, one baptism, one God and Father of all, who is over all and through all and in all." Likewise in Galatians 3:29 Paul summarizes, "And if you are Christ's, then you are Abraham's offspring, heirs according to promise."

Fourth, whom do we regard as having authority over us? This is a rather straightforward question. Different cultures and subcultures recognize a range of positions and titles. Fathers hold sway in every place but especially in cultures that emphasize filial piety. Teachers, employers, and judges yield power in their respective spheres. In particular settings, priests and witch doctors are revered almost like gods. In other contexts, cultural traditions and religious books (like the Qur'an) determine people's views of right and wrong, good and bad.

Finally, how do people think and talk about morality? Practically speaking, on what basis do people make ethical decisions? Law-oriented cultures often talk about guilt. Typically this describes people from Western cultures. They emphasize individuals' rights and are keen to avoid having a guilty conscience. A person's sense of guilt acts as a restraint against bad behavior.

Eastern cultures frequently utilize honor/shame language to discuss moral issues. A person may be criticized as having "no sense of shame" or "not wanting face." Appeals to "face" seek to nurture a sense of identity and reinforce group conformity. Group standards are decisive. "Face" indicates one's social status.

Other cultures could be described as having a "might makes right" mentality. For example, among certain tribal cultures, moral authority derives from one's power. People obey whoever inspires the most fear. Therefore, if people fear an evil spirit, then they will follow the commands of a local shaman or witch.

Tradition is an almost imperceptible authority in some places. Many people never call into question the correctness of a given tradition. Those in non-Western societies are less likely to challenge long-held beliefs than would most from Western cultures. Naturally, "tradition" may be a general "catch-all" term to sum up a number of ideas. Of course the categories mentioned above can have degrees of overlap. For example, ancestors may typify a group's honor and sense of identity. Some people may think ancestors have some sort of spiritual power. Therefore, one generation gives offerings to its dead ancestors. In some cultures, if people do not make sacrifices to their ancestors, then they lack filial piety. Accordingly, ancestor worship may be considered a moral action.

These five areas represent a few of the features that characterize a person's worldview. They are differing ways by which people categorize their experience. I have called them "organizing principles" because they implicitly organize our worldviews. They shape everything from the way we understand life to the manner in which we tell a story. Naturally this has implications for preaching the gospel.

Why does all this matter when it comes to contextualization? In any gospel presentation, we decide consciously or unconsciously what ideas we will emphasize. Our stories always have a perspective from which they are told. Perhaps one kind of presentation will highlight the following combination of elements: the individual, the world's diversity, God as judge, our differences, and law or guilt. This is simply one possible combination among many.

In order to realize the implications of what has been said, first remember that I have greatly oversimplified an infinitely complex dynamic by only listing five cultural categories. Each of these categories contains multiple subdescriptions. For example, with respect to identity, people may stress similarities or differences. Among authority figures, we mentioned fathers, judges, teachers, and others. For the sake of illustration, let me limit the amount of possible options. Assume that we limit "authority" to three subcategories (king, father, judge), "morality" to four choices (law, honor/shame, power, tradition), while the others are restricted to only two options. When you do the calculations, *there are a total number of ninety-six possible combinations!*

Don't get lost in the math—consider what this means. Depending on which cultural categories one uses to tell the gospel story, there are ninety-six different ways to organize the presentation. The way we choose to tell the story is what I have called our "implicit gospel." Even though we have grossly oversimplified cultural conditions, there are almost a hundred possible "implicit gospels" that we could preach. A hundred people may share the same theology; yet, because they emphasize a range of contrasting themes and metaphors, their message can sound quite different.

This phenomenon is easily understood if we think of popular movies and books. Stories have a plot, setting, and characters. Certain essential elements frame a story and so distinguish it from other stories. These features determine its key twists, transitions, subplots, and climax. Take, for example, Shakespeare's *Romeo and Juliet*. The play tells of the romance between two young "star-crossed lovers." Because of the conflict inherent to the story, they both tragically commit suicide. Popular movies like *Farewell My Concubine* and *Titanic* have similar elements in their stories. These romantic dramas also are full of turmoil where the relationship between lovers requires crossing social boundaries yet culminates in death. Despite their similarities, we could not casually retell their stories as if they were one and the same. They are very different stories. The writers use a variety of different principles to organize each narrative. Likewise, George Lucas' *Star Wars* movies tell us about a wide-scale civil war, but this doesn't mean the story is virtually equivalent to other movies about civil war, like *Gone with the Wind*, *The Founding of the Republic*, or *Glory*.

The Gospel and Our Implicit Worldviews

Why do I give these examples? It is because the gospel presents a story, thus a worldview. The gospel speaks of a fresh hope for humanity. It puts forth a worldview that rivals the prevailing norms of the broader culture. The biblical gospel narrates an alternative metanarrative for the entire world. This is the story around which biblical theology is concerned. This meta-story orders the various themes' connotations and emphases.

As seen in the previous chapters, the Bible uses a particular set of themes to frame the gospel. This good news has a distinctive plot that binds a multitude of biblical themes. The gospel's framework themes give structure to the story. Various motifs further illuminate the significance of the message. The themes we use in contextualization only have their intended meaning as they properly attach to the gospel's theological framework. Our story should in some way or another portray how the Creator God through Jesus Christ fulfilled his historical covenants to unite the world and ascend to the throne. God sets the world right, restoring the human family. This account involves specific historical events and points of emphasis. This story is not an abstraction, a philosophy separated from history.

What happens if we are not mindful of the "organizing principles" that shape our gospel presentations? Unwittingly we may tell a very different story than the one we consciously imagine. Our message itself may not necessarily be false. It may be full of right facts and doctrines. However, the way we organize the story could perhaps obscure or distort the gospel's own emphases.

Compare two ways of telling the gospel story. Let us first imagine a person who assumes that the gospel is primarily a set of ideas explaining how an individual can go to heaven. He also thinks the two main themes that frame the message are "law" and "God's love." Now imagine a second set of organizing themes. In this case, the gospel is presented as the story wherein God (as King) defeats his enemies, rescuing the human family (collective identity). He not only restores harmony to creation (unity); in addition, he glorifies himself and takes away human shame. What will listeners potentially hear from these two very different presentations? What might go unheard? What if we intentionally considered how to use those categories that are implicit to a culture? The way we organize our message has important implications. If we want our contextualizations to be faithful to Scripture and meaningful for a local culture, we will pay close attention to "organizing principles."

Syncretism emerges whenever we do not account for culture's influence. Denominational and organizational subcultures likewise have their own set of principles by which people divide and assess the world. As many have said, worldviews are more of something we *look through*, rather something we *look at*. No wonder it can be difficult to intentionally shape our worldview lenses in order to do contextualization.

KEY POINTS

- We all have a worldview from which we understand and explain our lives and the world around us.
- We all have basic assumptions and ways of thinking that help us make sense of the world. These constitute "organizing principles."
- "Organizing principles" could include elements like the fundamental nature of the world, human identity, and our views on authority and morality.
- Whenever we tell a story, such as the gospel, we implicitly use certain organizing principles. These principles provide a framework for our stories.
- The organizing principles we use will determine our "implicit" gospel.
- An "implicit gospel" is the message we indirectly communicate to others when preaching the gospel. Thus, our *implicit* gospel may have greater influence than the message we *explicitly* intend to tell.
- We need to consciously consider the influence of cultural organizing principles on our contextualization, whether at the level of interpretation or communication.

6

Process:
How Do We Move from
Biblical Text to Cultural
Context?

This chapter brings together all that has been covered so far in the book. Having discussed the various pieces of contextualization, we now need to take a few steps back and ask, "What do we do now?" How do we lift contextualization off the pages of the academic journal so that it influences people in real cultures? In what follows, I will suggest a model that can help people put theory into practice. In order to contextualize the gospel well, we have to understand how to integrate the various aspects of contextualization together.

It is not enough to say that Bible and culture are both important. Therefore, I begin by illustrating how exactly they interrelate. We can then understand the balance between them. Within contextualization, some components are firm and unchanging. Some aspects are flexible. Other parts are always fluctuating (i.e., those coming from contemporary culture).

The chapter then details a process or sequence that helps people contextualize the gospel in any culture. The model is a guide. It is not a formula that people can apply for quick and easy results. Contextualization seeks to express the gospel holistically. It begins with interpretation and biblical theology but always has in mind broader applications. The process requires creativity and integration. Therefore, it is best applied in cooperative dialogue with others. The model suggested here has a particular goal: produce contextualizations that are both faithful to Scripture and meaningful for a local culture.

Contextualization That Is Firm, Flexible, and Fluctuating

First of all, we should clarify the relationship between the gospel, other related theological topics, and culture. The purpose is twofold. On the one hand, we want to avoid *cultural* syncretism. We need to make sure contemporary culture does not trump Scripture when it comes to theology and evangelism. On the other hand, we also want to avoid more subtle problems like *theological* syncretism and "settling for truth." These problems were discussed in previous chapters. Even though we wish to affirm all biblical truths, we attempt to hold them in proper balance, consistent with the entire context of Scripture.

A contextualization model should be both *firm* and *flexible*. The gospel does not change, yet people in Scripture clearly use a variety of expressions to preach the gospel. As we saw earlier, there are consistent elements that distinguish gospel presentations. Moreover, our model should equip people to adjust their evangelistic approach according to the needs of a certain context. Cultures are always *fluctuating*. Any culture that is not in the midst of change is already dead. Cultures that are not in constant flux are suitable only for history books. If we only contrast the firmness of the Scripture with the fluctuations of culture, we will constantly struggle to grasp contextualization. Therefore, it is critical that we differentiate within the gospel itself *both* its firm and flexible elements. The threefold distinction (firm, flexible, and fluctuating) makes contextualization possible.

Figure 5: Contextualization Wheel: Framework, Themes, and Culture

Let me offer an analogy. Consider how a wheel makes a vehicle move forward. The wheel itself has two major parts—a rim and the rubber. The rim is firm; it gives the wheel its strength and shape. Lose the rim and you lose the wheel. The rim is the essential framework. The wheel's rubber fits around the rim. Rubber is flexible but only to a limit. There are inherent qualities to tire rubber such that we can't simple make it out of anything we want. I can't throw sugar and dirt together and expect to have rubber for a tire. Nevertheless there is some flexibility to how one can design the particular rubber on a wheel. Various designs are meant to fit different environments, whether hot, cold, mountainous, or flat pavement. Finally, there is the road. There is little that is constant about roads except that they always change. For example, drivers come across holes, curves, water, and hills. Also, the substance of the road itself can change! Tires respond differently to concrete, tar, gravel, mud, and sand.

Framework
("rim")

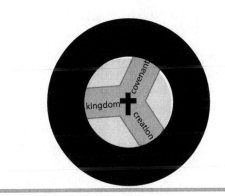

Figure 6: Framework Themes

The wheel analogy illustrates the major components of a gospel presentation. There are firm and flexible elements to the message we share. Yet that message must connect with the ever-fluctuating conditions of the culture. Earlier we saw that gospel presentations in the Bible have a *firm* framework. This is comparable to the wheel rim. The themes of creation, covenant, and kingdom consistently frame the message.

Themes
("rubber")

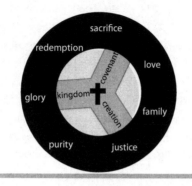

Figure 7: Explanatory Themes

Within that standard context, evangelists show *flexibility* in choosing theological ideas that explain the significance of the gospel. These motifs are analogous to the wheel rubber, which depends on the rim. These may include curse/blessing, honor/shame, redemption, justification, adoption, sacrifice, unity, law, and others. Emphasizing one theme does not mean minimizing the importance of another idea. Likewise, if a person's presentation does not mention justification or the sacrificial system, this in itself does not mean he or she denies those doctrines. We can draw an analogy. If a father tells his daughter that she did well on her math test, this does not imply that he thinks his son did poorly. Similarly, no one would ever accuse Paul of denying the Law's curse (see Gal 3) because he was silent about it in Lystra or Athens.

Problems emerge when one treats the rubber as a rim. That is, although many themes in some way belong to the gospel, they have distinct roles. They tell different parts of the biblical story. What happens, for example, if we treat the Mosaic Law as a framework (rim wheel) issue? One possibility is this: we will make all other issues revolve around that one single topic. As a result, other themes are regarded as less central or critical for a gospel presentation. We will regard someone's presentation as faithful so long as he or she ultimately arrives at that particular motif. Additionally, we might feel compelled to use themes that are too unfamiliar for unbelieving listeners. Although we want them eventually to know the entire Bible, we may need to choose another theme as a starting point in order to help them grasp our message. However, if we confuse the rubber and the rim, we may attempt to use a certain motif prematurely, before a listener can understand our meaning.

There is another possible consequence. One might quickly recognize that issues like circumcision and Sabbath keeping are no concern to non-Jews. Therefore, in order to discern the Law's relevance for Gentiles, we then might overgeneralize certain passages, such as Paul's discussions in Romans and Galatians. We begin to speak as if Paul were actually talking about a universal human law and not specifically the Jewish Law. Thus, our seemingly minor reorientation of themes sets us on a new trajectory, which has implications for theology and application.

Figure 8: A Firm, Flexible, and Fluctuating Model

The evangelists' audience greatly influenced the themes they used. Local conditions *fluctuated* (comparable to the road in the above analogy). From place to place, people had varying degrees of familiarity with Jewish teaching. Adjustments could also be made for people's education level and religious background (as in Acts 17). One can only imagine the reaction if Paul had quoted Greek philosophers in Jerusalem synagogues or cited the Abrahamic covenant (cf. Gal 3:8) when preaching at the Areopagus in Athens. Instead, what does Paul do when he could not directly appeal to the Abrahamic, Mosaic, or Davidic covenants? He uses a creation framework (Acts 14:15–17; 17:22–31), perhaps with shades of kingdom language (see 14:22; 17:31). The "rubber" around this "rim" included idolatry, offspring, the fatherhood of God, and righteousness (see 17:23,27–31).

One more analogy will suffice to explain the relationship between framework themes, explanatory themes, and culture. A contextualized gospel is like a Ferris wheel. (See Fig. 9) It has a stable framework and a rotating wheel with seats for passengers. The entire structure represents the gospel. Although it has mobile parts, the Ferris wheel (i.e., gospel) does not inherently change. In fact, the rotating wheel is essential to its nature as a Ferris wheel. The surrounding environment represents any culture in which we preach the gospel. The different seats represent particular points from which we understand the gospel and the surrounding culture. Our perspective on both may at times fluctuate. Likewise the cultural context may undergo changes. Nevertheless the gospel remains firm and flexible.

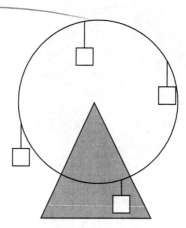

Figure 9: Ferris Wheel

THE PROCESS OF CONTEXTUALIZATION

How do we synthesize all this information into a practical model for doing contextualization? Our observations from previous chapters suggest a certain process. The first few chapters show us where to begin and what to avoid.

In chapter 1 we saw that biblical interpretation is the foundational starting point for contextualization. In other words, we cannot immediately assume that a conventional formulation of doctrine is the best starting point for contextualizing the gospel. After all, we must account for multiple contexts that influence the text's original meaning, a reader's interpretation, and its significance for the contemporary culture.

Chapter 2 warned us against a subtle habit of mind that undermines good contextualization. Deciding between right from wrong doctrines is insufficient. We need also to discern the major and minor points within the particular biblical context. Therefore, our model will need to include measures to hold in check the tendency to read one's own (sub)culture back into the ancient text. Specifically, the contextualization process begins with biblical theology rather than systematic theology. That is, we intentionally test our theological conclusions against the backdrop of the grand biblical narrative. A broad view of the entire biblical context is critical for establishing our boundaries and making connections between themes.

The next three chapters surveyed the major components of a contextualized gospel. Chapter 3 highlighted a pattern across the many gospel presentations in the Bible. They have a firm framework, which consists of three themes—creation, covenant, and kingdom. In chapter 4 we noted that evangelistic messages give priority to answering a distinct set of questions (Who? What?, Why?, How?). Although bound by Scripture, one still has a good deal of flexibility in deciding which answers to give. The fifth chapter reminded us that we all have a relative perspective on absolute truth. Cultural and personal backgrounds thus filter our perception of biblical truth. Although we cannot entirely set aside our worldview lens, we can certainly try to broaden our perspective. Therefore, the following model challenges people to be intentional in deciding what lenses they will use. Our gospel presentations should be framed by biblical theology and shaped by our contextual perspective.

The following section explains four stages in the contextualization process. They include:

Stage One: *Identify* Biblical Themes
Stage Two: *Interconnect* Cultural Themes
Stage Three: *Interpret* Biblical Meaning
Stage Four: *Infer* Cultural Significance

Chapters 3–5 began to demonstrate the first two stages. Chapters 7–8 will give examples of what it might look like to complete the last two stages. For ease of memory, there are two built-in memory devices. First, each stage begins with an action starting with the letter *I*. Second, the object being focused on alternates between the Bible and culture.

The first two stages attempt to identify and interconnect key themes within the Bible and a particular culture. Completing these stages requires a great deal of familiarity with both. Of course one does not expect new missionaries or new Christians to single-handedly formulate a fully contextualized gospel presentation. On the other hand, even people with long-term experience may never have given thorough reflection on certain aspects of Scripture or culture. In reality, contextualization inherently is not a one-person task. In any case, contextualization is the fruit of much prayer, study, experience, dialogue and, no doubt, failure. All this is to say that these stages are not only foundational, they are also labor intensive. We (with our ministry partners) need great breadth and depth of knowledge in order to find the interconnections between these two contexts.

Identify Biblical Themes (Stage One)

What is the end goal of stage one? *We want to identify how the Bible frames and explains the gospel.* The gospel tells a specific story with a particular plot. In stage one we study the Bible to discern what sort of flexibility we have in presenting this story.

From the start, our model takes measures so that contemporary culture doesn't subtly creep into and distort our understanding of God's revelation. This stage in the process makes a key contribution to the contextualization process. Specifically, it helps us determine the organizing principles that we can use (discussed in ch. 5). After all, on the surface we have no way to differentiate one cultural vantage point from another. Thus, this stage tempers or regulates the influence of our culture. Accordingly, we begin by examining the Scripture.

Later we can consider culture. First, we identify the gospel's framework as used in its original setting. Second, we will explore culture to discern the gospel's significance in a given context. Proceeding in this sequence is one way our model, at least to some degree, guards against cultural syncretism.

We first study the entirety of Scripture in order to grasp the coherency of the grand biblical story. Our goal is not mere familiarity; rather, we seek to identify the threads that unify the story. This is essentially the work of biblical theology. By reading broadly across the biblical text, we identify the essential framework for presenting the gospel. I have already argued for a threefold structure—creation, covenant, kingdom. In this interpretation process, we will see certain interconnections even between these three motifs. For the sake of clarity, I will call these "framework themes." There are also many concepts and images that explain the gospel's significance. I will call these "explanatory themes."

To accomplish our goal, we must give more than a half glance at the Israel story. So many contemporary gospel presentations give little attention to much—if not most—of the Old Testament. This is not the place to engage in a full defense of the Old Testament's value in gospel preaching; however, a few comments are necessary.

An objector might argue that modern-day "Gentiles" do not understand Jewish history and religion. Therefore, there is no need to overwhelm listeners with a lot of Old Testament background. One might even appeal to Paul's sermon in Lystra (Acts 14) or Athens (Acts 17) as proof. This objection fails to grasp a critical idea: the Old Testament is not mere background for the gospel; it belongs to the gospel. Galatians 3:8 (already discussed above) is clearly a case in point.

Furthermore, I don't think anyone argues that a modern unbeliever has to understand the entire Old Testament to become a Christian. Nevertheless we should take seriously how the Old Testament frames the gospel. Even Paul's sermon in Athens is thoroughly Jewish in that he immediately defends monotheism in an overwhelmingly polytheistic ancient world. In addition, we cannot ignore the fact that his letters to Gentiles rehearsed the gospel in thoroughly Jewish terms (see Romans, Galatians, Ephesians, etc.). The gospel is "in accordance with the Scriptures" (1 Cor 15:3,4; cf. Rom 1:1,2). All of Old Testament teaching centers on Christ (Luke 24:44). Thus, we need to so absorb the Old Testament story that it becomes, in effect, the only lens through which the gospel makes full sense to us. When we have done this, we can better guard against unbalanced interpretations arising from our theological, traditional, or cultural assumptions. The gospel is not an abstraction, a set of points removed from history.

We also need depth of understanding in order to discern how explanatory themes fit within the gospel framework. The "blessing" motif will suit a creation framework differently than it would within a kingdom setting. When talking about the Abrahamic covenant, one is more likely to talk about "all nations," "circumcision," and "justification" than various other topics. Similarly, we might want to know how "righteousness" relates to God as Creator on the one hand and Israel's covenant God on the other. The further we take a concept outside of its natural biblical context, the more likely we are to misuse it by giving it some emphasis foreign to its original meaning. In other words, we want the ability to move seamlessly from one theme to another. Accordingly, our explanation of the gospel will not sound overly systematic or formulaic. Ideally listeners will discern the gospel's inner coherency through the flow of our presentation.

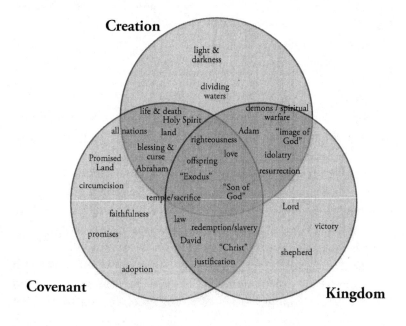

Figure 10: Three Biblical Circles

I anticipate some readers may feel a bit intimidated or overwhelmed when thinking about achieving this kind of biblical or cultural fluency. One must not forget that we are not talking about a static goal. By its very nature, the process of contextualization is ongoing. Previous ideas are revised, reinforced, or even rejected after further reflection. Culture constantly changes. Also, our personal understanding of the Bible and culture grows over time. Out of love for God, a Christian constantly seeks to deepen his or her understanding of God's revealed Word. Even so, being aware of what is needed for contextualization can help us be more intentional about how and what we study.

The graph left demonstrates one way that interpreters might relate explanatory themes within a gospel framework. The graph reminds us once again that all of these ideas help us understand the gospel. However, they connect to one another in distinctive ways that tell one kind of story rather than another. For example, the Bible sometimes uses shepherd imagery to describe a king. The "image of God" language, in its ancient biblical context, carries connotations especially associated with creation and kingship. Moreover, biblical writers often mention the Spirit in contexts related to both creation and covenant.

Some people may not like the above visual with its overlapping circles. Therefore, I have also included the graph below. If preferred, the same information could be written using columns and rows.

	Kingdom	Creation	Covenant
Light & Darkness		X	
Circumcision			X
Justification	X		X
All nations		X	X
Offspring	X	X	X

Figure 11: Kingdom, Covenant, and Creation

Interconnect Cultural Themes (Stage Two)

How do our findings above connect to the cultures in which we live? Stage one identifies the biblical gospel's framework and explanatory themes. Stage two uses these themes as a lens for studying culture. Our goal is to interconnect the biblical text and the cultural context. Our model allows us to identify thematic parallels between the two. We seek to find which *cultural* themes faithfully frame and explain a biblical gospel *presentation*.

Before overlaying the ancient and modern contexts together, we should first observe what is accomplished by working in this order—from biblical text to cultural context—in stages one and two. At an early point in the contextualization process, the Bible frames the agenda for what follows. How so? I list two ways. First, at the most fundamental level, the model establishes the grid through which to look at modern culture. That automatically gives a certain priority to Scripture in that it directs our focus when looking at culture. Second, the model more easily allows Scripture to determine which ideas are firm and flexible. Ideally this is because the grand biblical narrative (biblical theology) precedes systematic theology as well as our cultural study (stage two).

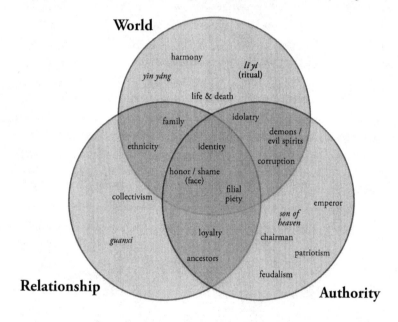

Figure 12: Three Chinese Circles

The graph above demonstrates one way to interconnect the themes of Scripture and culture. In order not to be abstract, I will use Chinese culture to serve as our specific context. Thus, "relationship" is a key cultural theme that captures a core idea in the covenant motif. The "world" may be a culturally clear way of talking about issues related to creation. Kingship obviously conveys the notion of "power" or "authority." In essence, relationship, authority, and the world become *framing ideas* for a contextualized gospel presentation in Chinese culture.

One can then identify an assortment of topics within these three macrothemes. Individuals will disagree about particular details and correlations. Still, the graph above can helpfully illustrate the process. Patriotism and the ancient concept of *tianzi* ("son of heaven") carry overtones related to authority and especially kingship. No doubt, there will be ambiguity and overlap in categorization. When this occurs, it is important that people discuss each idea's range of possible connotations. These are critical points of opportunity for us to gain understanding and more clearly communicate our intended meaning.

For instance, consider various Bible passages that concern covenant. In Romans and Galatians, some Jews misunderstood the Abrahamic and Mosaic covenants such that they thought Gentiles had to become Jewish to be fully acceptable to God. This idea naturally leads modern readers to discuss issues related to ethnicity and nationalism (even if it would be anachronistic to apply these terms back into ancient Israel). Since the one true God created the whole world, the doctrine of creation relativizes ethnocentrism or the sense of cultural superiority. However, notice what happens when one talks more about nationalism. There are increased overtones of national power that would more closely relate to authority and kingship.

Again, I have included an example of how one might organize the data from the circle diagram above in spreadsheet form.

	Authority / Power	World	Relationship
Harmony		X	
Collectivism			X
Loyalty	X		X
Ethnicity		X	X
Honor & Shame ("face")	X	X	X

Figure 13: Authority, Relationship, World

What about other topics with less clear parallels? For example, what if Marxism has influenced a particular culture? How should this element of the culture influence the cultural lens being developing in stage two? The question is especially important. If we do not know what to do, then one might unwittingly switch the order of stages one and two. In order to address the influence of Marxism, people could easily but mistakenly think that they should begin with Marxist culture rather than the Bible. Regardless of someone's intention, Marxism in fact might determine the framework of his or her gospel presentation.

We should instead consider the underlying concerns addressed within Marxist thought. For example, consider the goal of alleviating class distinctions. This theme could be placed within the "relationship" (cf. covenant) and/or "world" (cf. creation) circles. The Law established and/or highlights all sorts of social distinctions. Those with bodily ailments and handicaps did not enjoy the same opportunities given to priests. Israel had certain privileges not given to other nations. Many Jews in the New Testament misunderstood Israel's election as a nation and used it to exclude Gentiles. In addition, whether rich or poor, we are all made in the image of God and share the same ancestral parents. Accordingly, people from every class are called to honor God, but they fall short of his glory.

Similarly, Marxist thinking concerns a particular ideal notion of the world. According to some, such an ideal is achieved through revolution. With respect to this theme, Christians offer an alternative vision for the world. God will create a new heaven and new earth, over which he will reign as monarch. By this account, Marxist ideas could be mapped over unto the "world" (cf. creation) and "authority" (cf. kingship) circles.

The themes that frame the biblical gospel should also define our presentations. In stage one we use the firm and flexible gospel themes in the Bible so that we, in stage two, can identity how to frame a biblically faithful and culturally meaningful gospel presentation. The model helps us discern how the gospel most directly speaks to a specific culture, yet without forsaking theological balance. We are able to maintain a balance between themes within both the Bible and a local culture. By using the biblical framework as a grid for studying culture, we are forced to consider the interrelationships between themes within a given culture. We must not forget that concepts, images, and language have distinct connotations and interconnections within specific cultures. Our model slows us down to consider how ideas relate to one another. At the same time, our sequence ensures that we do everything in view of the gospel's biblical framework.

The approach suggested in this chapter engages contextualization and the gospel at a worldview level. The biblical writers, modern readers, and those who hear the gospel all have fundamental ways of thinking about the world. Our approach establishes a basic grid for understanding the gospel *story*, hence a biblically oriented view of the world. Moreover, this model does not oversimplify contextualization. By interconnecting themes at a worldview level, we resist various kinds of reductionism, whether concerning theology, culture, or methodology (e.g., certain "gospel bridges"). Worldviews are highly complex. In order to faithfully and meaningfully present the gospel, we need a model that integrates levels of perspectives.

Two Subtle Ways to Settle for Truth

Readers should be aware of at least two ways people might misapply this model; each leads to superficial contextualization. First, one can misuse one of the framework themes (creation, covenant, kingdom). Second, people might confuse framework and explanatory themes. This section also makes a few needed clarifications by explaining what this book is *not* saying.

Occasionally mentioning kingdom, creation, or covenant does not mean one is preaching the gospel like those in the Bible. First, consider the tract "Four Spiritual Laws" (4SL), popularized by Campus Crusade for Christ (Cru).[119] Under law 4, it describes the "self-directed life," wherein "self is on the throne." This is contrasted with the "Christ-directed life," such that "Christ is in the life and on the throne." Finally, the tract suggests a prayer whereby one can receive Christ. One line beseeches God, "Take control of the throne of my life."

Such kingdom language is really nothing more than a simple analogy. 4SL's imagery remains at a surface level compared to the Bible's own usage of the royal metaphor. In 4SL, one asks Jesus to take over a personalized "throne." Some could possibly misunderstand the imagery to say that Jesus is not yet King until we abdicate the "throne" in our personal life.

The precise way the tract uses this language is not particular to Israel's God and all that is implied by Jewish monotheism. The tract could just as easily draw another comparison; perhaps it could also say, "We act as CEOs over our lives, but we need to let Jesus be our CEO." With respect to the tract's point, nothing essential is lost. However, the Bible does not casually frame its gospel presentations. The gospel always and specifically aims to magnify what the God of Israel has done in history.

Similarly, "Creation to Christ" (C2C) uses monotheism but not necessarily in a way that is particularly unique to Israel's God in the Bible.[120] Also, part 4 mentions laws and sacrifices but not God's covenants, his specific promises, and his distinguishing works in history. Other so-called "gods" can similarly give commands and demand sacrifices. It is difficult to place C2C's God in a particular place and time within history. C2C's Old Testament presentation of God could also describe other gods. As with 4SL's use of kingdom language, so also C2C's usage of monotheism does not resemble the specific way the Bible frames the gospel.

Second, there is a danger in confusing framework themes and explanatory themes. If the former does not frame the latter, then we can run into a problem; namely, we might compromise the gospel by settling for truth. A few comments are sufficient to illustrate the point. Other examples were mentioned in chapter 2.

When using a law motif, people often so strongly depict God as a judge that modern readers can lose sight of the fact that God is King. A king is a judge, but a judge is not necessarily a king. God is more than a courtroom judge in the contemporary sense. God may well serve as a judge, but this is just one component among many within the biblical story. It is not a framework theme that supports the whole biblical gospel.

Many gospel presentations emphasize individual salvation. Of course this is an important idea. However, we need to understand the Bible according to its own narrative framework, using its basic unit of thought. The biblical writers repeatedly emphasize "nations," not merely individuals. The Abrahamic covenant shapes the entire biblical story like few other concepts, yet it concerns nations, not individuals. Of course nations contain individuals. A Westerner, for example, could potentially so focus on individuals that he or she forgets about the nations. We don't want to lose the group because of the individual when we could have both.

Interpret Biblical Meaning (Stage Three)

Stage three establishes the theological foundations for our contextualization. In particular, at this point in the process, we try to discern which biblical ideas are most helpful in contextualizing the gospel. Which biblical themes and concepts convey the gospel's message most clearly and meaningfully?

At this stage, we do *exegetical contextualization* (discussed earlier). In exegetical contextualization, we use a cultural lens to interpret Scripture. Since our goal is to understand truth in Scripture, we ultimately want an interpretive lens that is faithful to the Bible. Therefore, our approach to contextualization takes intentional measures to shape and focus the lens we use when interpreting Scripture.

Through a multilayered study of culture and the Bible, we gain a well-rounded perspective from which to approach Scripture. As one writer puts it, "A cross-cultural reading is more objective than a monocultural reading of the biblical text."[121] To be sure, culture is nothing more than a filter. The reader's culture by itself has no real authority. Nevertheless we humbly acknowledge that our cultural lens has an unavoidable influence on us. I specifically refer to our cultural *organizing principles* (already discussed in the last chapter).

How do we apply this step? What concrete steps do we take? I begin my explanation by stating each step abstractly. Afterwards I can illustrate what this process looks like using specific issues. We begin with an issue or concept within a contemporary context and then go to the Bible. In stage three we will again utilize the three-circle graphs from stages one and two. (See Fig. 14 for a visual summary.)

First, we put on a cultural lens by looking at the three-circle graph from stage two above. It indicated the cultural concepts that parallel to the gospel themes. Second, we then return to the first three-circle graph (from stage one), which shows the interconnection of biblical themes organized according to a gospel framework. By so doing, we seek to discover which specific biblical ideas best apply to which specific cultural issues. Finally, we achieve our goal. By doing this exercise, we highlight a group of biblical topics that seem especially applicable to a certain set of contemporary issues. When this stage culminates in a fuller presentation of the gospel, we will naturally use more terms from the Bible than from our culture.

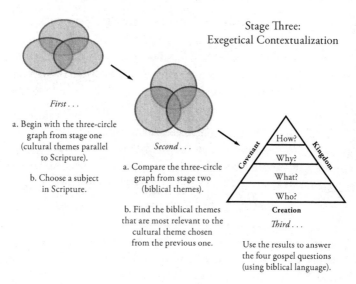

Stage Three:
Exegetical Contextualization

First . . .

a. Begin with the three-circle
graph from stage one
(cultural themes parallel
to Scripture).

b. Choose a subject
in Scripture.

Second . . .

a. Compare the three-circle
graph from stage two
(biblical themes).

b. Find the biblical themes
that are most relevant to the
cultural theme chosen
from the previous one.

How?
Why?
What?
Who?

Covenant

Kingdom

Creation

Third . . .

Use the results to answer
the four gospel questions
(using biblical language).

Figure 14: Stage Three Summary

A more specific example will illustrate how to use the three-circle graphs
from stages one and two. First, let us imagine that we want to address the
cultural problem of ethnocentrism. Of course we will want to consider the
various issues related to ethnocentrism in a local culture. Second, we look back
at the first three-circle graph (stage one, using a gospel framework). At that
point, we realize that a few biblical ideas are especially relevant. Comparing
the two graphs, we see that ethnocentricism belongs best within the "covenant"
and "creation" circles. The doctrine of creation highlights humanity's common
origin. In addition, we recall that the Jews misunderstood God's covenant with
Israel. They misused God's covenant to exclude Gentiles. Thus, other relevant
concepts may be "circumcision," "land," and "righteousness."

What exactly have we achieved? If we want to speak to the issue of ethnocentrism, we have now discerned a collection of biblical themes that will
guide our reflection, teaching, and ministry practice. Our next task then is
to seek out passages that discuss these topics. What do we expect to find? We
will often (but not always) see that texts focusing on covenant, righteousness,
circumcision, etc., will be very relevant when dealing with ethnocentrism.

What would result if we had simply looked up "ethnocentrism" in a
concordance or Bible dictionary? First of all, one won't find any mention of
the term in a concordance, since the word doesn't appear in the Bible itself.

If a dictionary even mentions the topic, the article will most likely be general, brief, and only list a select number of related verses. By contrast, the process in our contextualization model raises several possible strands of thinking, spanning a range of passages. Our attention will turn to various places of Scripture that a concordance or Bible dictionary might miss. Not only this, we will arrive at answers in a way that respects the biblical context.

Although our model can hasten sound, biblical contextualization, the process is not a shortcut around hard work. Readers still have to apply themselves to the work of exegesis—seeking to interpret the Bible's meaning according to its original context. The writer's underlying logic might not be self-evident. Biblical interpretation is not always easy. In fact, the labor grows more difficult as themes become more integrated. At this point, academic training may not be the most important tool at one's disposal. Instead character virtues like patience, perseverance, and humility can take us much further than the skills of a hasty seminary-trained missionary or pastor.

Let us test what has been said. The above process suggested a link between covenant themes and the issue of ethnocentrism. Accordingly, we will consider the biblical theme of God's righteousness, which is often associated with God's faithfulness to his covenant people. It is well known that Paul, in the book of Romans, focuses heavily on the motif of God's righteousness. What do we find?

In fact, we do observe a connection in Romans between God's righteousness and ethnic identity. For example, consider Romans 1:14–17, where Paul writes,

> I am under obligation both to Greeks and to barbarians, both to the wise and to the foolish. So I am eager to preach the gospel to you also who are in Rome. For I am not ashamed of the gospel, for it is the power of God for salvation to everyone who believes, to the Jew first and also to the Greek. For in it the righteousness of God is revealed from faith for faith, as it is written, "The righteous shall live by faith."

Verses 14–17 form one sentence in Greek. For now, simply note how Paul lumps ethnicity and God's righteousness together. The latter is sandwiched between references to ethnicity located both at the beginning and end of the sentence.[122] Also, compare Romans 2:9–11. Paul writes, "There will be tribulation and distress for every human being who does evil, the Jew first and also the Greek, but glory and honor and peace for everyone who does good, the Jew first and also the Greek. For God shows no partiality." In Romans 2, Paul slightly adjusts his verbiage from Romans 1:14–17, yet makes a parallel point. Rather than speaking of God's righteousness (as in Rom 1), Paul now says God is not partial.

Further notice Romans 3:21–30, especially verses 25–30. First, Paul emphasizes God's righteousness in verses 25,26: "This [Christ's sacrifice] was to show God's righteousness, because in his divine forbearance he had passed over former sins. It was to show his righteousness at the present time, so that he might be just and the justifier of the one who has faith in Jesus." He immediately applies God's righteousness to ethnic groups. In verses 27–30 Paul writes,

> Then what becomes of our boasting? It is excluded. By what kind of law? By a law of works? No, but by the law of faith. For we hold that one is justified by faith apart from works of the law. Or is God the God of Jews only? Is he not the God of Gentiles also? Yes, of Gentiles also, since God is one—who will justify the circumcised by faith and the uncircumcised through faith.[123]

The logic in verses 29,30 is telling. Paul equates justification by works (in vv. 27,28) with God's being partial toward a single ethnic group. Yet the one true God is righteous (vv. 25,26,29,30). Therefore, God keeps his promise to Abraham to bless all nations (cf. Rom 4). Salvation does not depend on ethnic identity.[124]

This brief review of Romans provides confirmation of the model's projections. Please note that we have only studied one specific passage. We have not examined a number of other texts that could potentially help us address the problem of ethnocentrism. Without question, God's righteousness concerns far more than ethnicity. The point I make here is simply that these two concepts are related. Once we identify some sort of relationship, our job is then to understand the various possible connections that exist between them.

After completing this third stage, what do we gain? First, this contextualization model offers a basic road map that points people in the right direction. The approach suggested in this chapter is not a quick-fix formula to solve all ministry problems. Rather, it is a guide to direct our labor more wisely. Second, this stage provides us with a biblical lens; therefore, this lens has authority when to move to assess local culture. In the example above, I pointed out the connection between ethnicity and God's righteousness. A similar approach can address more nuanced themes like Marxism (mentioned above). However, we must remember to let the gospel's framework (stage one) direct our analysis. Instead of talking about Marxism as a whole, we will speak to the relevant subthemes of Marxism (e.g., class distinctions, ideal world, etc.). Of course a more diversified cultural lens helps us to better reflect upon and thus interpret the *grand biblical narrative*. I give an example of this later in chapter 7. Our contextualization must accord at every level with God's word. In short, the present stage establishes the foundation for stage four.

Infer Cultural Significance (Stage Four)

In stage four we apply a biblical perspective (gained in stage three) to a specific cultural context. Beginning with Scripture, we ask ourselves, "How does the Bible assess our culture?" Likewise, how should the Bible change the culture? In short, this stage helps us draw inferences from the text to the cultural context.

Broadly stated, we now want to do *cultural contextualization*. In cultural contextualization, the Bible is the lens through which one interprets and assesses a culture. One moves from Scripture to culture. This fourth stage in the contextualization process uses God's authoritative Word to build a contextualized application. Ideally our *exegetical contextualization* (stage three) grounds our application. The Bible is not a mere filter; it has authority. Thus, it distinguishes right from wrong and defines what is primary and secondary.

What does this look like? How do we put this step into practice? (Fig. 15 offers a visual explanation.) Assume we want to start with a certain biblical concept, like covenants. Many people do not understand how to apply ancient biblical covenants to their life. It may seem to some that such covenants have very little relevance for their day-to-day lives. However, we can again use both three-circle diagrams above.

Look back at the second three-circle graph (from stage two), which mapped many contemporary cultural themes onto a gospel framework. We find that the circle labeled "relationship" (*guanxi*) corresponds with the "covenant" circle in the first diagram. We realize that covenants are relevant to a variety of contemporary questions. Thus, we can mention topics like group identity, loyalty, face, traditions, how to regard *guanxi* (relationships), etc. Chapter 8 will provide a concrete example of cultural contextualization, as explained by stage four.

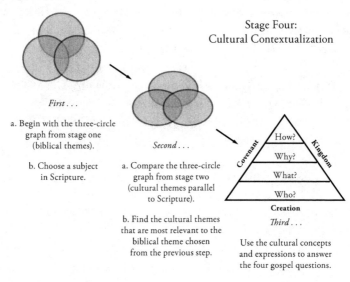

Stage Four:
Cultural Contextualization

First . . .

a. Begin with the three-circle graph from stage one (biblical themes).

b. Choose a subject in Scripture.

Second . . .

a. Compare the three-circle graph from stage two (cultural themes parallel to Scripture).

b. Find the cultural themes that are most relevant to the biblical theme chosen from the previous step.

How?
Why?
What?
Who?

Covenant

Kingdom

Creation

Third . . .

Use the cultural concepts and expressions to answer the four gospel questions.

Figure 15: Stage Four Summary

In completing this stage, the Bible should reshape our view of culture. Some aspects will be refined; other details reinforced. Nevertheless it is important to remember that contextualization is a dynamic rather than static process. One hopes that a person's understanding of Scripture and culture will consistently improve. Not only that, as people mature and have new experiences, so also will their perspective enlarge. As a result, we expect to continually reconsider, expand, and update our contextualizations.

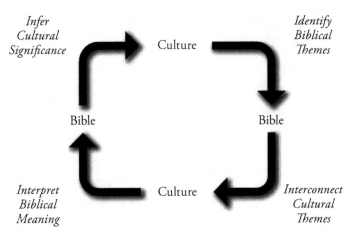

Figure 16: The Relationship between the Bible and Culture

Each Lens Has a Different Function

Before concluding the chapter, one last clarification is needed. In chapter 1, I defined contextualization broadly as the process wherein people interpret, communicate, and apply the Bible within a particular cultural context. However, this chapter distinguishes two types of contextualization. A key distinction between exegetical and cultural contextualization is the use of "lenses." The former uses culture as a lens to interpret the Bible. The latter uses the Bible to interpret or assess culture. At first glance it appears that my earlier definition of contextualization (in general) is essentially equivalent to exegetical contextualization. How do we make sense of the definition in view of these two types?

The above definition of contextualization suggests a center and a context. The Bible is the centerpiece of contextualization. Biblically faithful contextualization always acknowledges the Bible's authority over any particular culture. Additionally, Christians want to see aspects of contemporary culture ultimately transformed to reflect the biblical vision for the world. From beginning to end, the Bible should be the ground and the goal of contextualization.

On the other hand, our model recognizes that contextualization is never done in a cultural vacuum. Even if Christians focus their attention on the Bible, they always do so from within a social context. There is no conflict between the definition offered above and cultural contextualization. Why? One must not forget that even the biblical lens used in cultural contextualization (stage four) is still shaped by the cultural categories in the previous stages.

	Authority / Power	World	Relationship
Harmony		X	
Collectivism			X
Loyalty	X		X
Ethnicity		X(?)	X
Honor & Shame ("face")	X	X	X

Figure 17: What Kind of Lens to Use?

The above diagram illustrates an important distinction between exegetical and cultural contextualization. The two lenses (whether culture or Bible) serve different roles and so have different functions. In exegetical contextualization, culture inevitably filters our experience and so shapes our interpretation of the Bible. In cultural contextualization, the lens of Scripture does not simply filter perceptions. Instead it acts as the standard by which we assess the things we see in culture.

KEY POINTS

- The contextualization process follows a sequence that helps us avoid cultural and theological syncretism.
- Four stages in the contextualization process include: (1) Identify Biblical Themes, (2) Interconnect Cultural Themes, (3) Interpret Biblical Meaning, (4) Infer Cultural Significance.
  - In stage one, we identify how the Bible frames and explains the gospel. This framework focuses our study of culture in stage two.
  - Stage two uses the gospel's framework and explanatory themes from stage one to interconnect the biblical text and the cultural context.
  - Stage three establishes the theological foundations for our contextualization. It tries to discern which biblical themes and concepts convey the gospel's message most clearly and meaningfully.
  - Stage four applies a biblical perspective to a specific cultural context. We ask ourselves, "How does the Bible assess our culture?"
- The themes that frame the biblical gospel should define our presentations.
- Contextualizers need to have both depth and breadth of knowledge.
- The contextualization model proposed in the chapter engages contextualization and the gospel at a worldview level.
- A cultural lens acts as a filter for biblical interpretation; a biblical lens assesses local cultures.
- Contextualization requires collaboration among people from various backgrounds and skill sets.

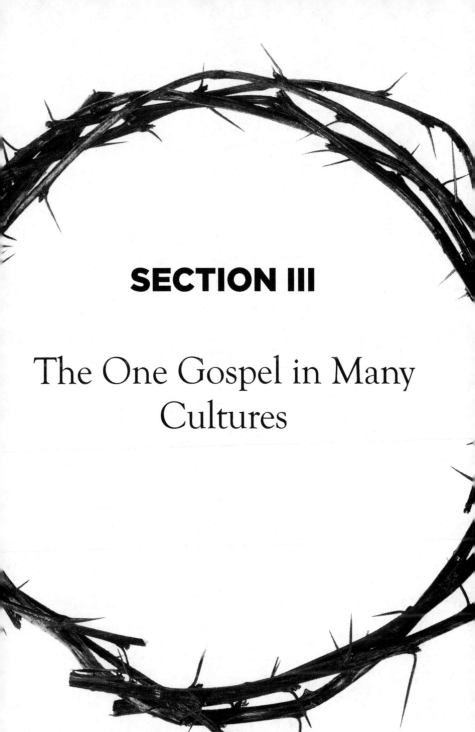

SECTION III

The One Gospel in Many Cultures

7

A Jewish Gospel among Gentiles: Using Acts 17 as a Test Case

Can We Preach a Jewish Gospel among Gentiles?

How did Paul frame a Jewish gospel among Gentiles? This is one of the most critical questions one must consider when doing contextualization. How we answer this question will greatly shape whether our gospel presentations are biblically faithful and culturally meaningful. Most of the examples of gospel preaching in the book of Acts have a distinctly Jewish flavor. Paul's sermons in Lystra (Acts 14) and Athens (Acts 17) are typically thought to be unique in that his listeners seem to be "full Gentiles" in the sense that they would not be considered Jewish proselytes and "God fearers" (as was Cornelius for example; cf. Acts 10). Accordingly, these passages play an important role in understanding what it means to contextualize the gospel about a Jewish king among modern-day Gentiles.

This chapter draws from Acts 17 in order to show that Paul's message among Gentiles has a number of markedly Jewish characteristics. In other words, Paul's gospel fundamentally is just as "Jewish" when he preaches to Gentiles as when he speaks to Jews. This idea is quite contrary to many people's interpretation. Accordingly, we should not draw from Acts 17 the lesson that one can leave behind the story of Israel when contextualizing the gospel today among non-Jews.

In demonstrating the point, I will simultaneously addresses two key issues, both of which are important for biblical contextualization. First, this chapter will show that Paul's gospel in Acts 17 is manifestly "Jewish." This is an exegetical-theological question. Second, Paul's preaching exemplifies for us what it means to "frame" the gospel. This issue is especially relevant to the matter of contextualization.

TWO KEY ISSUES FOR CONTEXTUALIZING THE GOSPEL

What is at stake in the discussion? In my experience, I find these topics represent two of the greatest obstacles that hinder efforts to contextualize the gospel throughout the world. On the one hand, Christians risk compromising the gospel by presenting a less than fully biblical message, one that largely omits the Old Testament, generally skipping from the Fall in Genesis 3 to the cross in Romans 3. Many times I have heard missionaries justify this practice to one degree or another. They object that the average Chinese, Indian, or tribal villager cannot be expect to "know all of the Old Testament" before being able to understand and accept the gospel. This exaggerated criticism is usually accompanied with a befuddled tone. They are unable to imagine teaching someone about the whole of Israel's history in a three- to five-minute gospel presentation.

On the other hand, Christian workers face the task of contextualizing their message in a way that is culturally comprehensible and yet is not compromised biblically. A plethora of books and articles consider which key motifs should inform any given gospel presentation. Which themes or doctrines are central and which images could simply be called "bridges" or "redemptive analogies"? In some respect, the discussion tries to answer a most basic question, "What is the gospel?" Yet the content of the gospel cannot be separated from questions about how to present the gospel. Accordingly, how we frame the gospel determines the actual message being communicated. It is possible to so misframe a host of correct doctrines that we misrepresent the central concerns of the gospel itself.

I have previously explained that gospel presentations in the Bible consist of two types of themes. There are "framework" themes as well as "explanatory" themes. In other words, various passages use diverse images both to frame and explain the gospel. Biblical writers consistently use three framework motifs: creation, covenant, and kingdom. All other images associated with the gospel can be considered "explanatory" themes. They fit within one or more of the above framework motifs; in this way, the two groups of themes are not distinct from one another. One should not create a false separation between them. Framework themes provide an order by which to relate the other motifs. The explanatory themes show the significance of the creation-covenant-kingdom framework. Within any gospel presentation, the two types of themes play different but essential roles.

It is critical that we observe and understand these two sets of themes. The gospel has a distinct framework that gives it firmness. In this way, the message does not change. We can also recognize the fact that not all gospel explanations in the Bible are precisely the same. There is a fair degree of flexibility when it comes to exactly how one might legitimately present the gospel. If we blur the distinction between framework and explanatory themes, we risk compromising the gospel by settling for truth. For example, one may make much of an important truth yet do so at the expense of other more central aspects of the gospel.

Paul's Gospel Proclaims a Jewish King (Acts 17:1–9)

Before looking at Paul's famous sermon in Athens, we need to first look at his lesser-known message preached in the previous context (Acts 17:1–9). While in Thessalonica, Paul goes to "a synagogue of the Jews . . . saying, 'This Jesus, whom I proclaim to you, is the Christ'" (vv. 2,3). His teaching received quite a response. A mob formed, "set the city in an uproar, and attacked the house of Jason," who had welcomed Paul and Silas (vv. 5–7).

What exactly did these Gentiles think Paul was preaching? How did they understand Paul's distinctively Jewish message? Verse 7 explains clearly. The mob complained, "They are all acting against the decrees of Caesar, saying that there is another king, Jesus." Even if they did not fully grasp Paul's precise meaning, the crowd certainly captured the crux of his message. This message (and a similar response) is exactly what we find in the four Gospels (e.g., Luke 23:2,3; John 19:12) as well as in the coming passage.[125]

When Paul proclaimed "Christ," the Gentiles heard the word "king." This is the essence of what it means for Paul in Acts 17 to preach a "Jewish" gospel among Gentiles. Do we see anything to confirm this conclusion from Paul's sermon in Athens? Yes. Unfortunately, key observations often go unnoticed and we miss how Paul contextualizes the gospel to non-Jews.

How Paul Frames the Gospel in Athens (Acts 17:22–31)

Paul's message at the Areopagus is not only very "Jewish," it also climaxes with the announcement of a king. First, we note the way Paul frames his message in light of Israel's story. Although not apparent to some people, his sermon is marked by a number of distinctly Jewish features. One might object that Paul does not overtly talk about Abraham and string together a series of citations from the Old Testament. Yet that is exactly what makes Paul's manner of contextualization so intriguing. The entire framework of the story he tells bears the weight of the gospel; it confirms that Paul is preaching the same good news in Acts 17 as is found in earlier chapters among Jewish listeners.

We have already see that Isaiah 40–55 is an extended polemic against idolatry, in which the prophet continuously correlates the one true God and the supreme King over Israel and the world. The God of Abraham would show himself ruler over the nations (cf. Isa 41:8; 51:2; 63:16). Previous chapters especially highlighted Isaiah 40:9 and 52:7, which explicitly utilize gospel language. Given Paul's use of the Old Testament (e.g., Rom 10:15; Gal 3:8), we should not hesitate to make the following conclusion: the gospel in the Old Testament is not different than that in the New Testament. The Creator God will fulfill his covenant promises to restore his kingdom in the world.

God Is the Creator

In Acts 17, Paul preaches this exact message. His audience in Athens consisted of pagan philosophers who obviously had little affinity for Jewish monotheism. These Gentiles accused him of preaching "'foreign divinities'—because he was preaching Jesus and the resurrection" (v. 18). Nevertheless Paul's message is unmistakably Jewish.

He begins with the Creator in verse 24. It is this "God who made the world and everything in it"; he is "Lord of heaven and earth." Paul clearly and utterly distinguishes the one true God from the rest of creation (vv. 24,25). The Creator-King reigns over the entire world, making "from one man every nation of mankind . . . [and] having determined allotted periods and the boundaries of their dwelling place" (v. 26). Paul, like the ancient prophets of Israel, effectively challenges the legitimacy of those false gods, whose idols are housed "in temples made by man" (vv. 24,29).

The Creator Is God of All Nations

Although Paul never explicitly mentions Abraham and Israel's covenants, the influence of the Jewish story cannot be missed. The plan of God to bless the world through his people clearly shapes the history that Paul recounts at the Areopagus. First, we should not miss the allusion in verse 26 to Deuteronomy 32:8.[126] Paul says that the Creator God "determined allotted periods and the boundaries of [the nations'] dwelling place, that they should seek God" (vv. 26,27). Similar to other Old Testament verses, Deuteronomy 32:8 explains, "When the Most High gave to the nations their inheritance, when he divided mankind, he fixed the borders of the peoples" (cf. Job 12:23; 14:5; Ps 74:17).

Furthermore, the broader context of Deuteronomy 32 is noteworthy, perfectly suited to the needs of Paul's own situation. Israel had been wandering, yet it was the Lord who found them in the desert (v. 10) and provided for their needs despite their idolatry (vv. 13–18,21). Verse 12 states, "The LORD alone guided him, no foreign god was with him." This was "the God who gave [them] birth. . . . [Namely, those who are] his sons and daughters" (vv. 18,19). Essentially Paul is rehearsing the story of ancient Israel to those whom he called "God's offspring" (Acts 17:29).

Additionally, Paul's sermon aims for the same effect intended by the Abrahamic covenant. In particular, he equalizes Jews and Gentiles by showing that the Creator is the God of all nations. First, Paul points to the fact that God "made from one man every nation of mankind" (Acts 17:26). Thus, even these pagans are considered God's offspring (vv. 28,29). As a result, there is not room for a sense of cultural supremacy. As Paul says elsewhere about the Jews (cf. Rom 2:17,23; 3:27), so also he says here that these Greeks should not boast (cf. 1 Cor 1:26–31; Eph 2:9). Paul wants to make it known, "There is no distinction between Jew and Greek; for the same Lord is Lord of all, bestowing his riches on all who call on him" (Rom 10:12). This is because "God shows no partiality" (Rom 2:11).

The Creator God Is King

Finally, Paul proclaims the kingship of God, who is "Lord of heaven and earth" (Acts 17:24). Paul makes it known that the Creator-King "commands all people everywhere to repent" (v. 30). Paul concludes his sermon just as in Thessalonica (v. 3). Specifically, he announces in verse 31 that God "has fixed a day on which he will judge the world in righteousness by a man whom he has appointed." This sort of judgment is the prerogative of a king. Who is this King? Paul says it is the man whom God raised from the dead, namely Christ.

Again, we see Paul appeal to the Old Testament without citing, as it were, verse and chapter. The key phrase in verse 31 directly recalls the hope of Israel as expressed in Greek: God will "judge the world in righteousness" (κρίνειν τὴν οἰκουμένην ἐν δικαιοσύνῃ, LXX, cf. Ps 9:8; 96:10,13; 97:9). To reinforce the point above, each of the psalms just cited distinctly proclaims the fact that God is King (cf. Ps 9:7,11; 96:6,10; 98:6).

Paul Answers Four Gospel Questions

Paul's message to the Athenians answers four gospel questions. First, who is Christ?—or, who is God? God is the one true Creator of the world. He is not like human idols, which are served by human hands and live in temples. He is the heavenly Father over the human family. Furthermore, the man whom God raised from the dead (i.e., Jesus) is the King through whom God will rectify the world.

We arrive at a second question: What does God in Christ do in the world? He made the world and gives life to everything in it. The Lord of heaven and earth made all nations from one man and now sovereignly works in the world so that they would know him. Although he has been patient with the ignorance of the Gentiles, he has appointed Jesus to be the means through whom he will establish justice. This is made clear in Christ's resurrection.

Why is this news important? The answer is apparent. Paul's sermon helps us understand who is our true Father and family. We have been ignorant of his sovereign and gracious hand in the world around us. In fact, we have worshiped created things rather than the Creator. The nations have tried to make gods after our own image. The divine King is able even to defeat death; thus, we can even hope for a resurrection of our own.

How should we respond? Paul clearly states that God "commands all people everywhere to repent" (v. 30). Thus, we should not "think that the divine being is like gold or silver or stone, an image formed by the art and imagination of man" (v. 29). As a result, we will give our allegiance to Christ, who will one day reign over all nations, having defeated every enemy, including death.

Contextualizing Our Presentation among Gentiles

What have we learned from the example of Paul? Paul's preaching in Acts 17 helps us to see how he contextualized the gospel. His message was characteristically Jewish, even when he spoke to Greek polytheists. Paul's gospel was framed according to three interrelated motifs: creation, covenant, and kingdom. These themes find their significance in the story of Israel. These framework themes ensure that Paul does not need to sacrifice the gospel's "Jewishness" in order to preach to Gentiles. When Paul spoke of "Christ," his Gentile listeners heard the word "king."

There are two ways in which we can contextualize the gospel. First, we can contextualize the presentation. Second, we can contextualize our goals while presenting the gospel. We should keep each of these areas in mind when framing our message. I will explain each in turn.

How should we seek to contextualize our *presentation*? First, observe that Paul's gospel summaries are more storied than systematic. Paul did not merely use stories; rather his message inherently is a story recounting the work of God in human history. Systematized presentations naturally tend to make the message abstract.

Second, we like Paul should emphasize God's story rather than our own. Although there are times that it is appropriate to tell our "personal testimony," one must be careful not to confuse our story with the gospel itself. God's story is much bigger than any individual's life experience.

Third, the gospel story is God-oriented rather than people-oriented. What do I mean by the phrase "God-oriented"? This is not another way of saying "God centered." When our theology is "God oriented," we tell the biblical story from God's perspective whereby he is the main character. A man-oriented presentation characteristically puts God in the passive voice: we are created, we sin, we are redeemed and will be with God forever. Told from God's vantage point, God created us, God is offended, God enters into covenant, God incarnates and defeats his enemies, God fulfills his promises and rescues his people.

Fourth, gospel presentations are thematic without being topical. In other words, we may talk about any number of subjects and use countless images and motifs. However, we must not reduce the gospel to a single topic within the larger story. The gospel is more than adoption, justification, and even God's love.

Fifth, we should follow the example of Paul, whose message was primarily historical rather than philosophical. Certainly Paul engages in a philosophical debate, albeit indirectly, with the best and brightest minds in Athens. Nevertheless Paul does so in order to speak about the one true God who reveals himself in history. Philosophical questions inform rather than frame his presentation. We too must be mindful not to preach God as an abstract being who is merely omnipotent, omniscient, and omnipresent.

Sixth, contextualization should be relevant without being reductionistic. Nothing is more relevant and practical than one's worldview. One's basic life assumptions and values determine everything we do. Paul's message is not limited to a single issue of interest to his listeners. Thus, in a modern context we should not filter everything we say simply through the filter of animism or *nirvana* (if either of these characterize the people we serve). There are far more factors that influence the lives of our listeners than either of these subjects. It may be far more urgent that people address so-called "secular" concerns than explicitly "religious" notions.

Seventh, gospel presentations focus *more* on knowing King Jesus than a theology of salvation (e.g., how a person gets saved). Although the two cannot be separated entirely, we must not forget to distinguish the difference. It is very possible for someone to emphasize a method of getting saved while minoring on the central truth of the gospel— Jesus is King. In Paul's sermon in Athens, he begins and ends with the kingship of God.

In summary, we contextualize gospel presentations by being mindful of the implicit narrative that both permeates the entire Bible and presumes the necessity of Israel's story. This is why biblical theology is so important. The grand biblical story interconnects countless themes in a balanced way such that proper emphasis is given to primary themes.

Viewed in this light, contextualization in many ways becomes far simpler and richer. Consider for a moment the fact that people do not need scripts or summary points in order to retell their own life story. They can move in and out of their story with ease. In telling their account, they could begin from any number of places and weave through the events in their life without trouble. In the same way, contextualization is done best when people internalize the grand biblical narrative. This sort of contextualization is more comprehensive and engaging. It is both biblically faithful and culturally relevant.

Contextualizing Our Goals among Gentiles

At one level, the goal of contextualization is obvious. We want people to follow Jesus as King. We want them to be saved from sin and death. From another angle, we can see that there are various possible aims that we wish to accomplish in the process. Accordingly, we not only want to contextualize our presentation, but also our goals. I will list a few of the objectives evident in Paul's sermon in Acts 17.

First, Paul seeks to clarify people's view of the one true God. He does not merely explain God's attributes in an abstract sense; he recounts the works of God in history. Thus, we see the scope of God's authority and providential care over the world. The Creator-King seeks the blessing of all nations (cf. Gen 12:3; Gal 3:8).

Second, Paul both humbles and encourages his listeners. He undermines the root of pride that festers up in ethnic or cultural superiority. People are prone to comparison. This tendency has devastating consequences. Communities suffer division. Fear grows. As conflicts escalate, so does the desire to exert power over others, whether intellectually, economically, or relationally. As my college pastor repeated many times, comparison is the thief of joy. It leads either to pride or insecurity.

Third, we can follow Paul's example by helping people find a proper sense of identity. What is their relationship to God? What is their relationship to others? In actual fact, the answer to the first question will be found by first addressing the second. The way in which we define "insiders" and "outsiders" will reveal our value system and those whom we recognize as authorities. What are the idols that unite our various groups and subcultures?

Finally, every biblical gospel presentation is a royal summons that calls listeners to give allegiance of King Jesus. It is not merely an assent to a set of doctrines. Of course the truths contained within the gospel story are critically important. On the other hand, we must never forget that the gospel funda-mentally aims at changing people's loyalty. Thus, this message transforms a person's worldview, group identification, and sense of honor and shame.

Proclaiming a Jewish King to Gentiles

In conclusion, Paul in Acts 17 demonstrates what it might look like to preach a Jewish King to Gentiles. He is not merely the King of Israel, he is King of the nations. Christ is not merely "my" personal Savior; he is the Savior of the entire world.

Some people may object that preaching such a "Jewish" gospel to Gentiles will sound foreign. Paul faced a similar challenge in his own day. Preaching monotheism and resurrection certainly sounded "foreign" (v. 18) to those in Athens. Ironically, Paul uses a "Jewish" framework to show that the gospel message is not at all foreign. After all, Israel's God is the only true God. Believing in the one true God is not actually "foreign." In fact, such preaching undermines exclusivist ways of thinking that define others as "foreigners."

Sadly, those people today who might oppose emphasizing "Jewish" aspects of the biblical story *ironically* may cause their own presentations to come across as foreign. Why? They could unintentionally preach a God abstracted from history. We must never forget that God has revealed himself in history to Israel. Therefore, if we skip over that Old Testament story, we cover over God's means of revelation.

KEY POINTS

- Paul's sermons in Acts 17 demonstrate one way that he framed and explained a Jewish gospel among Gentiles listeners.
- When Paul said the Jewish title "Christ," Gentiles heard him to mean "king."
- Paul preached a storied gospel, which is shaped by the three framework themes of creation, covenant, and kingdom.
- Even among Gentiles, Paul recounted the history of the world in a way that is informed by the story of Israel.
- Monotheism entails the kingship of God over all nations, which constitute one human family.

- People should consider how to contextualize both their presentation and their goals.
- The biblical presentation of the gospel summons people to give allegiance to King Jesus.
- If the Old Testament, particularly the story of Israel, does not influence our gospel contextualization, we unintentionally preach a God abstracted from history.

8

A Chinese Biblical Theology: An Example of Exegetical Contextualization

Rereading the Biblical Text within a Cultural Context

How might a Chinese cultural lens sharpen the contours of biblical theology? What happens when we intentionally interpret Scripture from a cultural perspective? The result can be called an "exegetical contextualization." *Exegetical contextualization* refers to one's interpretation of Scripture from a cultural perspective. It means locating the cultural context within the biblical text.

This chapter gives an example of exegetical contextualization. It uses a Chinese cultural perspective. Our goal is to *exegete* Scripture according to the author's original intent and, at the same time, to convey distinct emphases found within a contemporary setting. After highlighting a few key features of Chinese culture, the bulk of the chapter retells and reinterprets the grand biblical narrative in a way that is meaningful for Chinese people.

What results from this approach? Methodologically, we discover that contextualization via exegesis means listening for the echoes of culture within Scripture. Theologically, we gain a biblical theology as told from the perspective of an honor and shame culture. Missiologically, it is hoped that Christians around the world will be better equipped to contextualize the gospel. In seeing this model, others can develop similar examples suitable to their context.

Seeing the World through the Lens of Chinese Culture[127]

What do we see when we look at the world with Chinese eyes? Countless books and articles offer the reader insights into Chinese society.[128] I cannot here give a full review of China's history and culture.[129] For the sake of simplicity, the following section focuses on three major aspects of Chinese culture. In reality, human cultures are far more complex and resist reductionistic descriptions.

Nevertheless, even a brief introduction will familiarize readers with Chinese culture and sufficiently help them discern ways that a Chinese worldview could shape a contextualized biblical theology. Modern Chinese people see the world through the lens of honor and shame, have a high regard for relationships (*guanxi*), and long to get a share of the "Chinese dream." More simply, Chinese society is marked by a love of face, family, and fortune.

China has an honor/shame culture. Another way of saying this is that Chinese people are very concerned with "face"—gaining face, saving face, and not losing face. The concept is multifaceted. Essentially, "face" refers to one's social value as perceived within some group setting. "Face" is inherently public. One's face determines his or her group identity.

People gain or lose face for a number of reasons. Some are quite simple, even trivial, such as when a person is clumsy and trips. That can embarrass someone and so cause him or her to lose face. On the other hand, honor/shame has a moral dimension. One is "shameful" if he does not conform to the moral demands of the community. No one wants it said of him, "He has no sense of shame." Likewise, people praise (i.e., honor) those whom they judge as having good character.

Face is either "achieved" or "ascribed"; that is, it is either earned or inherited.[130] For example, one inherits the honor/shame of a friend group, family, name, or position. A no-named person can suddenly gain face by mere association, as when someone marries a famous actress. In addition, the public awards honor or shame based on what people do. The watching world applauds good grades and winning an award or sporting competition. Criminal activity and failing school bring social shame. We "give face" in various ways, including simple gestures of respect and words of praise. One's "face" is his or her "social currency."[131] To give (or withhold) honor to another person is to acknowledge (or deny) their position or worth. It establishes (or breaks) relationship and thus forms a person's identity. Identity is shaped both by the ways we are different and the same as others.

Face is not unique to Asia. It is a human phenomenon. In the West, the concern for public recognition takes different forms. Every community holds to varying standards of honor/shame. Americans, for example, speak of "people pleasing" and immerse themselves in social media like Facebook, Twitter, and personal blogs. Westerners typically stress *achieved* or *earned* face, thus *individuality*. Identity is often conceived in terms of how "I" am different than others.

Face determines relationship (*guanxi*) and vice versa. Foundational to Confucian philosophy is an emphasis on hierarchical social relationships. Moral behavior consists in properly ordering relationships such that "harmony" is achieved. Not surprisingly, Chinese people have prized social conformity for thousands of years. As the idiom goes, "The bird that sticks out is the one that gets shot."[132]

A person's *guanxi* has greater influence in determining his or her well-being than any other single factor. Relationships are managed through an informal but unmistakable custom of reciprocity where people exchange small and large favors or gifts as a way of cultivating mutual favor. One act of kindness puts another person in relational debt. Even if it is not discussed, all parties know the time will come when the gift giver may call for a favor in kind.

Since Chinese think primarily in terms of face and *guanxi*, less emphasis is given to "law" and "absolute truth," compared to the West. Morality cannot be separated from relationships that exist in concrete situations. The Chinese are keenly aware that right and wrong, to some degree, depend on the circumstances. Numerous examples could be drawn from daily life. For instance, people should not break the glass on someone's car, *unless* of course that person needs rescuing. Also, one has a greater obligation to family members than to a stranger.

One's family relationships are most important. Generally speaking, the parent-child relationship is prioritized above the marriage relationship. Children are to show filial piety to both their parents as well as their ancestors. It is a child's duty to perpetuate and honor the family name.[133] Elder parents frequently live with their grown children, who are responsible to care for them in old age. It is not uncommon that grandparents will have as much or more of an active role as the parents in raising a grandchild. Both parents probably have full-time jobs.

Identity is a collective idea: "I am who I know." Descartes said, "I think, therefore I am." A Chinese could paraphrase, "I belong, therefore I am."[134] History, age, and ethnicity shape how a person is seen in the eyes of others. One must respect his or her elders, whether living or dead. Ethnicity is more than one mere descriptor among others. The Chinese are proud of their long history. To be "Chinese" is to identify with an ethnic people whose glory extends for generations past. As a nation, they should act like a family. Literally, the Chinese word for "country" is *guo jia*, meaning "kingdom-family." Famously, China is called the Middle Kingdom (*zhong guo*, 中国), signifying its self-perceived place in the world. Naturally, this suggests that all people are divided into two types—insiders and outsiders. Anyone who is not Chinese is literally called an "*outside*-country-person," (*wai guo ren*, 外国人).

To twist the words of Karl Marx, money is the "opium of the people." The country opened to the outside world in the late 1970s, quickly becoming a socialist state with capitalistic characteristics. Increasingly, one feels inclined to switch the order. The population has grown wealthier since former President Deng Xiaoping urged his people to try their best to get rich for the sake of the country. There remains a huge gap that separates the wealthiest and poorest Chinese.

In keeping with traditional thought, education is regarded as the key to economic success (not counting one's *guanxi*). Children endure incredible pressure to study, study, study in order to get higher grades and eventually pass the nationwide *gao kao* ("high exam"), which can single-handedly determine if and where a student attends college. The education system is consistent with the need to learn Chinese characters. Memorization is emphasized more than creativity and critical thinking, which run counter to group conformity.

Chinese people take a rather pragmatic approach to life. They are less interested in systematic theories and focus more on concrete solutions to achieve their goals. Traditionally religion serves a practical function of gaining blessings in this life and after death. Political leaders in China have always assessed religions based on their social utility—how they help or hinder the ambitions of the state. It is not surprising that the one-child policy, which has been in place since 1982, has resulted in parents essentially treating their one child like an idol. The family's hopes for face and fortune hinge on its one and only son or daughter. For the sake of lineage and economics, sons are generally preferred over daughters.

A number of themes mentioned in this brief sketch of Chinese culture will appear in the contextualization that follows. Contextualizing biblical theology for a given culture requires that we find motifs that are in both the ancient text and the contemporary context. In particular, we can anticipate an emphasis on family, God's fatherhood, kingship, honor, shame, debt, loyalty, and group membership. Thus, the Chinese have a heightened sensitivity regarding ethnic identity, tradition, and the use of power by foreigners.

One final idea needs to be stated clearly. So many features of Chinese society find their root in an honor/shame orientation, broadly understood. These include moral and relational norms, collective identity, public policies, etc. If non-Chinese outsiders do not understand this facet of the culture, they will be less inclined to notice and appreciate occurrences of honor/shame in Scripture.

Shame is both the cause and the consequence of sin. This important point must be made in order to correct potential misconceptions. Shame is more than a subjective, psychological experience. Honor is more than medieval chivalry and heroism. Honor and shame each have objective and subjective dimensions.[135] Ultimately God is the supreme measure of honor. Because God's image bearers bring shame upon God's name, they themselves become shameful (see Rom 1:21–28; 2:23,24; 3:23). Conversely, God grants his people to have the same glory that he gives to Christ (John 17:22).

Interpreting the Biblical Text from a Chinese Context

Contextualized theology exists for the sake of a particular context. Accordingly, a good contextualization will use language, idioms, and word pictures that naturally communicate to the local listener, even if they perhaps sound awkward to outsiders. How then should one proceed to make a contextualization *for Chinese speakers* while writing this chapter *for English readers?* Much of what follows was originally written in the Chinese language and has had to be translated back into English. Some expressions simply lose their force in translation. Many cultural allusions are subtle.

If done well, a contextualization of the grand biblical narrative will sound different than a traditional reading; on the other hand, the content will all be quite familiar. To maintain flow to the story, I will use footnotes to make explanatory comments about culture and theology. Contextual theology is inherently complex, but it should also be coherent. Finally, given the sheer scope of the story, it is not possible to give citations defending every theological assertion. Readers can follow up for themselves using more focused sources.

We can divide the grand narrative of Scripture into six parts:[136]

1. One Family under Heaven (天下一家)
2. Losing Face and Fighting for Honor (丢脸争面)
3. King of All Nations (万民之王)
4. Setting the World Right (拨乱反正)
5. Honor through Shame (以辱为荣)
6. Avenging Shame and Restoring God's Kingdom (雪耻复国)

One can immediately identify key themes in each of the section titles, like family, honor, shame, and kingdom. These motifs are central to both the Bible and Chinese culture.

Also, note two more observations. First, the overall outline attempts to give a balanced account of the entire story. Thus, Israel plays as prominent a role in this contextualization as in the Bible. Second, observe how the story integrates various ideas together. Biblical writers often string together Old Testament allusions while at the same time addressing contemporary cultural concerns. The theology that results is both creative and relevant. In the same way, a contextualized biblical theology will be able to incorporate multiple themes. One must be conscious to avoid any sort of rigidity that is foreign to the biblical text itself.

The Creator God is Father and King (父王) over the world. This one true God gives life to every human being. He made the human family in his image. Therefore, we come under his name. In the beginning, God's family enjoyed perfect harmony and was without shame. He created the world to be his kingdom, even a temple in which he would dwell with his people. He put it in good order and ruled in righteousness. The human family is called to serve him as stewards over his creation, bearing the fruit of love and peace.

Humanity owes God a debt of love and honor.[137] We owe him filial piety—the respect due a parent from his children. Likewise, as citizens of his kingdom, we seek to spread his renown. True face (脸) only comes from a close relationship to our Father and King. By reflecting his worth in the world, we have a name and status that are truly praiseworthy. In fact, this is how we bring honor to our human family. We express our identity in the way that we represent God in the world. Loyalty and honor manifest love for God, our Father and King.

What happened? People have publicly dishonored God. In the eyes of the world, he has lost face. How? When we lack faith and so rebel against the one who gives life, we do not show God's infinite glory. We have all done wrong. In essence, it is as if we have spit in our Father's face. People would rather have autonomy than relationship, being unwilling to depend on their heavenly Father. We have no sense of shame. Humanity's relationship with God is broken. People refuse to bring glory to the family name.

As a result, our alienation causes us to lose face (脸, *lian*). We have become shameful. The constant brokenness in human relationships reflects the fact that we have fractured our relationship to God. The consequences are serious. We lack love and righteousness. His children disown him and bring disgrace upon the family. Therefore, God kicked our ancestors out of their home. We isolated ourselves. People have lost their true sense of identity. After all, we have lost all standing and honor. Consequently he cursed the world, allowing death, disease, and suffering to enter the world. Nature turned hostile. God will not tolerate our rebellion. We have brought on ourselves ruin and infamy. As the Chinese idiom puts it, our "names stink forever."

Consider our earliest ancestors. They began thinking about how to protect face. At their birth, they were not ashamed. In time, however, their actions revealed their real face. Therefore, when they heard God coming, they "hid themselves" because they were "afraid" of his presence (Gen 3:8,10). Even worse, people began competing for face.

Descendants are the fruit of their ancestors. "Dragons beget dragons, phoenixes beget phoenixes—each after its own kind."[138] Accordingly, we recall the conflict between two brothers, the sons of our earliest ancestors. One day they offered a sacrifice. God accepted the sacrifice of the younger son but not the older son. The older son became jealous of the younger. Comparison led to competition until there was only one brother. Anger gave birth to murder. God asked the older brother, "Where is . . . your brother?" He replied, "I do not know; am I my brother's keeper?" (Gen 4:9).[139]

Notice the older brother's implicit criticism. He does not want to be responsible for someone else. He does not want to answer to God. If God will not praise him, then he wants independence. We all are like this older brother. People want relationship with God yet with a subtle condition: so long as God gives us face, we are willing to have relationship with God.[140] We want God blindly to give us face. We want God to be like us—to have no sense of shame.[141]

It is a part of human nature to love face. This is not necessarily a bad thing. Everyone pursues honor and wants to avoid shame. This desire, however, has become distorted, bringing disorder. The love of face stains those who are made in the image of God. Loss of face and isolation bring fear. We lose our sense of security when other people do not think we have value. Fear grows where face is lost. We content ourselves with being "big fish in a small pond."[142] In this respect, people establish relationships simply for self-benefit. We see only ourselves and so deny even our family.

When families are corrupted, human societies fall into chaos. Consider the story of Babel. An entire community shared a common dream. They said, "Come, let us build ourselves a city and a tower with its top in the heavens, and let us make a name for ourselves, lest we be dispersed over the face of the whole earth" (Gen 11:4). The people have two interrelated motives. First, they want a great name: "Let us make a name for ourselves." Second, they want security: "lest we be dispersed over the face of the whole earth." However, God looks down on them. Genesis 11:5 says, "And the LORD came down to see the city and the tower, which the children of man had built." Although their tower aimed for the heavens, notice the condescending irony in verse 5, which states that "the LORD came down to see." In other words, they cannot reach the heavens. The story of Babel illustrates how we all "fall short of the glory of God" (Rom 3:23).

Humans try to use circumstantial face (面子, *mianzi*) to compensate somehow for a lack of enduring face (脸, *lian*).[143] This is impossible. *Lian* involves our character, our essential value as humans. We have formed countless factions, dividing into groups in which we might be respected. Trivial commonalities piece together a seeming unity, even if only temporarily. Common ground might include nationality, ethnicity, hometown, interests, traditions, and language. One thinks, "This is my country. That is your country," or "This is my home. That is your home." On the surface everything looks good. In reality the human family is scattered, cut off from one another, each in a different corner of the world. However, superficial characteristics create a mere fabrication, a hollow sort of harmony. Popular opinion controls us. We are concerned about our image, not God's. We constantly think about how we compare to others.[144] The world is full of hypocrisy and lip service.

Even if we reject God as Father, he remains the world's one true King. Accordingly, our disregard and disobedience can also be considered a "crime," even treason.[145] Humans are not willing to confess God as Lord. We have betrayed our King. In effect, humans launched a *coup d'état*. Over time, humans multiply and divide into factions. When we filled the earth, we colonized the world for our own self-interest.[146] As rebels, humanity lives as an enemy to God. Harmony has turned to hostility. Within God's kingdom, divorce and civil war are obvious marks that humanity does not seek God's face.

Where do we belong? Who are we? What do we depend on? These are critical questions. People naturally depend on their relationship network. Someone once said, "I am, because we are; and since we are, therefore I am."[147] People think their relationships (*guanxi*) can save them. Of course not all relationships are the same. Consider the following questions: Whom do we regard as our authority? Whom do we follow? In other words, to whom are we loyal? If we have a relationship with God, we *really* have *guanxi*. We *really* have face.

Out of fear, humans even began to worship false gods. With their own hands, they used wood and stone to make idols. In every land, all the nations created their own local god(s) to protect them from outsiders and from nature. As a result, people worship created things rather than the Creator. In short, people created false gods in their own image. Everyone worships himself or herself. We have brought shame upon God's name and cannot blot out this most fundamental offense against him.[148] Because there is only one God, he is the King of all nations. Idolatry therefore is not only betrayal; it is treason. How can God vindicate his honor, restore his kingdom, and bring reconciliation to his family?

The one true God takes the initiative to spread his renown among all nations, who are continually bent on seeking their own fame and wealth. God throughout history has sought to gather his children and restore human dignity. Long ago he chose to use a small and seemingly insignificant people to reestablish his kingdom in the world. God revealed himself to Abraham in Genesis 12, commanding him to leave his "country and [his] kindred and

[his] father's house" (v. 1). He promised to give Abraham a great name. In addition, God made a covenant with Abraham, saying, "In your offspring shall all the nations of the earth be blessed" (Gen 22:18; cf. Acts 3:25). Through Abraham's offspring, all nations will eventually join God's reconstituted family.

God's promise originally sounded especially strange. Abraham and his wife were very old and still had no children. Their bodies could not birth children. They did not completely understand God's word, so Abraham lay with his servant. She birthed a son, but God did not want to use Abraham's firstborn son. God's promise does not depend on ancestral lineage. Afterward Abraham sent the servant and her son away. The family God had promised Abraham would not come entirely through bloodline but rather through God's grace.

Abraham's descendants had to be loyal to the one true God, who always keeps his promises. When Abraham's wife was ninety years old, God allowed her to become pregnant with a son named Isaac. Only this God creates life. God tested Abraham, telling him to sacrifice Isaac, his only son (Gen 22).[149] Abraham believed God and so gave him glory. He was willing to offer his only hope for continuing his family line. Yet God stopped Abraham and provided him with a substitute, a lamb. This substitute protected God's promise and his family. Because he is faithful, God saves Isaac's life.

God's covenant with Abraham creates a problem. Since people have made God lose face, he should put us all to shame. However, he made a commitment to Abraham to save and bless all nations. How can God keep his promises and yet uphold his honor? He cannot simply overlook human evil. That too would be disgraceful. He also cannot break his covenant. That would also be shameful. How would God set the world right? For many years, this remained a mystery.

Abraham's family eventually became known as "Israel." At times it seemed as if God had forgotten his people. Because of a famine, Israel had to go to Egypt. God continued to multiply Abraham's descendants; thus, the Egyptian king began to fear them. That king decided to enslave them, using them to increase his own country's wealth. Nevertheless God defeated the false gods of Egypt and rescued them from oppression. God shows that he is not simply the God of one small area of land; rather, he governs the entire world. No earthly power can ultimately usurp his authority. He is the King of all nations.

As sovereign King, God redeems Israel from slavery; as Father to a new nation, he calls Israel his "firstborn son" (Ex 4:22,23). In addition, he declares to his people, "You shall be to me a kingdom of priests and a holy nation"

(Ex 19:6). In other words, God adopts them in order that they would bear his name among the nations. They do not exist for themselves. Rather, Israel had a God-given vocation. Collectively they were to be a mediator among the nations. Through Israel—Abraham's offspring—God would restore the harmony to the world.

God commands all nations to worship him, the only true God. Therefore, he gave Israel a law (礼仪). This law reveals the character of the world's true Father and King. From God's law, they were supposed to learn righteousness and a sense of shame.[150] God desired that Israel would be a nation of love and righteousness. Through his people, God lovingly manifests his glory to the nations. The one true God does not hide his face.[151] In contrast, he exposes the true face of false gods. He was gracious to his people, giving them both security and fertile land.

Sadly, Israel was unfaithful.[152] They cast aside the one true God as Father and King. They wanted a human king, like other nations. God showed tolerance and allowed them to have a king. The first king was taller and more handsome than other people. Despite all appearances, he was unfaithful. "Man looks on the outward appearance, but the LORD looks on the heart" (1 Sam 16:7). Therefore, God chose an unlikely man named David. David had no *guanxi* or *mianzi*, yet God made a covenant with David. Although David rose from humble beginnings and made many mistakes, nevertheless God promised that David's offspring would reign as King forever. Not only that, God adds, "I will be to him a father, and he shall be to me a son" (2 Sam 7:14). In essence, God narrows the means by which he will keep his covenant with Abraham. Through David's offspring, all nations will be blessed.

Over time, the people of Israel believed in themselves more than God. They confused religion, tradition, and relationship. They worshiped God only for the sake of private blessing.[153] During times of trouble, they would appeal to God for help.[154] They even asked false gods to bless them. Socially, people cared only for themselves, growing increasingly individualistic. The nation's leaders unjustly treated the weak and poor. The people of Israel were utterly shameless.[155] In Malachi 1:6, God even asks, "A son honors his father, and a servant his master. If then I am a father, where is my honor? And if I am a master, where is my fear?"

In short, Israel repeats the mistakes of their ancestors. They lacked filial love. They feared the surrounding nations and their false gods. They turned to idols, exchanging the glory of Creator God for created things (Rom 1:23). For the sake of food and wealth, they turned against one another. God had set Israel "in the center of the nations" (Ezek 5:5). She was supposed to be a light to the nations, being God's "middle kingdom."[156] Consequently God avenges himself. Israel was cursed and suffered exile. Once again God's people are forced to leave their home. Israel was put to shame. Foreign powers oppressed them. Even worse, the nations blasphemed God. God's chosen people are supposed to be the vessel through which God blesses all nations. Instead they are cursed. They preferred death to life, shame rather than the honor of God.[157] How does God vindicate his name?

Human unfaithfulness does not nullify the faithfulness of God. God is righteous; therefore, he always keeps his promise. He will not forsake his family. God reaffirms his covenant with his people. He promises to put his Holy Spirit within them. In effect, this means God puts his law into the hearts of his people.[158] They themselves would become the temple in which God dwells! Israel's exile would not last forever. God promises to wipe away their national humiliation.[159] However, he does not simply point to the resurgence of their nation. God will surprise his people and exceed our expectations.

Years later, God the Father graciously returns his children back to their motherland; however, various foreign powers continue to rule over them. At that time, the people of Israel were also called Jews. Their most powerful oppressor came from the West—the Roman Empire. The Jews resented foreign occupation. When the Roman Empire ruled, the Jews were full of nationalistic zeal. Many people wanted to overthrow the imperialists.[160] In order to show patriotism, people were very serious about the Jewish law. After all, so they thought, their shame was due to their having disregarded the words God gave to their ancestors. Never forgetting their national humiliation,[161] the Jewish people became more and more concerned with who was in and who was out. They divided the world into "insiders" and "outsiders."

Many ancient Jews misunderstood the essence of their law.[162] They used the law and their traditions to keep out "Gentiles," whom they essentially regarded as "foreign devils."[163] The family of Israel became exclusivistic. They thought their nation was the center of the world. Ancestral heritage, place of birth, land, human connections, and material blessings are no guarantee of God's blessing. His many blessings do not suggest Israel has "most favored nation status."[164] God does not show partiality (Rom 2:11). Rather, it is only because they have a relationship with their Father that they are set apart. It has always been this way. God's people are blessed to be a blessing. In reality, Israel, like the rest of humanity, forgot their calling.

Behind their zeal and nationalism lay an ironic tragedy. The Jews had indeed forgotten their earliest ancestors. On the one hand, they had not learned from the mistakes of the past. They continued to compete for face. Although coming from the same root, they sought each other's harm.[165] On the other hand, they did not follow their father Abraham's example. Abraham was faithful; therefore, God declared him righteous. Yet the Jews did not truly honor Abraham as a family ancestor. Otherwise they would listen to Abraham and worship the one true God. Even though the Jews loved their motherland, they disregarded their father. They had forgotten that God's one family consists of all nations. As a result, they essentially disowned their relatives.[166]

It was into this darkness that a man named Jesus was born. God himself came into the world he had made. Although God is spirit, he took on human flesh. The name "Jesus" means "God saves." Through Jesus, God will set his world right. In him, God fulfills all his promises. As David's offspring, Jesus is called "Christ" and the "Son of God." These titles were given to Israel's King. The story of Jesus is called the "gospel" (Mark 1:1). Jesus' life, death, resurrection, and future return can be explained in the following way[167]:

Jesus'	English	Chinese	Literal Meaning	Significance
Life	Reveals	服侍	"serve"	Jesus' mission (serves God and people), character (humble, loving); Isaiah's "suffering servant"
Death	Redeems	付债	"pay a debt"	Uses two common 付债 salvation metaphors. Jesus pays and thus bears our debt. sounds like 负债, i.e. to bear a debt.
Resurrection	Resurrects	复活	"resurrect"	Jesus defeats all his enemies, the last being death (1 Cor 15:25-26).
Return	Restores	复国	"restore a kingdom"	Then comes the end, when he delivers the kingdom to God the Father. (1 Cor 15:24)

Figure 18: Jesus' Life, Death, Resurrection, and Return[168]

This gospel story of Jesus Christ can only be understood within the larger narrative of the Bible.

Jesus reveals the glory of God. He sovereignly cast out demons, healed diseases, raised the dead, and rebuked those who dominated the weak. He even exerted power over nature. However, to everyone's surprise, he did not use armed force to overthrow Israel's political enemies. In fact, Christ turned his attention on those who were "insiders." He exposes the Jewish leaders' real face. They cared more about perceptions and power than they did the poor. Money was their real idol. Jesus says that people cannot serve both God and money.

By contrast, Jesus does not show partiality. He taught that people misunderstood God's covenant. His promises are according to faith and not family background. In fact, Jesus redefines "family." On one occasion,

> A crowd was sitting around [Jesus], and they said to him, "Your mother and your brothers are outside, seeking you." And he answered them, "Who are my mother and my brothers?" And looking about at those who sat around him, he said, "Here are my mother and my brothers! For whoever does the will of God, he is my brother and sister and mother." (Mark 3:32–35)

Abraham's true offspring do not trust in social connections. Their allegiance is to God. His words should affect people's hearts—not simply outward appearances. Jesus draws all people to himself (John 12:32). God aims to rescue humanity, not merely a local clan.

Christ came to establish righteousness. Because Israel historically had suffered humiliation, many Jews wanted God to vindicate them.[169] Some were willing to shed blood to make the Romans pay for their injustice.[170] Sadly, people misunderstood Jesus' intention. Jesus sought to vindicate his Father. Whether a so-called insider or outsider, all people dishonor God. Jesus was willing to suffer in order to reveal God's glory. Among Abraham's offspring, Jesus was unique. Like a faithful firstborn son, he wipes away family shame. How does he do this?

Eventually, social leaders turned against Jesus. Worldly powers could not force Jesus to deny God his Father. They conspired to torture and kill him on a cross. Although Jesus was perfectly filial, his own countrymen rejected him. This was all according to God's plan. All nations commit treason against the King of heaven and earth. We deserve judgment. God promised to use Abraham's offspring Israel to bless the nations, but Israel fell under a curse. He demands compensation, yet no one can pay the debt.

One begins to see the significance of Christ's death. Shamefully, God's enemies allowed his corpse to hang on a cross. According to Israel's law, "Cursed is everyone who is hanged on a tree" (Gal 3:13; citing Deut 21:23). By becoming a curse, Israel's Christ bears their shame. Therefore, as Israel's King, he represents them and removes the curse. Jesus sacrifices himself on behalf of his people. In this way, Jesus is our recompense. We owe the Father-King honor and our life. Christ pays back in full our debts—our honor debt and our life debt. Jesus represents humanity—perfectly glorifying God and removing human shame. Christ saves God's face.

As a man, Jesus is also able to represent humanity. He perfectly honored God our Father. Therefore, three days after his burial, God removed the curse by raising Jesus from the dead. Jesus' physical body came out of the grave, not merely his spirit. The world regarded Jesus as a criminal. However, through the resurrection, God the Father vindicates his Son, making him the King of all kings. Jesus' Father overturns the honor/shame standards of the world. In Christ, God defeats all his enemies, whether governments, spirits, even death. God reclaims his rightful place.

What does this mean for the world? God has glorified his Son; in the same way, Christ gives his glory to his people (John 17:22). Previously we lacked face. We were weak and oppressed. Various social powers, love of face, shameful desires, sickness, and fear enslaved us. However, Jesus now reconciles God and his people. In short, Jesus serves as a mediator. No matter one's background, position, achievement, network, or other identity, anyone can come under Jesus' name. Accordingly, God keeps his covenant and defends his own name. Because the one true God reveals his glorify, all nations will be blessed. He deserves worship.

If we are willing to repent and give allegiance to Jesus as Lord, then our King will grant us pardon. More than that, all who follow Jesus come under God the Father's family name. In this way, Jesus continues the family line of Abraham.[171] As God's children, we no longer boast about the people we know, our social standing, ethnic identity, or traditions. Instead, we "[boast] in the hope of the glory of God" and this "hope does not put us to shame" (Rom 5:2,5).[172]

How does all this change our lives? In short, we might say *yi ru wei rong* (以辱为荣).[173] The phrase can be translated two ways. First, it can mean, "to regard shame as honor"; second, it conveys, "to use shame for honor." What the world sees as shameful, God sees as honorable. Thus, the world sees Jesus' cross and the suffering of Christians as disgraceful humiliation. Yet God uses these means precisely to reveal his glory. God intentionally uses an unfaithful nation, Israel, to show his own faithfulness.

God views honor/shame through a different lens than that of any particular culture. The nations worship created things, but these idols are worthless. What the world sees as honorable, God regards as shameful. Many think "getting face" and "getting a name" are desirable, yet God regards such pride as lamentable. Accordingly, Paul is able to say, "But far be it from me to boast except in the cross of our Lord Jesus Christ, by which the world has been crucified to me, and I to the world" (Gal 6:14). Christians should expect God to use circumstances and methods of ministry that are painful, seem foolish, and draw the condescending sneer of culture. He wants to expose the superficiality of the world in order that people would "count everything as loss because of the surpassing worth of knowing Christ Jesus my Lord" (Phil 3:8).

The gospel announces that the one true God has made Jesus Christ the King of kings. This message demands a change in our fundamental loyalties in order to be saved from his judgment. The nations must forsake false gods. Following Jesus requires a change. Everyone lives in the midst of some community. We must exchange our old sense of belonging and gain a new sense of identity. Paul puts it this way, "I have been crucified with Christ. It is no longer I who live, but Christ who lives in me" (Gal 2:20). Being an outcast to one group means being included in another. Jesus makes a promise: "And everyone who has left houses or brothers or sisters or father or mother or children or lands, for my name's sake, will receive a hundredfold and will inherit eternal life. But many who are first will be last, and the last first" (Matt 19:29,30).

We join God's royal family when we love Christ. Those who identify with Jesus become our brothers and sisters. Family is not simply about sharing a bloodline. This new way of seeing the world brings new desires and leads to a new way of living. Christ's followers are willing to sacrifice their own interests for others. They do not idolize face. Instead, they strive to "love one another with brotherly affection [and] outdo one another in showing honor" (Rom 12:10). Humility gives freedom and joy. We will care more about honor that endures (*lian*) than that which passes with the clouds (*mianzi*). We now delight in God's honor and joyfully envisage Christ's return.

After Jesus' resurrection, he ascended to his Father, where he now reigns at the right hand of God. He promised to return in the future. He will set the world right. God will not forever tolerate human corruption, idolatry, shame, and faithlessness. Once and for all, he will avenge the insults of those who rebel against Christ and reject his people. In this way, the Father will completely rescue his children. This is why Paul writes, "Everyone who believes in him will not be put to shame" (Rom 10:11; citing Isa 28:16).

When Jesus returns, he will resurrect and renew our physical bodies. In death, our body "is sown in dishonor; it is raised in glory. It is sown in weakness; it is raised in power" (1 Cor 15:43). In fact, the entire creation longs for God to restore humanity's glory. His children and all creation will be liberated. God will create a new heaven and a new earth. The entire world will be our inheritance! There will be true peace and harmony. Creation once again worships the Creator.

This vision of the future reshapes how God's people today live in the world. Because of our firm hope, we should "consider that the sufferings of this present time are not worth comparing with the glory that is to be revealed to us" (Rom 8:18). Therefore, Christ's followers are not indifferent towards evil in the world. Because they delight in righteousness, they expose and confront all that is shameful. Because they believe Christ's promise, they do not tire in doing good, knowing their labor in the Lord is not in vain (see 1 Cor 15:58; Gal 6:9).

When God consummates his kingdom, our King will gather his family around him.[174] We will rejoice as those eating and drinking at a reunion feast (团圆饭). Our Father will finally establish a "universal brotherhood" (世界大同). We will celebrate the King's victory over his enemies. The poor, the crippled, the lame, and the blind will be among his honored guests. Our host invites all nations to eat at his feast. His people will joyfully proclaim Jesus as host of the feast. In Chinese, "耶稣作主席," which translates, "Jesus is Chairman."[175]

Echoes of Culture within Scripture?

What then shall we say? Does contextualization nullify biblical exegesis? Not at all. Indeed if it were not for contextualization, there would be no biblical theology. All theology is contextual theology.[176] All theology is revealed, expressed, and interpreted within a cultural context. God does not change, though the way that he speaks in history has varied. The writer of Hebrews makes this same point: "Long ago, at many times and in many ways, God spoke to our fathers by the prophets, but in these last days he has spoken to us by his Son, whom he appointed the heir of all things, through whom also he created the world" (Heb 1:1,2).

In *Echoes of Scripture in the Letters of Paul*, Richard Hays suggests a way of understanding Paul's method of interpretation that may help us to better do "exegetical contextualization." How does Paul interpret the Old Testament? Hays answers,

> *If we learned from Paul how to read Scripture, we would read as participants in the eschatological drama of redemption....* Through interpreting Scripture, we locate our present time in relation to the story of God's dealing with humankind. Paul believed that his stance at the turn of the ages gave him a warrant for his radically revisionary readings because it gave him a privileged perspective from which to discern the thematic unity of time past and future.[177]

We can adapt Hays' proposal for our purposes. First, if we learned from the biblical writers how to read Scripture, we will recall that the Bible was written for all humankind. Therefore, interpreting the Bible is not the exclusive privilege of any one particular culture or tradition. Second, when God inspired Scripture, he spoke to authors who were located within a specific context. The New Testament writers frame their reading of the Old Testament so as to highlight its meaning amid their contemporary circumstances.

Consider Mark 12:1–12. Jesus' parable is a blatant retelling of Isaiah 5. He speaks of wicked tenants who want to take over a man's vineyard and so decide to kill his son. Jesus then cites Psalm 118:22, "The stone that the builders rejected has become the cornerstone," making a Hebrew pun that connects the rejected "stone" (*'eb'n*, אֶבֶן) back to the murdered "son" (*ben*, בֵּן). As a result, the Jewish leaders "perceived that he had told the parable against them" (v. 12).[178] Exegetical contextualization likewise tries to explain Scripture in a way that helps people hear echoes of their own culture in the Bible.

Third, we see the unity of the church, both past and present. Our own experience enables us to identify with people in Scripture who have similar successes and failures as us. The missionary groans with the prophets when no one receives the gospel message. Pastors feel Paul's anxiety for the church daily (2 Cor 11:28). The Chinese family with one child can sympathize with Abraham as he climbs up the mountain with Isaac in Genesis 22.

Fourth, the one true God reveals himself in history. Therefore, in doing biblical theology, we must be careful not to take God's dealing with humanity and turn it into an abstraction. Christians must make radical claims that challenge social loyalties and relativize human idols. The gospel should revise the boastful ways that people talk about their past and future.

Finding China in the Middle of God's Kingdom

Biblical theology is not safe. If we keep theology abstracted from culture, we might avoid the risk of syncretism. After all, our theology would be immune to the contamination of culture. However, it is precisely here that any such theology would also cease to be biblical. God has revealed himself authoritatively in history. Having breathed the Bible into existence, the Holy Spirit now provides illumination so that we can interpret God's message according to its original meaning.

No doubt there are flaws in the way this essay has retold the biblical story. I do not claim for myself divine inspiration on par with the Bible. At times, the narrative above seems to juxtapose the experience of China and Israel. Whatever the similarities, we should not confuse the two. In the scope of redemptive history, the Chinese remain Gentiles who are "grafted in" (Rom 11:17).

Nevertheless, those concerned with the Chinese church should consider the value of making this sort of comparison. Various issues are at stake. For example, we have to decide how and if certain words and concepts can be used to convey biblical truth. For the sake of explanation, could we at times use the ancient Chinese concept *liyi* (礼仪) to explain the significance of the word "law" within the Jew-Gentile disputes? *Liyi* is a distinctly Chinese notion. It typifies Chinese cultural tradition and theoretically separates a true Chinese person from a foreigner. In addition, there are moral issues to consider. What about ethnocentrism and nationalism? As evident in the account above, monotheism directly challenges any such boasting. What biblical insights about honor and shame can be applied to the typical Chinese person whose sole concern is family and "face"? As these questions are answered, a great dragon will be released into the world for the sake of God's kingdom. Let the reader understand.

KEY POINTS

- Exegetical contextualization uses a particular cultural lens to interpret Scripture. This highlights for us aspects of the text that would be less clear if using another cultural lens.
- Chinese culture emphasizes face, family (relationships), and fortune. These motifs should shape a contextualized biblical theology.
- The major movements of the contextualized biblical theology in the chapter include:
  - Humanity is one family under God.
  - We have all lost face (*lian*) before God, yet seek to get face (*mianzi*) from the people around us. However, human praise (*mianzi*) cannot compensate for our face before God.
  - God takes the initiative to restore his kingdom and reconcile the human family. Accordingly, he establishes a series of covenants that reveal his faithfulness.
  - The Creator Father raised Jesus as King (i.e., "Christ"). He was perfectly filial toward his heavenly Father. Accordingly, he restores family honor and shares with us his glory.
  - God in Christ overturns the world's standards of honor and shame.
  - Ultimately, we await Christ's return. He will avenge the shame brought upon God's face and the human family and establish God's kingdom in the world. All nations will be blessed.

9

The Gospel with Chinese Characteristics: An Example of Cultural Contextualization

How Do We Preach the Gospel in China?

What does it mean to preach the gospel with Chinese characteristics? Countless authors have given their suggestions. Many agree concerning the key issues that should influence a Chinese contextualization. However, there are very few comprehensive proposals that could easily be called both biblical and "Chinese."[179] This chapter attempts to offer this sort of proposal, building on the previous chapters. It puts forward an example of "cultural contextualization," whereby one interprets culture through the lens of the Bible.

First, I will again provide a survey of Chinese culture. Although this may feel a bit repetitious in view of my last chapter, I think it remains necessary in order to show the whole process. In addition, I adjust my overview of Chinese culture to particularly suit the themes that will be emphasized in the contextualization that follows. Therefore, one can see how my description of Chinese culture prepares us to actually do cultural contextualization. Second, the chapter examines potential "false gospels" in Chinese society. Finally, I propose a gospel contextualization that draws upon major biblical themes and addresses significant problems in Chinese society. Regardless of cultural context, it is hoped that people will be able to utilize this process of contextualization to more effectively share the gospel in their own ministry setting.

Although theological ideas are contextualized for concrete social settings, this does not limit their value to a particular time and place. First of all, one can still benefit by observing the process used to develop a contextualized theology. Second, since cultures across the world share many common features, we can learn from those living in other contexts. Third, the Bible is written to all humanity. Its message is not restricted any one culture. Therefore, anyone who wishes to do theological contextualization will engage in many of the same questions, since they seek to interpret the same biblical text. Accordingly, this chapter articulates the gospel for the sake of a Chinese context, yet its relevance extends well beyond the Middle Kingdom.

Framing Our Answers to Four Gospel Questions

As we have seen, gospel presentations in the Bible have a distinct pattern. They are consistently framed by one or more of three themes—creation, covenant, and kingdom. In previous chapters, we identified three corresponding (though not equivalent) themes from Chinese culture. They capture something of the spirit of the three above-mentioned gospel themes. For Chinese culture, we could use one or more of the following motifs to frame our gospel contextualization—the world, relationship, and authority.

The biblical gospel answers four key questions. I'll review them briefly. There is a clear logic to the order of the questions. (1) "Who is Jesus Christ?" The Old Testament adapts the question to "Who is God?" (2) "What has Christ done?" This question aims to show what kind of a person he is. (3) "Why does Christ matter?" In other words, why is Jesus significant to us? This point largely deals with salvation. Traditionally, evangelicals have laid the greatest stress on this aspect of the gospel message.[180] (4) "How should we respond?" This fourth piece is not a part of the "gospel" itself, but the command to respond is typical of gospel presentations. Appropriate responses include faith, repentance, obedience, and praise. To be clear, gospel presentations may not necessarily follow this exact sequence in the flow of conversation. Nevertheless, the question order clarifies how to relate the various facets of the gospel according to its internal logic and stress.

How can we utilize this pattern found in Scripture for the sake of contextualization? First of all, these questions can serve as criteria by which to assess various evangelistic methods. Is the presentation sufficiently thorough? Does it give priority to Christ rather than simply emphasizing human salvation and response? It is easy to highlight inadvertently the latter to such a degree that Christ becomes little more than a bridge or a tool for human benefit.

Second, these questions alert us to the array of possible answers given in the Bible. Because there are multiple right answers to each question, one must be attentive to both biblical emphases and the needs of the contemporary culture. In other words, where is the greatest overlap between the biblical text and the cultural context? Scripture uses an assortment of motifs and metaphors. Chinese will inherently grasp certain of these themes more readily than the average American (i.e., honor/shame and collective identity).

For the purposes of this chapter, these four questions will guide our contextualization process and particularly our study of Chinese culture and the Bible. After becoming familiar with the important features of Chinese culture, one can then identify its "false gospels." Every culture and our various subcultures have substitute versions of the gospel. They offer alternative visions for what the world should be like, what are its problems, and what are the solutions.

A culture's false gospels also answer the four questions mentioned above. Thus, we first could ask, "Functionally, who is the savior-king in the culture?" Personally, one asks, "Functionally, who is the savior-king figure in my life?" Second, "What has this savior-king done in the past?" Again, the answer to this second question clarifies both what kind of a person the "savior" is as well as his significance (question #3). Therefore, it matters that one knows about this savior-king's character and power.

Third, "Why does it matter that attention be given to this authority figure?" What does he or she promise to do in the future? This question assumes a certain set of life problems that need to be solved. Implicitly, this false gospel speaks about some sort of ideal world.

Fourth, how should people respond, given this assumed view of the world and the offer made by the savior-king? Whatever the details, one thing is assured in this "gospel": people will only overcome the supposed threat if they will give their steadfast allegiance to a certain cause or person. What does the cultural gospel command of people? There is always a cost required.

Sketching the Contours of a Cultural Context

Within any large culture, there are countless subcultures. They each have a hierarchy of authorities, values, and standards of conduct. It would be impossible to give a comprehensive picture of Chinese culture. Sketches of culture are inherently limited by their abstraction. Aspects that are salient in one part of a country are hardly noticed in another. For example, when describing China, how can one generalize its view of religion? Minority groups in rural areas typically have a greater fear of local spirits and demons than Beijing urbanites, who are educated, atheistic, and work at professional government jobs. On the other hand, it would be easy to distinguish too sharply "near cultures." Near cultures often agree at fundamental points of worldview, even if their particular cultural expressions differ in detail or degree.

The contextualization proposed in this chapter focuses on a few themes prominent throughout China. Other books and articles give more detailed accounts of Chinese culture.[181] For now, we will review three spheres of Chinese social life. These include honor/shame, relationship, and economics. As in the previous chapter, we could restate them more simply in terms of face, family, and fortune. Each entails a variety of other subtopics.

According to a well-known expression, "People want face like a tree wants bark" (人要脸树要皮). "Face" is a Chinese way of talking about honor ("gaining face") and shame ("losing face"). Put simply, it refers to one's perceived social standing and value. As a social concept, face is gained and lost according to the standards of the watching public. This group could include one's family, coworkers, classmates, and fellow citizens, to give just a few examples. Certainly, one community will "give face" for something that would cause a person to "lose face" in another group. Anne-Laure Monfret quotes a Chinese person who describes the importance of face: "To lose face is like ceasing to exist in the eyes of others."[182] Not surprisingly, face determines one's identity within a given social setting.

Face is won, lost, or maintained in a variety of ways. One's public standing is partially determined by factors like family name, gender, one's relationships, position, and title. Face of this sort has often been called "ascribed" honor (or shame). By contrast, "achieved" face is the status gained due to individual achievements, whether moral or nonmoral.

For example, an athlete may get face by winning a competition. On the other hand, the bravery of a man who rescues children from a collapsing building would also win public praise. Of course comparable examples could be given with respect to shame (i.e., losing face). "Shame" and "losing face" could occur simply by not knowing the answer to a question and when losing a competition. Actions deemed immoral, such as criminal activity, are more serious threats to one's face.

Within the Mandarin language, one can even distinguish between two kinds of face, *mianzi* (面子) and *lian* (脸). *Mianzi* is a broader term, thus including more trivial and circumstantial reasons for having face. *Lian* more narrowly carries moral connotations. It refers to one's most basic worth as a person. All people are born with *lian*, which can be lost through bad conduct. One does not necessarily have *mianzi*. Every day it can be won, lost, and maintained.

Face is the lifeblood of relationships (i.e., *guanxi*). Quintessential relationships are found in the family. The Chinese notion of family extends well past the so-called "nuclear family" of the West. It even includes one's ancestors. The Chinese word for "country" (国家) combines the characters for "land/state" (国) and "family" (家). To adapt Descartes' famous dictum, "I am, because we are; and since we are, therefore I am."[183] This sort of collectivism contrasts the sort of individualism stereotypical of Western cultures. Chinese identity is largely determined by *whom* one knows. Accordingly, the Chinese conception of identity could be captured by the phrase "There is no me without you."[184]

One shares face with other people in his or her group. The head of the group, like a company CEO or nation's president, represents and embodies the honor of the group's members. There is a moral obligation therefore for everyone to seek and preserve face on behalf of those in their family, community, or peer group. Ties within relational networks are tightened by a constant exchange of favors (人情), which literally translates "person-feelings." The reciprocity of favors and gifts keeps people in relational debt to one another. One breaks relationship with another person if he or she did not repay this sort of debt. Naturally, Chinese tend to divide those around them into "insiders" and "outsiders." It is morally imperative to maintain harmony with insiders (the most important of whom are those within one's family). Chinese people are more practical than abstract in their thinking. When applied to relationships, this way of thinking can lead people to regard relationships as tools and means to be used for personal benefit.

What happens when one crosses from one social context into another? Problems emerge when different groups compete for authority. In a hierarchal society like China, the predicament is captured by the idiom "忠孝两难全" (*zhong xiao liang nan quan*), meaning something like "dilemma of divided loyalties." If familial relationships are primary, yet the nation is supposed to function as a large family, then to whom does one give his or her utmost allegiance—one's father or the king/emperor? Accordingly, tensions are heightened when talking about Christianity, which some see as an outside "Western" religion. Many Chinese people face a dilemma when they consider following Christ: how are they supposed to be loyal both to God and their family? In the Chinese mind, there is nothing more immoral than seeming to reject one's parents. For some, becoming a Christian might feel very "un-Chinese."[185]

Face and relationship are critical for those seeking fortune. When China opened to the world in 1978, economic reforms created a Chinese socialism "with capitalistic characteristics." Since that time, its citizens have labored to share in the wealth enjoyed by the West. This is sometimes called the "Chinese Dream."[186] Since 1982, the national policy restricting families to only one child has had tremendous social and economic implications. Any future hope for honor and prosperity by a family depends upon a single child. One bears the weight of both his mother and father's ancestors. In adulthood, this entails financially supporting two parents, two parents-in-law, in addition to one's own child.[187]

These dynamics coupled with China's massive population create a context in which everyone feels the strain of competition. Success is not measured simply by good effort. Instead, it is assessed by one's score on the *gaokao*, the national exam that decides if and where a student can attend college.[188] Any imperfection threatens the family's security and honor.[189] Fear of shame drives many to languish under the pressure.[190] The sort of stress, first felt in childhood, continues to some degree or another as people take to their careers, when they will fight to win respect for their family, company, and country.

A False Gospel in China

The world is full of false gospels. These so-called "gospels" are popular narratives that present themselves as both explanation and solution to the world's problems. What follows is just one example of a false gospel in China. Most certainly, individual beliefs and ambitions in particular contexts will vary, yet this pattern of thought is found in countless places.

The biblical gospel proclaims that Jesus is King; therefore, it is natural for false gospels to center on the question of authority. Whom do we recognize as having supreme authority? To whom do we give allegiance? How people answer these questions will have a tremendous impact on the direction of their lives, including what they hope in, what they struggle against, and whom they love.

Who Plays the Role of God?

One might say the god of Chinese culture exists in a "trinity." "Face" serves as a pseudo "Spirit," giving vitality and distinguishing those in one group from another. "Relationship" (*guanxi*) plays the role of the "Son," being regarded as a *functional savior* by most Chinese people. Ultimately, there is no material gain (i.e., the "Father") except through the "Son" and the empowerment of the "Spirit." Like the rest of humanity, millions bow their knee to the altar of wealth and security.

For a typical Chinese person, this god incarnates in the form of one's parents. This is not surprising given the fact that Chinese tend to identify strongly with their group. The most central group is their family. In Chinese history, social harmony has been a means of survival.[191] This begins with the family, in which one develops his or her views of authority and morality. Huo Shui concludes, "Family is the primary building block for social structures and for human interaction."[192]

Confucianism has shaped Chinese culture as much or more than any other religion, philosophy, or ideology. Three of the five foundational relationships, according to Confucian thought, are familial, the most prominent being the father-son relationship.[193] Fengyan Wan cites the Chinese classic *The Book of Filial Piety* (孝经), capturing the essence of a child's moral education:

Filial piety is the foundation of all virtues and the fountainhead whence all moral teachings spring.... Our bodies—from a single hair to a bit of skin—are derived from our parents, we must not in the least injure or wound them. This is the beginning of filial piety. We establish ourselves in the world and are considered successful by cultivating virtues and observing morality, so as to leave a good name for posterity and to bring glory to our parents: this is the ultimate realm of filial piety. Hence filial piety begins with the service of our parents, proceeds to serve the emperor and is consummated in establishing ourselves in the world and achieving virtue and hence success.[194]

Rappa and Tan add a key idea:

The family was the state in miniature, the state the family writ large. Max Weber calls China a "familistic State." From the Han dynasty onwards, the imperial laws upheld the absolute authority of the father in the family and reinforced other hierarchical family relations prescribed in the state ideology.[195]

Consequently, since political power is vested within a family model, it benefits the state to reinforce the importance of parental authority.

Contemporary writers expand our understanding about the way Chinese children see their relationship with parents. Although children readily acknowledge that authority changes depending on the situation, it has been found that, regardless of context, mothers are consistently regarded as the *moral* authority compared to those outside the home.[196] The need to protect "face" bolsters an ethic that centers on child-parent relationship. Therefore, one always seeks to maintain the appearance of keeping core social values, such as harmony and filial piety.[197] Even if a child were to disagree with his parents, the concern for face ensures that his actions will be bound by a consideration for his parents, whom he must publicly honor.[198] K. K. Hwang supports the point with his analysis of empirical data. For Chinese people, he concludes that it is more important to pursue "social face" (a positive social impression) than to seek "moral face," though of course one would not want to "lose" moral face.[199]

What Do Chinese Parents Do?

Parents give life to their children. Mothers and fathers make sacrifices to protect and provide for the child's physical and educational needs. As Amy Chua puts it, "Chinese mothers get in the trenches, putting in long grueling hours personally tutoring, training, interrogating, and spying on their kids."[200] In reality, one's life and fortune are the fruit of a long line of ancestors. There are no mere "individual" accomplishments.

Within this framework, children are in debt to their parents (and, more generally, ancestors).[201] This debt is relational. A child owes the elder honor and loyalty. Of course this relational debt has financial implications. All things considered, Chinese typically regard relational debts as being more important than financial debts.[202] Yeh and Bedford echo comments made by many others:

> Belief in reciprocal filial piety is based on the idea that children should repay their parents for their lives, and the expense and trouble of raising them. . . . The fact of the debt can never be in question, so the existence of the obligation is likewise unquestionable.[203]

Recently, Amy Chua indicates that she is well aware that Chinese parents enjoy a leveraged position over their children.

> Chinese parents believe that their kids owe them everything. . . . The understanding is that Chinese children must spend their lives repaying their parents by obeying them and making them proud. By contrast, I don't think most Westerners have the same view of children being permanently indebted to their parents. Jed [her non-Chinese husband] actually has the opposite view. "Children don't choose their parents," he once said to me. "They don't even choose to be born. It's parents who foist life on their kids, so it's the parents' responsibility to provide for them. Kids don't owe their parents anything. Their duty will be to their own kids." This strikes me as a terrible deal for the Western parent.[204]

Hwang succinctly adds, "Parents are the origins of one's life. People have the utmost filial obligation to repay the unending debt to their parents."[205]

Why Does This Matter?

A number of characters within Chinese-American literature illustrate the problem felt by Chinese children. Erin Khuê Ninh first restates the previous point: in a culture that stresses filial piety, a child has a debt, which is "incurred by birth and binding the subject, by virtue of living, to an ever-increasing principle."[206] She then recounts the anxiety felt by the characters, who are crushed by the burden of being Chinese daughters. They are in constant fear of transgressing the unknowable, changing, and seeming arbitrary standards of a sovereign parent. The "familial norms of filial obedience are devised in such a way as not to be attainable—and are, something like the proverbial carrot on a stick, effective precisely *because* they cannot be attained."[207] Ninh summarizes the plight in which the Chinese girl finds herself:

> Propriety is therefore the norm most appropriate to sovereign power, for what remains is simply that that which her parents deem acceptable is acceptable (proper), and that which they deem unacceptable is unacceptable (improper). Such a norm does not offer even the pretense of an outside referent, an objective measure. It is the prime number of norms: divisible only by obedience.[208]

One of the women longs for "perfect filiality," while another says, "In all of my imaginings, I was filled with a sense that I would soon become *perfect*. My mother and father would adore me. I would be beyond reproach."[209]

What is at stake? Without face (*mianzi, lian*) and relationships (*guanxi*), how can one ever expect to get married, have kids, find a job, buy a house, and provide food and security for one's family? Some have compared face to a "credit card," a form of "social currency"[210] Those who lose face by not conforming to cultural norms will risk social "bankruptcy." When one lacks face and relationships, one ceases to exist. Lawrence Yang and Arthur Kleinman graphically describe the problem.

> Those who fail to cultivate *guanxi* networks are assigned a severely disadvantaged status, a solitary state viewed as "disastrous." To represent the "social death" linked to such persons (and their associates), Northern Chinese terms use "death" (*si*) as a modifier (e.g., *sipi*—"dead skin"; *sixing*—"dead characters") to describe the closed opportunities of such individuals' social networks. One especially illustrative term—*si menzi*—means "dead (closed) doors." By contrasting the popular phrase of using one's connections to obtain resources, or "going through the back door" (*zou homen* [sic]), *si menzi* is a metaphor that describes a relationship leading to no further resources.[211]

What can save a person from this death? There is no other way under heaven by which one can be saved except by having a name.

This "salvation" begins with family, a person's most basic relational context. If one cannot manage the relationships in his own household, how will he relate to those in society? To maintain face (*lian*), one must pay careful attention to how he treats those closest to him. Most significant are blood relatives. Previously, I mentioned that Chinese children, when they become adults, are responsible for providing financially for their parents. A recent Chinese law further illustrates the central importance of parent-child relationship. Adult Chinese children are now *legally* required to visit their parents on a regular basis.[212]

How Should People Respond?

It is as if parent and child were bound by a covenant. In exchange for life, protection, and provision, a child is obligated to show filial piety. For a Chinese person, the parent-child relationship determines one's identity and worth. It implies a promise and a threat—either honor or shame. Obedience is about face. If one does not show proper respect to one's parents, then he or she is a failure. He utterly loses face.

From childhood onward, Chinese children are constantly under the threat of losing face. Naturally, they feel tremendous pressure. They have a sense of needing to pay this debt back. Morality inherently involves face. Our view of right and wrong is connected with our sense of honor and shame. When a person does wrong, we sometimes say that person "has no sense of shame" (不知廉耻). People try hard to prove their identity and worth. Consequently, grown children labor diligently and make countless sacrifices to secure a sense of contentment, security, and success.

How Does One Pay an Infinite Debt?

Consequently, Chinese adults become slaves to their parents.[213] The debt children owe their parents quickly enslaves them. Life decisions are oriented in two directions. Looking backwards, people have a sense of obligation to pay back a debt. Looking to the future, the fear of losing face binds them. They know they should pay back their parents; however, these kids intuitively know *they can never pay back their parents.*

There is a reason children remain in debt: parents define what constitutes "filial piety." For so many Chinese parents, showing proper respect will include a number of things: a name, face, money, car, kids, house, etc. By providing their parents with these things, children show *renqing* (人情), literally translated "human feelings" or, more loosely, "favors." *Renqing* practically expresses one's concern for another person. Reciprocity is essential for the ongoing existence of a relationship. Accordingly, people *owe renqing* (*qian renqing*, 欠人情). Within parent-child relationships, the child owes a debt that can never be repaid. Parents determine the payback.

Parents make sure their child knows his or her position. If they were to show too much satisfaction with their children, if they praised their kid too much, then the child might get the sense he had fulfilled his duty. He or she would feel a little less urgency to do what parents command. To some degree, parents would relinquish control over their kids. Therefore, mothers and fathers withhold their approval. At the very least, their expressed contentment towards the child is restrained or measured. At times, one hears a parent praise their children. Sadly, however, that commendation is often followed quickly with a "but," after which the child hears one or two small corrections for further improvement.[214] By withholding their full approval, parents ensure that they will retain control. Children remain desperate and in debt. In effect, they become slaves to their parents, to whom they owe complete allegiance.

What else might a person do who wants to be freed from this debt and slavery? One popular option is to get wealthy, but not for the sake of bringing face to the family. Rather, getting rich is simply another means of winning face for oneself. Money not only brings freedom from the demands of parents; greater wealth could also mean turning the tables. In that case, it is now the parents who appease the whim of their adult child, hoping to get a little reward in return. Whatever the motive, Chinese people simply exchange one form of slavery for another. If money does not own a person, he or she can quickly fall slave to a car or house. There is another direction that one might go. A common alternative to these options is nationalism or even ethnocentrism. Such ideology essentially is a kind of family pride enlarged to a national scale.

How Should We Honor Our Father?

When people read the metaphors of Scripture, it is only natural that readers will draw from their own life experience to interpret such language. For example, the Bible calls God "Father." Of course many people will wonder if God is like a Chinese father. How are they similar? How are they different? False gospels typical blend what is true with what is false. If Christians are to preach the gospel faithfully in China, they will need to help people identify ways the culture distorts a major motif in Scripture—family.

The gospel summons people to change their allegiance. For Chinese this raises the question about how they should relate to their parents. In Matthew 10, Jesus sends out the twelve disciples, giving them a warning:

> Do not think that I have come to bring peace to the earth. I have not come to bring peace, but a sword. For I have come to set a man against his father, and a daughter against her mother, and a daughter-in-law against her mother-in-law. And a person's enemies will be those of his own household. Whoever loves father or mother more than me is not worthy of me, and whoever loves son or daughter more than me is not worthy of me. And whoever does not take his cross and follow me is not worthy of me. Whoever finds his life will lose it, and whoever loses his life for my sake will find it. (Matt 10:34–39)

Chinese will immediately recoil at the high cost of Jesus' invitation to follow him. Becoming a Christian is more than praying a prayer or doing a ceremony. Clear gospel preaching always exposes idols.

Christians are not immune to the influence of the false gospel summarized above. As we see in Galatians, compromise can also creep into the church precisely when one seeks to obey God.[215] Chinese may ask, "What does it mean to honor our mother and father?" Jesus only complicates the question when he states, "For whoever does the will of my Father in heaven is my brother and sister and mother" (Matt 12:50; cf. Mark 3:35). In addition, we also have to ask, "Who defines the meaning of 'honor'?" A contextualized gospel takes seriously the fact that honor can have many shades of meaning.

Reinterpreting Chinese Culture from a Biblical Perspective

We are interpreting Chinese culture through the lens of Scripture.[216] We have discerned critical perspectives and problems within contemporary Chinese culture. They are characterized using a variety of key biblical themes, which are interwoven throughout the canon. In order to contextualize the gospel in China, it is imperative to identify ways in which the story of the biblical text finds expression in the Chinese cultural context.

The various motifs are interconnected. One's sense of identity, honor, and shame grows out of one's relationships, the most important being those in one's family. The way people relate to their families will shape the way they interact with others in society. Acceptance by one group entails adopting its honor/shame standard, which necessarily means a person will be excluded from other groups. Group members must conform to certain expectations of behavior. Conformity is a mark of allegiance. Essentially, these obligations or duties are the cost of belonging to the group. If one falls into debt, he or she runs the risk of being rejected, isolated, and put to shame.

To preserve the truthfulness of a gospel presentation, we need to define our terms. In the contextualized gospel presentation that follows, a number of ideas will be redefined in light of Scripture. For example, one must consider how to answer Jesus' question, "Who is my mother, and who are my brothers?" (Matt 12:48). In both the Bible and in China, this is a fundamental measure of what is right, wrong, good, and bad.

In John 8:31–59, Jesus' polemic engagement with the Pharisees is full of imagery intended to reinterpret and redefine their understanding of reality. First, Jesus suggests they are slaves in need of freedom (John 8:31,34–36). In response, the Pharisees claim that Abraham is their father (8:33,39) and possibly even insinuate that Jesus is an illegitimate son, "born of sexual immorality" (8:41). Jesus counters, not only by calling God his Father; he also explains that their actions prove that the devil is their father, not Abraham (8:39–47). In the end, Jesus says one's identity (a child of whom?) and status (a slave or free person?) are determined by whom he or she honors. Jesus declares,

> I do not have a demon, but I honor my Father, and you dishonor me.
> Yet I do not seek my own glory; there is One who seeks it, and he is
> the judge. . . . If I glorify myself, my glory is nothing. It is my Father

who glorifies me, of whom you say, "He is our God." But you have
not known him. I know him. If I were to say that I do not know him,
I would be a liar like you, but I do know him and I keep his word.
Your father Abraham rejoiced that he would see my day. He saw it
and was glad. (John 8:49,50,54–56)

Moreover, Paul explains the gospel using similar imagery and redefines
the same concepts.[217]

A Chinese Contextualization of the Gospel[218]

The contextualized gospel presented in this section answers the four questions
mentioned above: "Who is Christ?" (or "Who is God?"), "What has Christ
done?" "Why does he matter?" and finally, "How should we respond?" I will
briefly summarize some of the main points that follow. God, as the Creator
of the world, is Father of the human family. He sent Jesus to be King over
all nations, whom he is reconciling to his heavenly Father. God restores his
kingdom in the world by defeating his enemies through the life, death, and
resurrection of Christ. Believers can join God's family.

Therefore, Chinese Christians are not enslaved to parental expectations
and the cultural demands that usurp God's role as heavenly Father. People
should repent of familial idolatries and give their allegiance to Christ, who
graciously shares his glory with us. In the previous chapter, I gave a narrative
account of the grand biblical story. I will not rehearse it here. Instead, I will use
a more analytical approach. The purpose of this section is simply to highlight
a number of ways one could answer each of the four questions in a way that
is both faithful to the Bible and meaningful to Chinese culture.

Who Is the God of Jesus Christ?

When preaching the gospel among Chinese people, one could describe God
in at least three ways: Creator, Father, and King.[219] He is the one who brings
harmony out of chaos, separating light and darkness, deciding between life
and death. He is the measure of all that is good and right. As Creator of the
world, the one true God is not limited to any particular place. He is not like
the local idols of folk religions. He does not live in statues or temples. In

addition, he is not partial to any single nation. God not only orders the cosmos, he also sovereignly sustains the world. He creates beauty and provides food. The Creator is sovereign.[220] Because he is Creator, God is also Father of the human family (人类大家庭).

God creates humanity in his image. As his children, we were originally intended to bring him face. He wants us to reflect his glory in our family relationships. Of course God is also the King of the world. We owe him supreme allegiance and love.[221] God shows his power and kindness in history. He rules as a loving Father. Naturally, he requires filial respect and honor. In short, we owe God our *renqing* (人情), our sincere affections. We honor the Father-King when we reflect his rule over creation.

In Jesus, God the Father manifested himself in the world. Accordingly, God's people regard Jesus as King of all kings. Jesus is often called "Christ" and "Son of God." These titles signify Jesus' royal status (王位).[222] Thus, one might say Jesus is the true "son of heaven" (*tianzi*, 天子). Jesus was perfectly filial towards his heavenly Father. As the offspring of Adam, Jesus is also human and thus able to represent the human family. He is the perfect image of God. Not only this, Jesus is the offspring of Abraham and David. As such, Jesus is the fulfillment of God's promises. Jesus is the means through which God will bless all nations, establishing his rule over the entire world.

What Has God Done in Christ?

In Christ, God defeats his enemies. Jesus demonstrates the sovereignty of God over every power that opposes God's kingdom—whether demons, disease, dominions, or death. In this way, he reveals his glory and exposes humanity's sinful shame. The life, death, and resurrection of Jesus overturn common notions of wisdom, love, family, justice, honor, and shame.

At first the crowds welcomed Jesus. Not only was Jesus an excellent teacher, he was also able to heal the sick, feed the hungry, and cast out demons from people. He was even able to raise the dead. No matter whether one was an insider, an outsider, a rich man, a poor woman, a social leader, or had a disease, Jesus was willing to help them and eat with them. It has been said, "What you do not want done to yourself, do not do to others."[223] However, this was not Jesus' way. Instead, his life and words taught, "Whatever you wish that others would do to you, do also to them" (Matt 7:12).

Jesus challenged many of the prevailing values of his culture. He even redefined "family." Once, when Jesus' mother and brothers wanted to speak with him, he said, "'Who is my mother, and who are my brothers?' And stretching out his hand toward his disciples, he said, 'Here are my mother and my brothers! For whoever does the will of my Father in heaven is my brother and sister and mother'" (Matt 12:48–50; cf. Mark 3:31–35).

In God's eyes, family is not merely according to bloodlines. Jesus warned his listeners that families would be divided because of him (Matt 10:34–39). On the other hand, he gave his followers a promise: Jesus said,

> Truly, I say to you, there is no one who has left house or brothers or sisters or mother or father or children or lands, for my sake and for the gospel, who will not receive a hundredfold now in this time, houses and brothers and sisters and mothers and children and lands, with persecutions, and in the age to come eternal life. But many who are first will be last, and the last first. (Mark 10:29–31; cf. Matt 19:29)

God will give them a family made up of people from all nations.

At other times, Jesus deeply offended the Jewish leaders, saying that they were not really Abraham's offspring (John 8). In addition, he preached a seemingly revolutionary message. Christ proclaimed the kingdom of God. He showed how God's kingdom stood in sharp contrast to the political powers of his day, whether those in Israel or from Rome. Foreigners had long oppressed the Jews. Naturally, they dreamed of a king who would rescue them. However, Jesus' proclaimed an entirely different kind of kingdom. When his own disciples began to seek power and face, he exhorted,

> You know that those who are considered rulers of the Gentiles lord it over them, and their great ones exercise authority over them. But it shall not be so among you. But whoever would be great among you must be your servant, and whoever would be first among you must be slave of all. For even the Son of Man came not to be served but to serve, and to give his life as a ransom for many. (Mark 10:42–45; cf. Matt 20:25–28)

God's power is manifest through weakness, suffering, and loving enemies.

Jesus confronted injustice, prejudice, ethnocentrism, unfaithfulness, and greed. He exposed people's true face. Jesus undermined various cultural customs. Why? Israel's teachers customarily used cultural traditions to disobey God, give themselves face, and control the common people. Social leaders misused God's words. Some saw religion as a ways of getting face, gaining power, and growing their wealth. They used God's blessings as a way of excluding others. Ethnocentrism and nationalism fostered hatred against the nations, who had mistreated Israel in the past. Jesus exposed their culture (*wenming*, 文明) as hypocrisy and vain propaganda.

According to conventional standards, Jesus had little "face" (i.e., *mianzi*). His hometown was small. He received no formal theological training. Jesus was not like normal people. He did not try to climb the social ladder (攀附权贵). He did not people please, seeking to win the praise of man. Instead, he was humble. Despite Jesus' fame and accomplishments, Jesus often wanted to avoid the public spotlight.

In return, his countrymen turned against him. No one likes to lose face. They falsely accused him, treating him with contempt. The Jews slanderously asked him,

> "Are we not right in saying that you are a Samaritan and have a demon?" Jesus answered, "I do not have a demon, but I honor my Father, and you dishonor me. Yet I do not seek my own glory; there is One who seeks it, and he is the judge. Truly, truly, I say to you, if anyone keeps my word, he will never see death." (John 8:48–51; cf. 5:23,24)

The world's threats could not make Jesus deny his Father. Rather than settling for social acceptance (*mianzi*), he sought the face (*lian*) of God. Finally, one of Jesus' closest friends betrayed him, helping the political leaders execute Jesus. His disciples abandoned him. Originally, God created Israel to be blessing; instead, they now were under a curse (cf. Deut 28–29; Gal 3:10–13). They rejected God by murdering their true King. What God considered glorious, the world regarded as shameful. During Jesus' life, he said to all,

> If anyone would come after me, let him deny himself and take up his cross daily and follow me. For whoever would save his life will lose

it, but whoever loses his life for my sake will save it. For what does it profit a man if he gains the whole world and loses or forfeits himself? For whoever is ashamed of me and of my words, of him will the Son of Man be ashamed when he comes in his glory and the glory of the Father and of the holy angels. (Luke 9:23–26)

God uses what is shameful in the world's eyes to reveal his glory.

Death cannot hold Jesus (Acts 2:24). Three days later, God resurrected Jesus, vindicating Jesus as King of kings, Lord of lords. God had stripped the political leaders of their strongest weapons—fear, shame, and ultimately death. Through the cross, God condemned evil (e.g., sin). In Jesus' resurrection, shame was put to death. God overturns injustice. The heavenly Father will avenge the shame brought upon his name and restore his kingdom. "He disarmed the rulers and authorities and put them to open shame, by triumphing over them in him" (Col 2:15). Through the resurrection, God brings about a new creation. He begins to remove shame and evil from the world. In essence, God through Jesus Christ creates a new humanity (Eph 2:15). In this way, God is righteous. He keeps his promises. God is not partial, but rather blesses all nations.

Why Does Christ Matter?

Humanity has a debt that it cannot pay; therefore, the world lives under a curse.[224] Humans are made in God's image, created to reflect his glory in the world. We owe God our love and loyalty. This is the first and most fundamental human debt—the debt of filial piety to our true Father. However, since our first ancestors, people have preferred independence above relationship with their Father and King. Our rebellion dishonors God. Our betrayal shows we have no sense of shame. Consequently, humans feel a sense of isolation, having all lost *lian*.

The human family is fragmented against itself. Each group divides the world into "insiders" and "outsiders." People throughout human history seek security and contentment through the groups in which they belong, whether their family, country, ethnicity, or social network. This way of seeing the world ensures that individuals will have a sense of identity among people like themselves. Within these relationships, persons compete for face, which is gained and lost according to how well one adheres to the group's values. In essence, we humans have invaded God's kingdom, segmenting the world into colonies to serve our own purposes.

The human lust for *mianzi* is in fact a longing for *lian*. Humans intuitively know we should not be fractured as we are. We fear the continued isolation that comes from being separated from God. Seeking *mianzi* is a cheap substitute for lasting *lian*, which is found in relationship to God. *Lian* is the sense of value one has as a human who has been made to reflect the face of God in the world. We know there is safety and joy in relationships. However, we have distorted identities, giving allegiance to various persons or groups that promise to accept us, to give us face.

In Romans 6, Paul explains that all people, apart from Christ, are slaves to sin. We are unable to obey God from the heart (cf. Rom 6:16–18). In essence, this means people are enslaved to their shameful, evil hearts (无耻的心). We have all "loved the glory that comes from man more than the glory that comes from God" (John 12:43; cf. Rom 2:29). Jesus once said,

> They do all their deeds to be seen by others. For they make their phylacteries broad and their fringes long, and they love the place of honor at feasts and the best seats in the synagogues and greetings in the marketplaces and being called rabbi by others. But you are not to be called rabbi, for you have one teacher, and you are all brothers. And call no man your father on earth, for you have one Father, who is in heaven. Neither be called instructors, for you have one instructor, the Christ. The greatest among you shall be your servant. Whoever exalts himself will be humbled, and whoever humbles himself will be exalted. (Matt 23:5–12)

God knows when we try to use religion, ceremony, or relationships for personal benefit. Therefore Jesus quotes Isaiah 29:13 to describe his opponents, "This people honors me with their lips, but their heart is far from me" (Mark 7:6; Matt 15:8).

Therefore, we also have a second debt. We owe him our lives, because we have defamed his name. In essence, we spit in his face, as it were, before a watching world. We ourselves have become utterly shameful and now deserve to be put to shame. There is no greater shame than death. It exposes our ultimate weakness and the folly of our claim that we are self-sufficient. With boldness, every person proclaims before God, "I believe in myself!" God will vindicate his name. Death is the final humiliation in the face of our boasting.

Jesus perfectly glorified God. Through his life, death, and resurrection, Jesus completed the mission God gave him. Before God the Father, Jesus has face (*lian*) that can never be lost. Even though social leaders condemned him, God "highly exalted him and bestowed on him the name that is above every name, so that at the name of Jesus every knee should bow, in heaven and on earth and under the earth, and every tongue confess that Jesus Christ is Lord, to the glory of God the Father" (Phil 2:9–11). Because he represents humanity as a "second Adam" (cf. 1 Cor 15:45), he pays humanity's honor debt.

At the cross, Christ pays our life debt. His death is the compensation we cannot pay.[225] He sacrificed himself as a sin offering. Thus, he vindicates God's name, which had been defamed among the nations (Ezek 36:23). As a result, God gathers his people, forgives their debt, and grants them his Holy Spirit (Ezek 36:25–28; cf. Jer 31:31–34; Gal 3:13,14). Through the Holy Spirit, God frees his people, changing their hearts and enabling them to glorify God. They can finally do what is right—give God face. The first Adam brought death, curse, fear, and enslavement. Christ brings life, blessing, joy, and freedom (Rom 5:12–21; 1 Cor 15:22–28,40–49). In his death, Jesus hung cursed with the nations. In his life, all nations are blessed with him (Gal 3:10–13).[226]

We can explain the way that Jesus redeems us from slavery using Chinese language. Sin can be conceived as both a debt to be paid and thus a burden to bear.[227] How do we combine these two metaphors? "To pay a debt," in Chinese can be translated as 付债 (*fu zhai*). Also, 负担 (*fu dan*) translates the word "burden." Combining the two phrases, one can translate 负债 as "to bear a debt." Conveniently, there is also an obvious rhyme in the characters 付 and 负. Accordingly, we summarize how Jesus accomplished our redemption on the Cross—by bearing the burden of our debt to God.

God makes us his children and restores humanity's honor. Jesus, as the "firstborn son," reconciles the Father and the humanity. We are no longer the King's enemies (Rom 5:10; Phil 3:18). Instead, God adopts us as a heavenly Father (Rom 8:12–25; Gal 4:1–7). From all nations, he restores the human family such that we "become children of God, who were born, not of blood nor of the will of the flesh nor of the will of man, but of God" (John 1:12,13). According to ancestral lineage, we will die. Through the blood of Jesus, we gain life. God regards his people as having Jesus' own honor. In this sense, one could say we "borrow his face" (跟他借面子, *gen ta jie mianzi*).[228] If we follow Christ, the Father loves us like he loves Jesus. In John 17:22,23 Jesus prays to his Father: "The glory that you have given me I have given to them, that they may be one even as we are one, I in them and you in me, that they may become perfectly one, so that the world may know that you sent me and loved them even as you loved me."

God the Father is not like so many human parents. He does not depend on our face, our gifts, our status, or our abilities. Even though he does not need us, he loves us. His words and commands are a delight, not a burden (Ps 119: 24,47; 1 John 5:3). Jesus said, "Come to me, all who labor and are heavy laden, and I will give you rest. Take my yoke upon you, and learn from me, for I am gentle and lowly in heart, and you will find rest for your souls. For my yoke is easy, and my burden is light" (Matt 11:28–30). People in life make many promises that never come true. However, Jesus has shown himself sovereign by defeating his enemies. He is able to do what he promises (cf. Rom 4:18–21). Because Jesus is Lord, there is hope. "Whoever believes in him will not be put to shame" (Rom 9:33; cf. 10:11; Isa 28:16).

Harmony and blessing characterize God's kingdom. God will create a universal brotherhood (世界大同). God will judge human sin and evil. Rebels will no longer rule the world. Politicians have always devised plans to construct a "harmonious society." One example is the "Eight Honors and Eight Disgraces" (八荣八耻) campaign introduced in 2006 by Chinese President Hu Jintao.[229] In contrast, Jesus brings into existence a world of the "eight blessings" (八福), which are signified in the Beatitudes of Matthew 5:3–10.[230] When Jesus returns, God will make a new heaven and new earth (Rev 21:1). Paul exclaims, "The creation itself will be set free from its bondage to corruption and obtain the freedom of the glory of the children of God" (Rom 8:21). Isaiah describes this ideal state, "The wolf shall dwell with the lamb, and the leopard shall lie down with the young goat, and the calf and the lion and the fattened calf together; and a little child shall lead them" (Isa 11:6).

How Should We Respond?

How do we enjoy these blessings? God commands all nations to trust Christ as Lord. Because God is King, faith is an ongoing act of allegiance. Because

God is Father, our faith is equivalent to filial respect. Since God is the world's only true God, true faith means forsaking idols and false gods. In other words, following Christ necessarily entails repentance. We need a change of mind and a new heart. True repentance produces obedience. Obedience itself does not save people. True obedience is not found in ceremony or tradition. Instead, faith implies a new perspective about face. Our view of honor and shame naturally produces loving works.

Conversion changes our group identity. When we trust Christ, we belong to a new family and enter a new kingdom. Becoming a Christian does not mean rejecting our family and country; rather, we enlarge our sense of family and nation. Who do we most want to please? Who do we want to accept us? The answers to these questions reveal our sense of identity. Faith in Christ determines our "in group" and "out group," not bloodline, political views, gender, or denomination. Paul thus says,

> For consider your calling, brothers: not many of you were wise according to worldly standards, not many were powerful, not many were of noble birth. But God chose what is foolish in the world to shame the wise; God chose what is weak in the world to shame the strong; God chose what is low and despised in the world, even things that are not, to bring to nothing things that are, so that no human being might boast in the presence of God. And because of him you are in Christ Jesus, who became to us wisdom from God, righteousness and sanctification and redemption, so that, as it is written, "Let the one who boasts, boast in the Lord." (1 Cor 1:26–31)

Boasting reflects our sense of belonging. We forsake exclusivistic pride.

The gospel also provides the solution to the ancient Chinese dilemma concerning loyalty (忠孝两全). Should one give foremost allegiance to the king and nation or to one's father and family? The gospel makes clear that God is both King and Father. Likewise, one does not have to choose between being Chinese and being a Christian. The world is God's kingdom; humanity his family. In Ephesians 3, Paul intermingles different motifs to make this point. God is the "Father, from whom every family in heaven and on earth is named" (Eph 3:14,15). He sent Christ "that he might create in himself one new man. ... So then you are no longer strangers and aliens, but you are fellow citizens with the saints and members of the household of God" (Eph 2:15,19). It is for this reason that the early church father Tertullian called Christians a "third race."[231] Christ's kingdom includes all nations. In him, "There is neither Jew nor Greek, there is neither slave nor free, there is no male and female, for you are all one in Christ Jesus" (Gal 3:28).

Finally, believing the gospel of Christ means accepting his mission. Christians desire all nations to make much of Christ. God's people long to see righteousness in the entire world. Taking up this mission has a cost—suffering. People do not like us to expose their true face. Having a righteous community requires we challenge selfish and arrogant people. Because God's children identify with Christ, they are willing to suffer with Christ. Paul encourages us:

> We are children of God, and if children, then heirs—heirs of God and fellow heirs with Christ, provided we suffer with him in order that we may also be glorified with him. For I consider that the sufferings of this present time are not worth comparing with the glory that is to be revealed to us. (Rom 8:16–18)

Being accepted by Christ will mean rejection by the world.

Conclusion

This chapter offers an example of a "cultural contextualization." In order to avoid abstraction, it assumes a specific social setting. It demonstrates one possible way that people can communicate the gospel in a Chinese context. Of course there are many ways to talk about the gospel. However, gospel presentations tend to follow a particular pattern, answering four key questions. In order to communicate the gospel, it is helpful to know some of the more popular "false gospels" in a culture.

In our study of Chinese culture, we identified a number of key themes. Specifically, the chapter highlights the relationship between Chinese parents and their children. Biblical metaphors like debt and slavery helpfully illustrate fundamental cultural problems. A variety of similar theological contextualizations and evangelistic tools could be developed. Broadly speaking, gospel conversations and evangelistic tracts could focus on questions like, "Who is my family?" "Where do I belong?" and "Why do we want face?" Likewise, we could begin with questions Chinese have traditionally raised, such as "Should we honor the emperor or our father?" "What does it mean to be filial?" and "What is the basis for true harmony?" In summary, the chapter has argued via demonstration that contextualizing the gospel requires us to take seriously the dictum "Context is king." Interpretation and application begin with recognizing one's context. "Cultural contextualization" intentionally uses the biblical text in order to interpret cultural context.

KEY POINTS

- A "cultural contextualization" will use a biblical perspective to interpret and assess a local culture.
- Accordingly, we can identify the false gospels that exist within a culture. Every culture tells some sort of counterstory that tries to rival the true gospel.
- One way to contextualize the gospel in Chinese is to focus on the parent-child relationship.
- In this way, the presentation is framed using the key themes of relationship (*guanxi*) and authority.
- Debt, slavery, and freedom are also major subthemes in the presentation. In effect, Romans 6 and Israel's exile are influential in shaping the way the chapter explains Chinese culture and its need for the gospel.
- A contextualized gospel for Chinese people will highlight the importance and influence of face and identity.

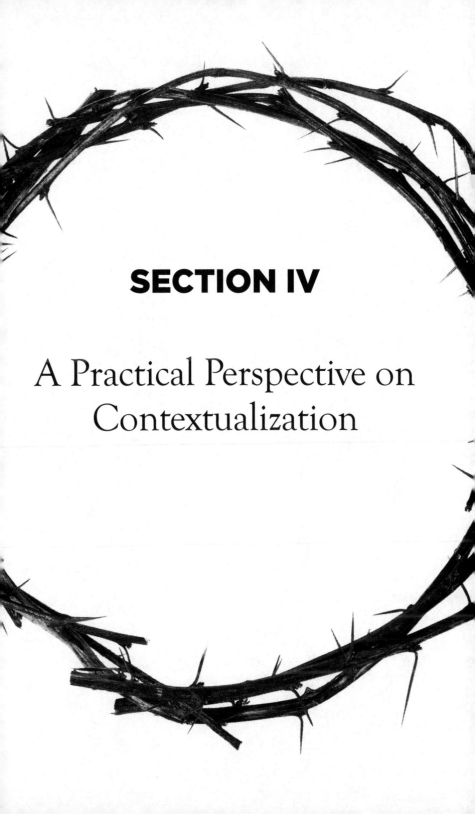

SECTION IV

A Practical Perspective on Contextualization

10

Contextualizing Our Ministry: Implications for Strategy and Training

How do we contextualize our ministry? How does the view of contextualization discussed thus far apply to things like discipleship, leadership training, and mission strategy? This entire book has focused on a specific question: how do we contextualize the gospel? Our understanding of the gospel should influence our Christian practice. That topic is far too broad for this book.

Therefore, this chapter is only an introduction to that discussion. I will suggest a range of possible applications. I first highlight a number of obstacles to contextualization. They concern not only head knowledge and skill sets; they also include issues related to character. Second, I offer a few types of application that stem from the model of contextualization presented in the previous chapters. I hope readers will freely develop and expand upon my comments. Third, I specifically consider the question of training priorities. How do we teach people to think comprehensively about matters of theology and culture?

Obstacles to Contextualization

Many Christians lack adequate biblical knowledge to contextualize their ministry. At one level, I refer to a consistent trend I observe among Western missionaries. Missionaries generally are not expected to have the same level of formal educational training as is required of, for example, a typical American pastor. I once heard a seminary professor point out the fact that doctors, lawyers, and other vocations not only undergo strenuous initial training; additionally, they spend their entire careers in ongoing, continuing education. They refresh and update their knowledge base and skill sets. For many, their motive is nothing more than the love of money.

Christians are given the charge of interpreting, sharing, and applying God's word in the world. Eternal matters are at stake. The demands upon one's life are many. In many respects, missionaries must do a little of everything that a pastor does, if not more, yet in a second culture and language. They have to convey and apply the gospel among people who have strikingly different worldviews. They address problems typically unheard of in their home country. While there is no reason that every missionary needs a PhD, I do suggest that evangelicals need to reconsider the sufficiency of current methods of theological training, both in terms of rigor and breadth.

With respect to biblical knowledge, contextualization requires that we have proficiency in a few key areas. First, Christians need greater familiarity with the *grand biblical story* (i.e., the Bible's metanarrative). As I converse with ministry partners as well as my students, I have regularly seen an inability to recount clearly and comprehensively the big story that unites the sacred text. People often know Genesis 1–3, scattered stories in the Old Testament, and much of the Gospels. Without question, they are most comfortable recalling Paul's letters. However, if you ask someone to retell the Bible as one large, unified story, most of the Old Testament would be passed over. We cannot expect that a piecemeal understanding of the Bible will be sufficient to do contextualization that is meaningful, comprehensive, and faithful to Scripture.

Second, Christian workers need more training in *biblical theology* and not simply systematic theology. "Biblical theology" is more than simply theology that is biblical. I recently spoke with two seminary professors (both with PhDs) who did not even know that biblical theology was a field of study in its own right. What is the difference between biblical theology and systematic theology? To put it most simply, systematic theology starts with the reader's questions and topics (like the church, salvation, end times, etc.). It then proceeds to examine the full range of passages related to the subject. Systematic theology tries to synthesize the various relevant verses.

On the other hand, biblical theology starts at a more fundamental level. Biblical scholars here try to discern the theological categories and problems inherent to the original author within the narrow confines of his context.[232] Thus, if one is doing a study of John's Gospel, he or she will have very little to say about justification by faith; however, readers will find that a lot of creation imagery frames John's Gospel. Ideally, biblical theology informs and grounds systematic theology. If we skip the former, we run the danger of assuming answers too quickly and then seeking Bible verses simply to justify those conclusions.

Third, Christian missionaries need strong *interpretation* skills. Biblical interpretation (i.e., exegesis) is not the same thing as doing theology. Theology is (or should be) the result of interpretation. Theological doctrines are the conclusion of the interpretation process. I was once "confronted" by a friend who accused me of teaching "advanced hermeneutics" or "advanced interpretation." After much confusion, I finally asked what he meant by these terms. I discovered that what he meant wasn't actually "interpretation" or "exegesis." He simply meant "theology." I have seen this confusion again and again. As a result, people think they are "interpreting" the Bible when in fact they are simply finding verses to "proof text" their already assumed conclusions.

Seminary programs should also consider making the biblical languages a standard part of their missionary training curriculum. Missionaries have to navigate the meaning of words across multiple languages. Having a strong foundation in the original languages is an important guard against various errors. Some challenges are not obvious. For example, the Chinese Union Version (和合本) is the standard translation used among Christians in contemporary China. However, in Romans 1–11 alone I found around fifty different places where the original Greek words for "because" and "therefore" were omitted from the translation.[233] In fact, sometimes the word for "because" was translated "therefore" and vice versa. These words have opposite meanings!

We undermine both contextualization and biblical authority when we do not distinguish theology and interpretation. Why? If local Christians do not have this specific skill set, they cannot easily check the teaching they hear from pastors and missionaries. The complex conclusions of systematic theology overwhelm the average layperson. When teachers defend a particular doctrine, their explanations are frequently fragmented collections of verses separated from their natural literary context.

This results in at least two consequences. First, congregations become discouraged at the prospect of understanding the Bible for themselves. Second, they must overly depend on whoever among them has the most education. The pastor's interpretation *functionally* assumes the authority of the Bible itself. In more traditional cultures, people are slow to challenge authority figures. Generally, biblical interpretation is rendered all but impossible since any teaching that disagrees with the "traditional" reading is rejected or at least viewed with great suspicion.

Obviously, local language proficiency is critical for contextualization. With it, we develop relationships and discern ministry needs. Missionaries need to be lifelong language learners. In order to develop healthy contextualization, we must progress beyond a basic level of language. Instead of settling for religious terminology, people would do well to press forward in theological language. In addition, one gains more of an insider's perspective when he or she understands word connotations and how to connect logical ideas. Thus, developing abstract language helps missionaries discern and discuss worldview level issues. Memorizing formulaic presentations is not enough.

Contextualization is undermined when people lack depth in cultural understanding. Cultural knowledge cannot be assumed even among long-term workers. Recently, a group of new missionaries with a major missions agency went through prefield training. In the process, one of the missionaries asked the speaker about how honor and shame influences one's ministry in East Asia. The speaker, who had spent many years in East Asia, was in a leadership position in charge of preparing the new missionaries for service in Asia. The speaker was a bit stumped. Not knowing what to say, he turned the question around and asked the question to another one of the new missionaries (who had only recently read an introductory book about honor and shame). The speaker never gave an answer; instead, he simply said that, whatever we do, we shouldn't compromise the gospel. The point of the story is this—it is inexplicable that a missionary with long-term experience in East Asia and in charge of training should *literally* have no insight to give newcomers to the field.

Contextualization also suffers when we lack a range of other skill sets. For example, missionaries need to consider their own communication skills. The ability to do analysis and be creative enables us to see the world through others' eyes. A number of social, theological, and practical problems require that people learn to think outside the traditional box. One must be flexible, ready to adapt methods and strategies. Missionaries need to be aware of a natural tendency to uncritically do "what everyone else has always done."

Given the breadth of skill and knowledge needed to contextualize our ministries, organizations could give more thought to how leaders are selected. Is there genuine diversity on your leadership team? Do the same types of people tend to rise to positions of authority? Perhaps we need to rethink our profile of an ideal strategist. In their different ways, various people can make effective strategy decisions, whether he or she is a theologian type, a pastor figure, a networker, or the most pragmatic of church planters.

This above list may look daunting to some. It can easily discourage people. However, there is good news. Contextualization is not a one-person job. No single person has all the skills I've mentioned. We need realistic expectations. Our discussion on contextualization reminds us that we need other people. We belong to the church. We need other members of the body of Christ.

This realization leads us to consider some of the character-related obstacles to contextualization. Contextualization fails when people lack patience, teach-ability, and humility.
Laziness looks for ministry shortcuts, not worldview change. Truth and application are kept in abstract terms, which are easier to manage. Idleness and apathy are contrary to initiative taking. They get in the way of people taking care of their responsibilities and paying attention to details. We cannot expect to contextualize the gospel when we are unwilling to admit our insufficiency and thus to cooperate with others. In this sense, one must be willing to "lose face."

Contextualization requires a proper perspective on oneself and ministry priorities. The Christian worker must guard against his or her having a sense of superiority, whether concerning culture, education, or other reasons. Provincialism of any kind is a harbinger for syncretism. For instance, denominationalism, factionalism, social hierarchy within the church tend to create a narrow-mindedness that resists outside influence and the changes that it brings. Naturally, those who do contextualization will find that many of their friends and coworkers misunderstand them. Their peers may wonder whether contextualization is synonymous with compromise. As a result, another obstacle to contextualization is the unwillingness to suffer. When people are unwilling to give up comforts and the sense of being understood, they will inevitable reaffirm the status quo. Groupthink sets in; stubbornness can get confused with bold faithfulness.

In short, the greatest obstacle to contextualization is a lack of love. Love does not limit the context of one's concern to self and, by extension, one's own in-group. In addition, contextualizing the gospel is a labor of faith and hope in the God who does not change regardless of culture. The process requires hard work, sacrifice, and long-term vision.

Broad Applications

The model of contextualization explained in this book has at least five general applications. I list them primarily for the sake for guiding our reflection and conversation after readers have put down this book. Every ministry is con-textualized in some way, whether for the better or worse. Perhaps these five categories of application will help keep us from getting muddled up about a rather complex topic.

Contextualization influences every area of ministry. First and most obvious, the model presented in this book equips people to create new contextualiza-tions. This is an ongoing need of any ministry. Second, the proposed model helps people better interpret the Bible. By understanding the relationship between culture and Scripture, Christians can have a more humble perspec-tive to ask better questions of the text and themselves. We need flexibility as well as firm convictions.

Third, Christian workers are equipped to analyze culture. The insights gained then shape ministry strategy and give particular focus to gospel pre-sentations. Furthermore, greater understanding of culture reduces ongoing culture shock and fosters longevity in missionary service. Fourth, the preceding discussion establishes a framework for assessing our ministry. In particular, the various topics and subpoints can be turned into diagnostic questions that can then be applied to various contextualizations, like evangelistic tracts.

Finally, our contextualization model will influence how we train church leaders and missionaries. For one thing, we will consider how to remove or minimize some of the obstacles to contextualization listed above. Churches and mission agencies will see the importance of ongoing education and development. Contextualization is not something that only missionaries do. Even within one's own culture, people can and should do contextualization. Sometimes ignorance towards our own culture distorts our view of other cultures. Accordingly, one way to better contextualize in a second culture is to better understand our home culture.

Building a Training Program

As a way of concluding the chapter, I want to use an analogy to draw together what has been said. How do we train people to learn both theology and culture for the sake of contextualization? A training program resembles the plan by which one builds a house. First, we establish a foundation. *Interpretation skills* are of foremost importance. The Bible provides an authoritative perspective on the world. Worldviews of any sort are full of details. By developing this discipline of biblical exegesis, we build our foundation on stable ground. Second, we erect the framework of *biblical theology*, which gives the gospel its essential structure.

Third, we move to *culture*—the interior of the house. Culture can be learned in a number of ways. In addition to living in other cultures, one can study history, anthropology, philosophy, and other social sciences. I suspect most people typically think of contextualization in terms of this third aspect. As a result, people consciously or unconsciously select organizing principles according to their tradition, home culture, personal preference, or perhaps their agency's ethos. In effect, the principles we use to organize our gospel presentation implicitly give a house its design. These organizing principles are invisible, but their influence is pervasive. By analogy, our knowledge and use of culture subtly determine things like floor layout, room size, window placement, and the direction the house faces, whether north, east, south, or west. It is important to observe that having different designs and themes does not necessarily undermine the house's sturdiness. In fact, without these sort of cultural principles, the gospel becomes an abstraction at best. Without good contextualization, our presentation perhaps is just an empty building, a mere "house" and not a "home."[234]

What will be the final result of our efforts? In this process, we slowly construct a systematic theology, one with a solid foundation and framework, and suitable for the context. One could regard systematic theology as theology contextualized around specific themes. Most of us who have received seminary training are mainly used to studying systematic theology. This habit of learning and teaching inevitably leads some people to assume our theological "house" has already been built. Therefore, having assumed a particular understanding of the gospel, they see no need for contextualization. In fact, systematic theology is the result of contextualization, not its starting point.

The various doctrines of systematic theology (e.g., soteriology, ecclesiology, eschatology, etc.) depend upon the foundation of exegesis. Certainly, we may present the gospel in diverse ways, *yet* each approach must conform to the gospel's inherent framework.

KEY POINTS

- Our contextualization model has a number of implications for the way we do ministry.
- There are a number of obstacles to contextualization. These could include a lack of biblical and cultural knowledge, underdeveloped skill sets, and even a person's character.
- Contextualization is not a one-person effort. It requires much collaboration.
- Contextualization teaches us that we need to have diversity within our leadership teams.
- Our view of contextualization should cause us to reconsider the way we train missionaries and leaders.
- A training model that takes contextualization seriously should first of all emphasize interpretation (exegetical) skills and biblical theology.
- Contextualization, and missionary training in general, should integrate a variety of disciplines as a way of helping people better grasp a myriad of cultural dynamics.
- Systematic theology is a product of contextualization, not its starting point.

11

Cultural Lenses: Can We Use Contemporary Culture to Interpret Scripture?

We are predisposed to see, as the emphasis of a text, the kind of things that are also emphasized in our own cultures. This is because we naturally try to organize biblical teaching into the mental categories native to our worldview. In order to make sense of the world, it is only natural to use familiar patterns of thinking. One's assumptions are countless and unconscious.[235]

In order to interpret and apply Scripture, it is critical that we balance our particular perspective by becoming aware of other ways of seeing the world. Let me reiterate a quote that captures the spirit of this chapter quite well. One theologian rightly states, "[A] cross-cultural reading is more objective than a monocultural reading of the biblical text."[236] Inevitably people from some cultures will grasp aspects of biblical teaching more easily than those from other cultures (and time periods).

However, the existence of such varied ways of judging and prioritizing human experience would seem to render contextualization nearly impossible. Even when people share common cultural backgrounds, biblical interpretation is already difficult enough. After all, we are trying to understand a text from the point of view of the writer within his own historical setting. Everyone reads Scripture from within a certain cultural milieu.

Naturally, the various interpretations that result will have differing points of emphasis. Trying to reconcile these competing ideas only complicates the interpretive process. Interpreters will be tempted to accuse one another of eisegesis, whereby people force a meaning into the text that is actually foreign to the author's intent. Likewise, readers will be quite unaware of their own eisegesis, since they naively presume the biblical author categorized the world in the same general ways that they do. One should not assume that these differing interpretations contradict; they may simply have distinct points of emphasis.

At one level, general revelation and the basic structure of the world ensure that people can find common ground for communication and interpretation. Regardless of time or place, people understand concepts like family, author-ity, law, honor, morality, and relationships. Biblical authors use a number of these kinds of "human" categories (perhaps in the form of metaphors) to communicate significant truths.

In that sense, people's ability to understand special revelation is quite dependent on their experience and/or general revelation. For example, the doctrine of salvation alone employs various concepts, including slavery, glory, fatherhood, sonship, law, shame, righteousness, mercy, loyalty, and sacrifice. God reveals himself so that people from all nations might know him. One therefore can expect the Bible to speak in some manner that makes sense to people in every culture.[237]

On the other hand, many people struggle to grasp the meaning of multiple biblical motifs. We cannot expect twenty-first-century Americans to easily grasp the significance of ancient Near Eastern kingship, the covenant concept, and collective identity (as opposed to the individualism endemic to Western society). Some biblical passages will cause a typical Eastern reader to have more tension than that found in the average Western reader. For example, Genesis 2:24 says, "Therefore a man shall leave his father and his mother and hold fast to his wife, and they shall become one flesh." Those who are more individualistic will hardly feel the weight of Jesus' words, "If anyone comes to me and does not hate his own father and mother and wife and children and brothers and sisters, yes, and even his own life, he cannot be my disciple" (Luke 14:26).

Every cultural perspective has inherent blind spots that hinder biblical interpretation and thus contextualization. Humans have basic limitations and differences that will always make communication difficult. What can be done to account for the plethora of global perspectives? At the same time, how do we also center our interpretation (and eventual application) on the author's original meaning? In one sense, all people living today face the same challenge. How do we cross thousands of years of history to regain the perspective of the biblical writers? Ultimately, this chasm cannot be overcome.

Reading the Bible across World Cultures

This chapter offers a counterintuitive solution to our dilemma. I suggest that we can actually use contemporary cultures *as a means* of interpreting the ancient biblical text.[238] Perhaps this could be called "reaching back by reaching out." It is important that people learn about and even internalize ways of thinking that are typical in other parts of the world. In so doing, they gain two things: (1) a measure of objectivity, and (2) a broader understanding about what it means to be human. As a result, we are forced to examine and question many of our assumptions. It is possible to gain fresh insights about the biblical text as our understanding of other human cultures expands.

Although no contemporary culture is identical to the ancient cultures depicted in the Bible, there are certainly differing degrees of overlap. In some respect, East Asian cultures today resemble the Ancient Near East better than would those of Chicago and a Los Angeles suburb. In other instances, one may hear the echoes of Scripture most clearly when reading from a traditional African perspective. Those same themes may be less pronounced to someone in London or Paris. Inasmuch as similarities exist between modern and ancient cultures, contemporary readers from different parts of the world will have certain advantages and disadvantages when interpreting the Bible. Of course these advantages are not absolute. They are relative to the topic and theme. Human cultures complement one another.

The diagram on the following page illustrates a process of interpretation whereby one can better grasp the biblical context by reaching across the world's contemporary cultures. The world's cultural history can be mapped as a globe. We want to think in two directions. The earth's surface represents modern-day societies. The earliest human communities are located at the earth's core. As we move from the center through the earth's layers to the crust, we see the evolution and interweaving of human cultures. There are no neatly defined lines to demarcate one culture from another across successive periods. Yet one can still speak in broad categories, trends, and characteristics. There is both continuity and discontinuity.

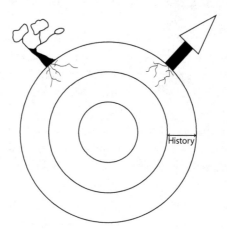

Figure 19: Two Cultural Trees

More recent civilizations (nearer to the earth's crust in the diagram) are birthed out of the cultures that came before them. Otherwise said, contemporary cultures are amalgamations. They fuse together cultures from history in ways that are incomprehensible. Vast differences aside, the younger societies have many aspects in common with the world's ancient civilizations. Therefore, China can be described as an "honor" culture, rather than a law-guilt based culture, even though law-related concepts (e.g., judges, order, politics, etc.) are not at all foreign.

In some respect, the world's earliest cultures typify what is most basic to *human culture*. The generations that follow are simply creative adaptations and expressions of essential humanness. We could make the point from a more theological perspective. Every culture distinctly manifests the same image of God, according to which humanity is created.

Contemporary cultures are represented as trees. They are living, varied, and rooted in the ground of history. Naturally, some trees have shallow roots; others go much deeper. They all spring from the earth below, from which they get nutrients. In the picture presented here, the roots represent the ways in which modern cultures emerge from previous civilizations. The process is natural but complex, mysterious but reasonably comprehended at the risk of abstraction.

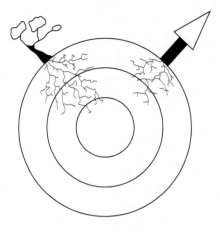

Figure 20: Deep Historical Roots

People can understand a culture's influences if they are willing to dig into its past. People are accustomed to researching recent historical events and figures. It is not so difficult to understand the influence of the civil rights movement on twenty-first-century America. It is more challenging to see how sixth-century Egyptian society precisely weaved its way through medieval Europe to eventually shape present-day American culture. Although it is difficult to make conclusive judgments about the ancient world, scholars can unearth a range of useful insights with collaboration and effort. Of course historical and cultural research takes place around the world. As people trace their roots back in time, they find increased interaction among the mother civilizations to the modern world. For example, the Silk Road famously spanned Asia. As a result, countless cultural exchanges no doubt spawned new communities and ways of thinking that continue to influence us today.

Simply put, present-day cultures, at one level or another, share common ancient histories. Inasmuch as the world's people share common backgrounds, various themes will reappear again and again in cultures both across time and geography. For example, ancient cultures are often depicted as being collectiv-istic and honor/shame oriented. Such descriptions do not deny that ancient cultures also have individualistic or law-oriented features. Not surprisingly, wherever one looks in history or around the world, humans still continue to be concerned with things like group identity, reputation, and related matters.

Learning about contemporary cultures equips us to better interpret Scripture; however, this does not mean that culture provides authoritative "revelation." This chapter brings the world and revelation together in a manner similar to Albert Wolters' proposal. He writes,

> Because [Christians] believe that creational structure underlies all of reality, they seek and find evidence of lawful constancy in the flux of experience, and of invariant principles amidst a variety of historical events and institutions. . . . In every situation, they explicitly look for and recognize the presence of creational structure, distinguishing this sharply from the human abuse to which it is subject.[239]

Of course there are no guarantees that people with a multicultural perspective will actually be better theologians; after all, "the everyday components of our lives—our family, our sexuality, our thinking, our emotions, our work—are the structural things that are *involved* and *at stake* in the pull of sin and grace."[240] The point is simply this: all things being equal, a multicultural approach is advantageous for seeing things in the text that are actually there in the Bible. Much will be missed with only a monocultural view. Therefore, when it comes to interpreting the Bible, there should be a less clear distinction between missiology and theology. Missionaries and missiologists should be among the world's finest theologians. Likewise, theologians would be helped not only by reading books about the Ancient Near East but also by visiting or living in the modern-day Middle East and Far East.

In the model presented here, moving horizontally across cultures gives people varying degrees of access to see past civilizations and worldviews. Thus, Americans who travel to China can quickly realize the importance of collective identity, "face," and hierarchy to the Chinese people. Such priorities echo those of ancient biblical cultures. As one better understands these values and the internal logic of this kind of worldview, Christians will "have eyes to see" key themes and motifs within passages that previously seemed so familiar. Suddenly their new awareness and appreciation for the way people think around the world become key tools to digging deeper into the biblical authors' original meaning.

There are certainly objections that could be raised. They serve as needed warnings. First, we should not equate any modern culture with an ancient biblical culture. Chinese culture differs from those of Abraham, David, Jesus, or Paul. The point being made is that these cultures have *overlapping themes of emphasis* or "creation structures" (to use Wolters' phrase). Even if particular details differ between them, readers are at least made aware that these values and categories of thought should be considered.

A second concern is eisegesis, whereby the reader's own assumptions (not shared by the original author) force an interpretation into the text. Frankly stated, this is a danger for *every* interpreter, *even more so* for the person who only uses a monocultural perspective. In fact, one can counter that a multicultural perspective actually helps to minimize eisegesis, because he or she is more aware of a broader range of issues that have concerned humans throughout history.

Finally, a third concern is that of relativism. Does this model collapse into relativistic interpretations and water down the absolute authority of God's revelation? No, not at all. Interpreters should always seek the meaning of the text as intended by the biblical writers in their contexts. All *biblical* interpretations are bound by this common locus.

Reconsider the proverbial analogy of the blind men who all touch different parts of the elephant. Lesslie Newbigin rightly points out that the word picture is self-defeating because the narrator, rather than proving relativism, actually presumes an absolute perspective and a common object of study.[241] There are only so many parts of the elephant that can be touched. If the blind men talked with each other, they would in fact get a very sound understanding of what they were all touching. Everyone has his or her own blind spots. Yet collaboration opens one's eyes to see far more than would ever be possible alone.

I will briefly highlight a few implications. First, this model presented in this chapter makes a good case for prioritizing the work of long-term missionaries. Short-term work does not afford the kind of reflection and internalization needed to grasp the way locals see the world. In fact, brief exposures to another culture can easily reinforce pride in one's own culture. This can fuel prejudice and narrow-mindedness. An overemphasis on short-term missions must not become a detriment of long-term funding, training, and placement. It is the long-term worker who will typically have deeper relationships with locals. Thus, they have the greater opportunity to develop contextualized theologies.

Second, it is imperative that we encourage and develop global theologies, not being content with only Western (i.e., *traditional*) theological formulations. Doing this requires tremendous humility, cooperation, intentional training, and a shift in priorities. Third, any particular cultural perspective by itself is insufficient to holistically interpret Scripture. Fourth, it follows that we should purposefully use other cultural perspectives to interpret Scripture. Fifth, the model illustrates the importance of the doctrine of humanity and of general revelation. Sixth, second-culture people (including second-generation children) could potentially be key people to assist the contextualization process. Seventh, we humans are more alike than we think. This observation ought to both humble and comfort us. It should also make us more open to the insights of others around the world.

Why Are Christians Talking Past Each Other?

We could talk endlessly about points of theology; yet, we eventually need to address underlying, deeper-level issues. What happens when one does not take seriously the significance of other cultural perspectives? He or she very easily could begin either to patronize or resent those from other cultures. Again, taking seriously other people's views does not at all mean wholesale agreement. In fact, when we truly engage others' ideas, further disagreements often result precisely because their differences become clearer. At times, initial protests against another worldview (or its resulting theology) will subside as one gains better understanding.

The purpose of comparing views is not to choose one over another. To begin with that as the goal is simply to beg the question, to assume that one faces an either-or dilemma. Instead, we hope to discern whatever truth *does* exist among the various choices. Habitually forging dichotomies can be fatal to theologizing. After all, two seemingly contradictory alternatives may in fact be true, but from different vantage points.

Take for instance the frequent contrast made between law-guilt and honor/shame. Writers commonly treat law-guilt as an objective category (thus most important for theology). At the same time, they might treat honor/shame as a mere social or psychological category (rather than a major theological concern). Accordingly, theologians often give their most rigorous attention to issues of law-guilt. Honor/shame is overlooked as a mere cultural metaphor useful for contextualization but not essential for theology. It is easy to miss the obvious point: *law is just as much a social metaphor as honor or shame.*

The following section compares seven areas that are typically used to contrast a "Western" and an "Eastern" worldview. One should not suppose that these seven exhaust all possible differences. In addition, the following are simply general characterizations. Analyzing cultures requires some degree of abstraction. There are always exceptions and varying degrees of conformity between individuals and their culture. Nevertheless, the descriptions represent broad trends as identified by scholars in various fields. Scores of books and articles have discussed issues related to each of the highlighted categories.

The purpose of this section is simply to illustrate how Scripture can support seemingly dichotomous ways of thinking. Since this is simply an introductory discussion, I will not attempt to present a thorough defense of each view. However, it is hoped that this section will spur fruitful reflection among theologians and missiologists. In particular, what aspects of our theologies and contextualizations need refinement and expansion? Although this chapter focuses on the contrasts between East and West, other comparisons from other parts of the world could just as well be used to one's benefit.

First of all, Easterners and Westerners, stereotypically speaking, have two views of history respectively—cyclical and linear. Eastern cyclical thought is most pronounced in Buddhism, with its notion of *samsara* or reincarnation. Western thinking is often linear and emphasizes logically sequence. Western theologians are quick to contrast a "Christian" view of history and Eastern views.[242] According to a linear construction of history, creation marks the beginning of a long but purposeful process that culminates at a definitive end; namely, Christ's return, God's judgment, and the new creation. The universe is not random. Christians deny the futility of fatalistic views of history. It is difficult to find Christians who disagree with this general assessment of history. But is this the only way to conceive of history?

Is cyclical thinking contrary to Scripture? Biblical theology gives good reason to temper standard Christian objections. At one level, the cyclical nature of the world is the fundamental assumption of Ecclesiastes.[243] In addition, scholars have long recognized that biblical authors frequently use typology to convey their meaning. Paul for instance says that Adam was a "type [τύπος] of the one who was to come" (Rom 5:14). In 1 Corinthians 15:45, Christ is called "the last Adam." Some also "view Adam to be a type of Noah in the

Genesis narrative itself."[244] The tabernacle and its gifts and sacrifices "serve a copy and shadow [ὑποδείγματι καὶ σκιᾷ] of the heavenly things" (Heb 8:5). The OT sees "Israel as a new Adam/humanity,"[245] yet in another sense Israel simply repeats the fall of Adam.

The pattern is seen elsewhere. Exodus language is used in the Prophets (pointing to the end of exile and the salvation of God's people) and in the New Testament.[246] This typology is also evident in rabbinic literature.[247] Beale speaks of

> segments of the OT where there are repeated narrations of Yahweh's commissioning people to fill certain offices (e.g., judges, prophets, priests, kings, and other leaders), the repeated failure of the one commissioned, followed by judgment, and the cycle starts again in the following narrative.[248]

In the Davidic covenant (2 Sam 7; 1 Chron 17), there is hope that the cycle will end. David himself becomes a type-figure for Israel's kingship and ultimately for Jesus himself. Furthermore, Wright summarizes what many other scholars have also observed in Matthew's Gospel:

> The life of Jesus *recapitulates* key elements in the earlier story of Israel. For a moment, as Jesus stands on the mountain giving the famous sermon, he is Moses. For a moment, answering his critics about his actions on the Sabbath, he is David. For a moment, as he calls and names the twelve disciples, he is perhaps Jacob, bringing the twelve patriarchs into the world. For a moment, healing the sick and raising the dead, he is Elijah or Elisha. And so on.[249]

More could be said than this brief overview allows.

From one perspective, the Bible presents history as cyclical. God accomplishes his purposes through a series of events in which later events echo past ones. In a sense, history continues to repeat itself. This is not a vicious cycle that amounts to fatalism. Rather than thinking in two dimensions (either as a line or a circle), one can think of a spiral or cone. There is progress with each cycle; nevertheless, the circular fashion in which God works is unmistakable. In light of these observations, perhaps one could say Jesus brings final salvation, such that the new heaven and new earth finally breaks the cycle of birth, sin, and death.

A second contrast could be made and concerns one's view of humanity, naming whether a culture is generally individualistic or collectivistic. Traditional Western theology and gospel presentations have especially highlighted individual salvation.[250] By comparison, it is less obvious that theologians have allowed a collectivistic worldview to strongly influence their theologies. In some cases, there seems even to be strong resistance to collectivistic readings.[251] This neglect is difficult to justify.

Scripture gives great attention to the question "Who are God's people?" or "Who are Abraham's offspring?" One immediately thinks of the Jew-Gentile controversies highlighted in Acts 15, Romans, Galatians, and Ephesians 2–3. Jesus had a similar dispute in John 8:31–58. The fundamental distinction in the OT narrative is Israel and the nations. The nations disperse from the Tower of Babel (Gen 11), are made disciples via the Great Commission (Matt 28:18–20), and gather to worship Jesus in Revelation 5:9; 7:9.

Individual identity is not merely determined by how one is different from others; it also consists in how one is similar to others. Identity is formed by one's membership in a group, such as a family, country, school, team, friend group, etc. Individuals exist within relationships. In Matthew 25:31–46, Jesus taught that the way we treat his people is the way we treat him. Paul hears the same message from Jesus on the road to Damascus (Acts 9:4,5). The church is a body with many members (1 Cor 12:12–27; Col 1:18,24). Fundamentally, is the church "one" entity or a "collection" of parts?

Some people see oneness where those from other cultures see separation. It is impossible to be dogmatic by claiming that the Bible is only oriented to individuals rather than collectives. Both views could be pressed to unhealthy extremes. In fact, both have a place in forming a robust biblical theology.

A third set of differences has already been addressed—law-guilt versus honor/shame. A few additional observations and comments are still needed. Are legal categories central and honor/shame peripheral? An Eastern worldview sheds light on a number of passages. In Romans for example, Paul gives unmistakable priority to honor/shame when he writes, "You who boast in the law dishonor God by breaking the law. For, as it is written, 'The name of God is blasphemed among the Gentiles because of you'" (Rom 2:23,24). In Greek the verb in verse 23 is ἀτιμάζεις (dishonor); "breaking the law" is a noun set within a preposition (διὰ τῆς παραβάσεως τοῦ νόμου). Verse 24 reinforces the interpretation. Law breaking is simply a *means* of the essential problem—not giving God "face." Unrighteousness in Romans 1 is not defined in terms of law breaking but rather in overt honor/shame language (1:18–28). Sin is "fall[ing] short of the glory of God" (3:23). Those who are justified "will not be put to shame" (9:33; 10:10,11). The faith that justifies gives glory to God (4:20). Being justified, one "[boasts] in hope of the glory of God ... and hope does not put us to shame" (5:2–5).[252] Indeed, God does everything for the sake of his glory (cf. Rom 15:8,9).[253] Rather than setting law and honor in tension, those engaged in contextualization and theological study do better to find how they are interrelated. More has been said on this topic elsewhere.[254]

Fourthly, Westerners and Easterners tend to have different approaches to the question of knowledge and reality. Western education and scientific inquiry highlight the importance of analysis, abstract thinking, and logical coherence. Naturally, the European and American church has contributed greatly to a systematic understanding of Scripture. This emphasis is reflected in theological education. A typical Western seminary student spends at least two or three courses in studying systematic theology.

Many Easterners, on the other hand, are less inclined to such speculation, whether philosophically or in religion. In *Analects* 2:2, Confucius teaches, "Until you are able to serve men, how can you serve spiritual beings? Until you know about life, how can you know about death?"[255] Chinese have a pragmatic approach to life. They first seek to know if an idea works for some practical end. Thus, religion is viewed as a means of getting blessing in this present life. Chinese philosophy stresses harmony.

Those with more pragmatic tendencies also serve the church by drawing our attention to parts of the canon that can easily get overshadowed by the Pauline Epistles. Proverbs, for example, is full of practical advice for living a righteous life. Psalms and Ecclesiastes give sober reflections that challenge Christian idealism. More pragmatic theologians will help us better see connections between Paul's theology and the latter half of his letters, where he *applies* the former. When the global church interprets Scripture together, Christians help one another not to settle for merely right ideas but also to glorify Christ in right practice.

A fifth contrast concerns moral truth. Western apologists affirm absolutism and reject relativism. The latter is a common perspective in Eastern societies.

Once again, Christians would not disagree that God himself is the absolute standard by which one measures truth, right, wrong, good, and evil. Relativism generally asserts that truth and morality depend on circumstances and culture. One cannot claim dogmatically that what is right for you is right for me. It would seem that relativism has no place in biblical interpretation and must be resisted in contextualization.

Even here, it is important to take the time to understand the values that underlie relativistic thinking. The word "relativism" need not imply utter and direct contradiction. For instance, we all easily recognize that deciding between right and wrong, practically speaking, depends on one's situation and relationship. Sexual relations are right in marriage but wrong with someone else's spouse. In the OT, God approves of Israel destroying her enemies, yet Jesus' command to love our enemies also means that it is wrong to take revenge (cf. Rom 12:19). In one sense "none is righteous" (Rom 3:10), yet in Psalm 14, from which Paul quotes, the psalmist then adds "God is with the generation of the *righteous*" (Ps 14:5).

Meaning is relative to context and perspective. Hence, 1 Chronicles 21:1 says Satan incited David to take a census, whereas 2 Samuel 24:1 says the Lord moved David to do it. Scripture commands us both to honor and hate our parents (Ex 20:12; cf. Luke 14:26). We should always preach the gospel (2 Tim 4:2), except when we shouldn't (cf. Matt 14:13,23). We should always rejoice and yet "weep with those who weep" (Rom 12:15; cf. Phil 4:4). Famously, Jesus "relativized" the OT Sabbath laws. The fruit of the Spirit includes self-control, yet Paul says, "But if they cannot exercise self-control, they should marry. For it is better to marry than to burn with passion" (1 Cor 7:9). Discerning the relative value of absolute truths will help us better to distinguish sin from what is simply weakness. An Eastern perspective contributes a dose of humility to the Christian life. Critical realism steers the interpretive process away from a naive dogmatism that merely affirms correct answers but has little regard for context.

Sixth, Western and Eastern habits of thinking influence the interpretive process itself, not only the result of one's theologizing. As Richard Nisbett points out, Westerners are prone to dichotomous, either-or thinking whereas Easterners tend towards harmonizing ideas, identifying both-and relation-ships.[256] Chinese seek a "middle way" (*zhongyong*) between the two extremes. In research, it was found that Chinese judged a "more plausible proposition as less believable if they saw it contradicted [the alternative] than if they didn't." In contrast, Americans were likely to believe the "more plausible proposition more if they saw it contradicted [the alternative idea] than if it didn't."[257] Neither tendency is necessarily desirable.

Within Western Christian history, how many controversies and divisions derive from a lack of appreciation for both-and thinking? Countless disputes polarize two options, whether concerning the divine/human nature of Christ, God's sovereignty and human responsibility, the place of works and faith, or the divine/human authorship of the Bible. On the surface of things, if there were ever a contradiction, it would appear to be when Paul says, "One is justified by faith apart from works of the law" (Rom 3:28), yet James says, "A person is justified by works and not by faith alone" (Jas 2:24). Both East and West can benefit from one another. Perhaps a number of tensions within Western theology would be eased as Western Christians become proficient at both-and thinking. Likewise, as Easterners understand Western thinking, they may find themselves guilty of syncretism, thus compromising biblical truth.

Finally, it would not be surprising to find Eastern and Western Christians diverge in their appreciation for biblical genres. Chinese education emphasizes memorization. Students must spend considerable time not only memorizing classic works; also, simply learning the Chinese language requires extensive time and practice since it is a character-based system. Lacking an alphabet, every single character must be learned through rote memory. Chinese have a high regard for tradition and history.

By contrast, Western pedagogy stresses logical problem solving and debate. Creativity and novelty are valued. Not surprisingly, people spend a lot of time in the West on systematizing theological points and developing new ministry methods. Without question, this effort has benefited the church. Western Christians have a high regard for Paul's letters (as they should). Relatively speaking, there is less stress laid on narrative books and the OT wisdom literature. The Bible utilizes a number of genres. We must be careful not to create a canon within a canon, centered on our preferred genre. Theological provincialism naturally results whenever churches do not seek to think outside the local and traditional box. Unfamiliarity breeds uniformity and conformity, undermines the unity of the global church, and compromises biblical theology.

Context Is King All Over the World

Contextualization starts with interpretation, which centers on the Bible. This chapter, indeed the book, has tried to show that the maxim "Context is king" can be interpreted and applied in two distinct ways. The first is simple and familiar to most readers. Those who interpret the *Bible* seek to find the author's meaning within his original context. The biblical authors lived in a context quite foreign to our own. In that sense, reading Scripture itself is a cross-cultural experience.

There is a still another way in which "context" influences (perhaps even "rules") the way we read the Bible. When reading the Bible, we must recognize the simply fact that, to some degree, we are all products of our own culture. I am not at all implying some sort of "deterministic" theory of interpretation. Far from it. I simply highlight an unavoidable fact. Our cultural contexts inherently influence the kind of things we will tend to see and emphasize. We all have a cultural lens. No one reads the Bible completely free of presuppositions that have arisen from (for better or worse) his or her cultural background.

Since the Bible is God's revelation for all humanity, one expects that a global perspective on things would open our eyes to new insights that previously lay in a cultural blind spot. Fundamentally, we are humans, made in the image of God and not simply "Westerners" or "Easterners." Accordingly, this chapter has suggested a way to use present-day cultures to better understand ancient Scripture. Interpreters are urged to seek a broader understanding of the *human* context, both globally and historically. By so doing, they become acutely aware of themes that are in the Bible but have never figured prominently in their daily life. A multicultural perspective can help reconcile various tensions in Scripture. As a result, the church will be equipped to develop *contextual* theologies that are both biblically faithful and culturally meaningful.

KEY POINTS

- In order to interpret and apply Scripture, it is critical that we balance our particular perspective by becoming aware of other ways of seeing the world.

- General revelation and the basic structure of the world ensure that people can find common ground for communication and interpretation.

- Likewise, people's ability to understand special revelation is quite dependent on their experience and/or general revelation.

- Every cultural perspective has inherent blind spots that hinder biblical interpretation and thus contextualization.

- We can use contemporary cultures *as a means* of interpreting the ancient biblical text.

- Simply put, present-day cultures, at one level or another, share common ancient histories. Inasmuch as the world's people share common backgrounds, various themes will reappear again and again in cultures both across time and geography.

- Thus, contextualization is a cross-cultural *and* cross-historical process.

- It is imperative that we encourage and develop global theologies.

- The chapter examined seven common discussed differences between "Eastern" and "Western" cultures. In the process, we see that both perspectives offer a measure of truth that can help the church.

Appendix 1

The gospel we preach shapes everything else we do. Therefore, in the following pages, I provide a comprehensive evaluation form that can be used to evaluate gospel presentations. Although I especially have in mind evangelistic tracts, websites, and videos, one could use it to evaluate any sort of gospel presentation. The form has three sections:

1. Observations
2. Assessment
3. Relationship to the Culture

Humility requires that we not "assume" that a certain gospel presentation is both biblically faithful and culturally meaningful. Therefore, the following evaluation form can help churches and mission organizations thoughtfully and thoroughly consider the relative value of using certain presentations as opposed to others. The observation and evaluation questions are designed to spur discussion. Accordingly, it is best if the evaluation is completed within the context of a group.

EVALUATION FORM FOR ASSESSING GOSPEL PRESENTATIONS

I. OBSERVATIONS

A. Impressions

1. In two or three sentences, restate the main idea of the presentation (try to use its phraseology and/or key themes).

2. How does the presentation begin (major themes, verbiage, etc.)?

B. Use of Scripture

1. What are biblical passages are used in the presentation?

2. What passages are most prominent or emphasized?

3. What is the range of texts used (genre, authors, etc.)?

C. How does the presentation *frame* the gospel? In other words, what theme or motif structures the entire presentation?

1. Creation (e.g., Creator as Father, humanity as family, etc.)?

2. Covenant (e.g., Abraham, David, etc.)?

3. Kingship (e.g., Israel's King, defeats enemies, etc.)?

4. Other?

D. What metaphors, analogies, and imagery are used? In other words, what cultural and/or biblical themes fill in the framework (previous question)?

_____

_____

E. Priorities

1. How does the presentation answer the following four gospel questions?

   a. "Who is Christ?" (Similarly, "Who is God?")

   b. "What has Christ done?"

   c. "Why does Christ matter?"

   d. "How should we respond?"

2. How does the presentation prioritize the answers to these four questions? In other words, which answers receive the greatest stress and attention? List below.

    a. _____

    b. _____

    c. _____

    d. _____

F. **What is the presentation's "implicit gospel"? In other words, in what ways does a cultural worldview shape the presentation? Write observations as needed.**

    1. Social Unit: Who is primary?
       Individual or group?   N/A

    2. Nature of the World: Which is primary?
       Unity or diversity?   N/A

    3. Authority: Who has authority? _____

       (e.g., king, father, judge, teacher, tradition, book, other)

    4. Identity: What is the basis for identity?

       Differences (e.g., achievements, good deeds, unique features, etc.) or similarities (e.g., relationships, origin, status, etc.)?

    5. Morality: Decisions about good, right, and correct use of what kind of language?

        a. Law (e.g., judge, guilt, innocence, condemnation, crime, etc.)

        b. Honor/shame (e.g., conformity, face, glory, praise, embarrassment, etc.)

        c. Power/fear (e.g., spirits, demons, etc.)

        d. Purity (e.g., cleanse, wash, filthy, etc.)

        e. Tradition (e.g., ancestors, customs, etc.)

        f. Other?

        g. Which of these are primary? Least used?

G. The assumed reader/listener of this presentation has what kind of background?

H. What themes and topics are *not* included? (This is an open question for the sake of observation and reflection. No presentation can say everything. This question itself is *not* intended to convey a value assessment.)

II. ASSESSMENT

  A. Use of Scripture

1. Is it faithful to the biblical author's context? Are individual passages applied in the way the biblical author originally used them in their original context (e.g., themes, terms, concepts, etc.)? Explain.

2. Is it balanced and/or comprehensive? Does the presentation use passages from throughout the Bible in a balanced way? Explain.

3. Practically speaking, does the presentation favor one or two particular themes in a way that makes it difficult to use other themes or ideas from Scripture? (This question does *not* ask if the presentation *contradicts* other ideas.) Explain.

4. Does the presentation primarily retell the biblical story as a whole (biblical theology)? Or does it focus more on narrower themes (systematic theology)?

5. Does the presentation's "framework" reflect the way the Bible uses this framework? Or is it used simply as a cultural bridge? Explain.

6. Does the presentation present the gospel in clear, concrete, historical terms? Is it a bit too general, philosophical, or abstract? Explain.

7. Even if the theological conclusions (doctrines) are correct, are they explicit in the Bible or are they simply correct (or possible) inferences? Are there statements that are more speculative in nature (rather than explicit)? Explain.

8. How is the resurrection used (e.g., as a passing reference or a proof)? Does it state or develop the resurrection's theological significance?

9. What strengths does the presentation have that are not mentioned above?

10. What would you want to change or adjust about the presentation?

B. The Evangelist

1. What *theological assumptions* might the presenter have that would make it difficult to use this presentation? (Perhaps due to their denominational background, theological training, etc.)

2. What *cultural assumptions* might the presenter have that would make it difficult to use this presentation? (For example, if the presentation comes from a missionary who is foreign to the local culture.)

3. How easily can someone reproduce the presentation? Does it need to be memorized? Are there built-in ways to recall and present the information?

III. RELATIONSHIP TO THE CULTURE

A. What are basic features of the cultural worldview? Write observations as needed.

1. Social Unit: Who is primary? Individual or group? N/A

2. Nature of the World: Which is primary? Unity or diversity? N/A

3. Authority: Who has authority? _____
   (e.g., king, father, judge, teacher, tradition, book, other)

4. Identity: What is the basis for identity?

   Differences (e.g., achievements, good deeds, unique features, etc.) or similarities (e.g., relationships, origin, status, etc.)?

5. Morality: Decisions about good, right, and correct use of what kind of language?

   a. Law (e.g., judge, guilt, innocence, condemnation, crime, etc.)

   b. Honor/shame (e.g., conformity, face, glory, praise, embarrassment, etc.)

   c. Power/fear (e.g., spirits, demons, etc.)

   d. Purity (e.g., cleanse, wash, filthy, etc.)

   e. Tradition (e.g., ancestors, customs, etc.)

    f.   Other?

    g.   Which of these are primary? Least used?

B. Reflect on the following topics and discuss with others.

    1.   Culturally, one should keep in mind what things about the following aspects of the local culture?

        a.   Literacy? Education?

        b.   Influence of gender?

        c.   Use of story?

        d.   Use of art in the culture?

        e.   Perceptions and practice of religion?

        f.   Challenges and opportunities created by the local language?

C. Aesthetically, what does the presentation convey to local readers (via images, words, colors, etc.)?

Appendix 2

The following is one example of a contextualized gospel presentation. It summarizes the theology presented in chapter 8 ("A Chinese Biblical Theology"). It was originally designed and written for a Chinese context.

Rather than summarizing a few key doctrines, the presentation surveys the grand biblical Story, dividing it into six stages. This division reflects the major movements of the Story in a balanced way that respects the critical role of the Old Testament and its relationship to the New Testament.

Also, observe how the presentation's language intermingles various themes that are not only in the Bible but also meaningful in an East Asian context. Some of the most noteworthy themes include honor-shame, kingship, purity, and loyalty.

Finally, this is not a conventional "gospel tract." Instead, it is designed to serve as a "gospel guide." In other words, by introducing the overarching gospel narrative, this presentation accomplishes two purposes. First, it guides conversation with non-Christians. Second, it can facilitate evangelistic training for Christian believers. One simple reason many people do not share the gospel is because they cannot make sense of it in terms of the grand biblical Story.

For a translation of this guide and other similar presentations, go to jacksonwu.org.

DOES THE CREATOR-KING HAVE "FACE"?— A SHORT GOSPEL PRESENTATION[258]

Where do we belong?
That depends on our relationships and our face.
But what does all this mean?
The following historical story answers these questions.

One Family under Heaven

In the beginning . . .

The one true God created the world and all living things. He brought order to his creation, making it be a place of blessing.

He made male and female according to his image. We share in God's face. God is humanity's heavenly Father. He calls them to represent him in the creation. Thus, we owe God honor.

The Creator-King designed the world to be the place where he would dwell with his people. He wants all things to enjoy his holiness. God determined to bless the world through relationships. As people honored him, they would also enjoy unity with one another. God's kingdom was to be a place of righteousness.

The one true God planned to use the human family to fill the earth with his glory. If only they would love their Father and King, there would be harmony in the world.

Losing and Seeking Face

What is wrong with the world?

Since our earliest ancestors, we have loved created things more than the Creator. We forsake our Father for food, face, and fortune. Although humans were created to reflect God's glory, they have dishonored God's name.

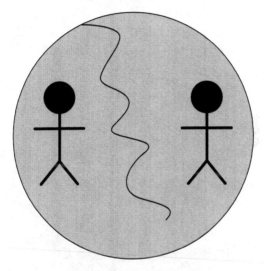

Because people have lost face before their Father and King, humans are alienated from God and one another. Shame stains the human family. Human rebellion brings about the curse of discord and death. People owe God their life. In fear, people seek face, hoping to find security and joy. We trust in ourselves and our relationships rather than our Father. We misuse relationships for personal gain.

The King's family has betrayed him. They choose to set up rival factions and occupy his kingdom. When people violate and offend the King, they commit what is called "sin."

King of All Nations

But there is good news.

The Creator-King planned to reverse the world's curse. He made a covenant with a man named Abraham, promising to bless the world through his offspring. From Abraham, God created a nation, Israel, to be a light to the nations. He showed his power and grace by rescuing them from slavery. He provided them with land, food, and a law.

God's royal law was intended to reveal God's nature and will. In this way, the law glorifies God by helping people to envision a society where justice reigns. It exposes human sin and teaches his people to live holy and righteous lives.

God wants to live among his people. Therefore he commanded them to build a temple to symbolize his presence with them. He established Israel to be a kingdom of priests, a holy nation who worshiped the one true God (Ex 19:6). God planned to use his relationship with Israel to bless the nations.

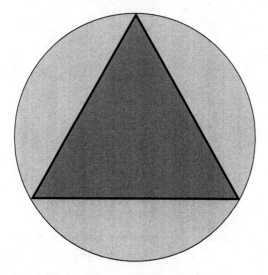

However, Israel failed to honor their covenant. Their religion became a mere tradition. They had hard hearts. They preferred the praise of people over the praise of God.

God's people became shameful and so concealed the truth of God's glory among the nations.

Setting the World Right

However, God is righteous.

He does not forsake his promises to this people. He will indeed restore his creation and be Father to all nations. The heavenly Father sent his Son, Jesus, to be the world's one true King. Through him, God fulfills his covenant to

Abraham. From Israel, God raised up a Savior, called "Christ." This Son of heaven sets the world right.

Jesus declared the good news, "The time has come, God's kingdom is near! Repent and believe this good news" (Mark 1:15).

Not only did he teach what God's kingdom is like, he also healed the sick and cared for the socially disadvantaged. People often love only others like themselves, but Jesus loves all people. He opposed God's enemies, whether demons, disease, unjust authorities, and the like.

Jesus challenged society's traditional thinking. Therefore the leaders of Jesus' day opposed him, provoking the common people to reject him.

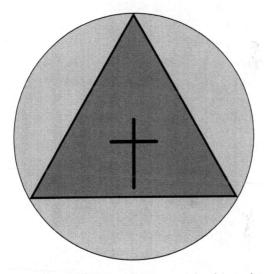

Although he had committed no crime, people ultimately condemned him, crucifying him on a cross. Even though he deserved people's allegiance and honor, they humiliated him. Their selfish hearts were defiled, refusing to give God glory.

However, this was all according to God's planned will. God had always planned that Jesus would repay the debt humanity owed God.

Although people are hostile to him, our king—Jesus—willingly bears the burden of humanity's depraved offenses, taking away their curse.

Jesus' entire life even unto death perfectly glorified the heavenly father. To everyone's surprise, this is how Christ gained victory!

Honored through Shame

The heavenly Father turned the tables.

Jesus was buried, and after three days God raised Jesus from the dead. From humanity's first ancestors to the present, death seems to rule every aspect of the present world. However, Christ overturns the powers in the world that oppose God. Jesus through resurrection defeats death to become the Lord of life. Any who pledge loyalty to him will no longer be slaves to fear.

God through the resurrection vindicates Jesus and so declares his people righteous. Although we lost face, God in Christ restores our face. God the Father causes all who are loyal to Christ to come under his name. He thus rebuilds the human family. They are called the "church."

Jesus cleanses them from corrupting filth. Therefore God's Holy Spirit dwells among his people. They are God's temple, the place where God dwells. Through his Spirit, God changes people's hearts such that they imitate Christ, giving them freedom to live holy lives. God's children are regarded with honor as a royal priesthood.

The Creator-King turns their view of the world inside out. God commands all people to give allegiance to King Jesus, repenting of shameful behaviors and attitudes. Christ's followers become his ambassadors among all nations. They proclaim, "Be reconciled to God!"

Yet God overturns the world's standard of honor and shame. The world does not understand His people, such that many even reject them. What God sees as glorious, the world sees as shameful. What God sees as shameful, the world sees as glorious.

Avenging Shame and Restoring God's Kingdom

God's people have a wonderful hope.

After his resurrection, Christ ascended to God the Father. God's children await Christ's return from heaven, God's throne room.

All who are in Christ are glorified with him. They will receive resurrected bodies, made into the likeness of Christ. The human family, once estranged, will be reconciled. The entire world will dearly love one another with all sincerity.

God through Jesus will ultimately defeat his enemies, especially death. He will condemn those who will not give their allegiance to him. In this way the Father-King will wipe away the disgrace and injustice that his people have suffered.

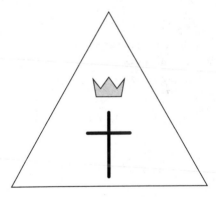

Our Creator-King will make a new heaven and new earth. According to his original plan and promises, he remakes the world to be the Temple in which he dwells with humanity. Every tribe and nation will become a universal brotherhood.

God restores harmony. The earth will be filled with the knowledge of the glory of God as the waters cover the sea (Hab 2:14).

The Creator-King truly has face!

How Should We Respond?

Change your mind

This story is the story of the entire world, including every nation, tribe, and individual. We share a common history, problem, and need. There is but one hope for us all. Idols and ideologies cannot save us.

We must see the world as God sees the world. We must call this story our own story. We must recognize as true what the one true God has done in history through Jesus Christ.

Accordingly, we forsake old principles and assumptions about how the world works and who is in charge. We must see others and ourselves through the lens of God's revealed word, which is found in the Bible.

God calls upon all people—including you—to repent of everything that does not reflect his holiness, anything that does not glorify his name.

Give your allegiance to Jesus Christ.

Have a new heart

How do you know that you are a child of God?

God's Spirit gives true believers a new heart. God's people seek to love him with all of their heart, mind, and strength. Like their heavenly Father, God's children delight to see God honored.

Naturally their aim is to love others as themselves. They desire righteousness, purity, faithfulness, generosity, and unity, among other virtues. God grows humility in their hearts rather than pride.

Christ is their greatest joy. They do not pursue the praise (*mianzi*) from people; instead they long to see the face (*lian*) of God.

Whose face do you seek?

Seek a transformed life

In humility, those who follow Christ regard themselves as his servants. Whether they eat, drink, or whatever they do, they want to do it for the glory of God. Christ's love compels genuine obedience; it is not merely the result of tradition or obligation.

God has given his children a mission. Because they bear his name, they should reflect his glory in the world. The story found in the Bible teaches them how to live a Christlike life. For his sake, God's people gladly accept the

Appendix 2

cost of following Christ. This includes various kinds of suffering, including the loss of relationships and perhaps even one's life.

However, those who believe this good news with their hearts gain a new family—one which consists of all nations. Those who belong to Christ's church love one another, regarding themselves as members of Christ's body, of which he is the head.

By the power of the Spirit, God's people proclaim God's kingdom. Together they strive for holiness. In this way they display a glimpse of the world as it will be when Christ returns to create a new heaven and new earth.

Who Are You?

If you enter ingo this great story, then God will change your identity!

If these things are true for you,

... then God has brought you into his family. Fundamentally, your identity does not come from your birth family, nationality, culture, social status, or achievements.

... then God has made you holy. You are no longer a slave to shameful desires. In the world, you are his royal representative and not a rebel to God.

Where Do You Belong?

If these things are true for you,

... you belong to God's kingdom family. In this present age, we are aliens and strangers. By grace we belong to Christ's church, a people marked by faith, hope, and love. As a community, we worship the one true God, studying the Bible, praying to God, and serving those in need.

Because of Christ, we truly have relationship (*guanxi*).

Since Jesus now rules as king, are you willing to believe
this good news and follow him?

Appendix 3

BIBLE VERSES THAT EXPLICITLY MENTION THE GOSPEL

Our view of the gospel cannot be limited to verses that explicitly mention the word "gospel." Yet they should be fundamental to our understanding. Accordingly, I have provided a listing of every instance where the biblical writers use Greek and Hebrew words that mean "gospel" or "preach the gospel." As can be seen, they generally fall within one or more of three major themes: creation, covenant, and kingdom. In many passages there is some ambiguity. However, the surrounding context often provides a few suggestive hints.

I have tried to comment on select passages in order to clarify why I classify verses the way I do. Of course people will disagree at times with the way I label a particular verse. Despite disagreements in such places, readers will see a definite pattern emerge. Consistently the biblical writers and preachers use these three themes (creation, covenant, and kingdom) to frame their gospel presentations.

HOW DOES THE BIBLE FRAME THE GOSPEL?

The chart lists the Bible passages that explicitly use the noun "gospel" or the verb "preach the gospel" in the original Hebrew Old Testament, Greek Septuagint (LXX), or Greek New Testament.

x – indicates that a passage uses the theme
x? – indicates that a passage probably uses the theme

Text	Creation	Covenant	Kingdom	Comments	Unclear
Old Testament					
2 Sam 31:9			x		
2 Sam 1:20			x		
2 Sam 4:10			x		
2 Sam 18:19			x		
2 Sam 18:20			x		
2 Sam 18:22			x		
2 Sam 18:25			x		
2 Sam 18:26			x		
2 Sam 18:27			x		
2 Sam 18:31			x		
1 Kings 1:42			x		
2 Kings 7:9			x		
1 Chron 10:9			x		
Ps 40:9				Kingdom; Covenant?	
Ps 68:11			x (cf. v. 24)	Covenant (v. 26?), Creation (v. 32)?	
Ps 96:2	x (v. 5)		x (vv. 10, 13)	Covenant (v. 13, "faithfulness")	
Isa 40:9	x		x (context)		
Isa 52:7			x	Creation? (cf. ch 51) Covenant? (cf. ch 51:2ff)	

Text	Creation	Covenant	Kingdom	Comments	Unclear
Isa 60:6			x?	vv. 3, 10–14, 16	
Isa 61:1			x		
Jer 20:15				No relationship; concerns child's birth	
Joel 2:32		x?	x?	context	
Nah 1:15			x	2:2; echoes Isa 52:7	
New Testament					
Matt 4:23			x		
Matt 9:35			x		
Matt 11:5				Kingdom ? v. 19 ("Son of Man")	
Matt 24:14			x		
Matt 26:13					x
Mark 1:1	x?		x?		
Mark 1:14			x		
Mark 1:15			x		
Mark 8:35			x	v. 29 "Christ"; vv. 31, 37 "Son of Man"; 9:1 "kingdom of God"	
Mark 10:29			x	vv. 23, 25	
Mark 13:10				Kingdom ? (context)	
Mark 14:9					x
Mark 16:15	x?			People debate whether this verse belongs in the original manuscripts.	

Text	Creation	Covenant	Kingdom	Comments	Unclear
Luke 1:19		x (vv. 32–33, 54–55, 69–70, 73)	x (vv. 32–33)	"Son of God" (v. 35) is title of a king	
Luke 2:10			x (v. 11)	Context is also an indirect clue	
Luke 3:18			x (v. 15)		Covenant? 3:8
Luke 4:18			x		
Luke 4:43			x		
Luke 7:22			x	v. 28; "Son of Man"	
Luke 8:1			x		
Luke 9:6			x (9:2)		
Luke 16:16	x?		x		
Luke 20:1			x?	Context and its Old Testament imagery connotes a kingdom idea	
Acts 5:42			x	Cf. 5:31	
Acts 8:4			x (8:12)		
Acts 8:12			x		
Acts 8:25			x?	8:12	
Acts 8:35			x?	8:12; background of Isaiah (vv. 32–33)	
Acts 8:40			x?	context	
Acts 10:36			x?		
Acts 11:20					Kingdom? (repeats titles "Lord" and "Christ")
Acts 13:32		x	x (context)		

Text	Creation	Covenant	Kingdom	Comments	Unclear
Acts 14:7		x?	x?	That they "continued to preach the gospel" implies the gospel in the above context.	
Acts 14:15	x				
Acts 14:21			x		
Acts 15:7		x?			
Acts 15:35					x
Acts 16:10					Kingdom? 17:10 derives from the calling in 16:10
Acts 17:18	x?		x?		
Acts 20:24			x?		
Acts 21:8					x
Rom 1:1		x	x		
Rom 1:9		x (context)	x (context)		
Rom 1:15		x (context)	x (context)		
Rom 1:16			x		
Rom 2:16			x?		
Rom 10:15			x (context)		
Rom 10:16			x	10:15; "obey"	
Rom 11:28		x?			
Rom 15:16		x?	x		
Rom 15:19			x?		
Rom 15:20			x	Cf. context of Isaiah (especially 52:7)	
Rom 16:25		x?	x?	See language of context	
1 Cor 1:17					x
1 Cor 4:15			x	4:20	

Text	Creation	Covenant	Kingdom	Comments	Unclear
1 Cor 9:12			x?		
1 Cor 9:14			x		
1 Cor 9:16			x?		
1 Cor 9:18			x?		
1 Cor 9:23			x?		
1 Cor 15:1	x	x	x	context	
1 Cor 15:2	x	x	x	context	
2 Cor 2:12			x	2:14	
2 Cor 4:3	x	x (context)	x (4:5?)		
2 Cor 4:4	x	x (context)	x (4:5?)		
2 Cor 8:18					x
2 Cor 9:13				Kingdom ? ("obey")	
2 Cor 10:14				Kingdom ? (language of context)	
2 Cor 10:16				Kingdom ? (language of context)	
2 Cor 11:4				Kingdom ? (language of context)	
2 Cor 11:7				Kingdom ? (language of context)	
Gal 1:6				Kingdom (vv. 4, 11)	
Gal 1:7				Kingdom (vv. 4, 11)	
Gal 1:8				Kingdom (vv. 4, 11)	
Gal 1:9				Kingdom (vv. 4, 11)	
Gal 1:11				Kingdom (vv. 4, 11)	
Gal 1:16					x
Gal 1:23					x
Gal 2:2					x

Text	Creation	Covenant	Kingdom	Comments	Unclear
Gal 2:5					x
Gal 2:7		x?	x?		
Gal 2:14		x?			
Gal 3:8		x		directly cites Abrahamic covenant	
Gal 4:13					Covenant? (cf. Ch. 3)
Eph 1:13	x? (vv. 4, 10)	x			
Eph 2:17	x (v. 15)	x			
Eph 3:6	x? (v. 9)	x	x? (7, 10)		
Eph 3:8	x?(v. 9)	x	x? (7, 10)		
Eph 4:11					x
Eph 6:15			x?	battle language in context	
Eph 6:19			x	v. 20, "ambassador"	
Phil 1:5					x
Phil 1:7					x
Phil 1:12					x
Phil 1:16					x
Phil 1:27			x?	Greek: "behave as citizens worthy of . . . " (trans. ESV note); likewise, uses "Christ" title	
Phil 2:22					x
Phil 4:3					x
Phil 4:15					x
Col 1:5	x?		x (vv. 13, 16)	implicit in context?	
Col 1:23	x				
1 Thess 1:5	x? (1:9)				

Text	Creation	Covenant	Kingdom	Comments	Unclear
1 Thess 2:2	x? (1:9)				
1 Thess 2:4	x? (1:9)		x?		
1 Thess 2:8			x? (2:12)		
1 Thess 2:9			x? (2:12)		
1 Thess 3:2					x
1 Thess 3:6					x
2 Thess 1:8			x	"obey"; vv. 5 (kingdom), 6, 8, 9	
2 Thess 2:14					Kingdom? ("called")
1 Tim 1:11			x	"entrust"; v. 17 (King)	
2 Tim 1:8			x?	1:9, 10, 12	
2 Tim 1:10			x?	"Savior"	
2 Tim 2:8		x	x		
2 Tim 4:5			x	Cf. 4:1, 8	
Philemon 1:13					x
Heb 4:2	x	x			
Heb 4:6	x	x			
1 Pet 1:12					Covenant? (v. 10)
1 Pet 1:25	x?		x?	1:17, 20, 24–25	
1 Pet 4:6					Kingdom? (4:5, 6, 11); Creation? (4:7, 19)
1 Pet 4:17	x (v. 19)		x?	"judge"	
Rev 10:7	x (v. 6)		x?	"servants"	Covenant? ("mystery")
Rev 14:6	x		x	14:3, 7	
Total	**25**	**26**	**93**		

Appendix 3-Analysis of Gospel Themes

Notes
(Endnotes)

Introduction

1   For a helpful essay arguing that our gospel should be biblically "faithful" and cultur-
ally "meaningful," see Bruce Riley Ashford, "The Gospel and Culture," in *Theology and Practice of Mission: God, the Church, and the Nations*, ed. Bruce Riley Ashford (Nashville: B & H Academic, 2011), Kindle loc. 3099–3492.

2   Jackson Wu, *Saving God's Face: A Chinese Contextualization of Salvation through Honor and Shame* (Pasadena, CA: WCIU Press, 2013), 10–39.

Chapter 1: Context Is King

3   N. T. Wright, "Simply Jesus" (sermon). Willowcreek Community Church, South Barrington, IL, http://media.willowcreek.org/weekend/simply-jesus/ (assessed 6 November 2011).

4   This section draws heavily from my discussion in Wu, *Saving God's Face*, 21–24.

5   David J. Hesselgrave and Edward Rommen, *Contextualization: Meanings, Methods, and Models* (Grand Rapids, MI: Baker, 1989), 200.

6   Ibid., 33–34.

7   Susan S. Baker, "The Social Sciences for Urban Ministry," in *The Urban Face of Mission: Ministering the Gospel in a Diverse and Changing World*, ed. Manuel Ortiz and Susan S. Baker (Phillipsburg, NJ: P & R, 2002), 75. Baker cites Louis J. Luzbetak, *The Church and Cultures: New Perspectives in Missiological Anthropology* (Maryknoll, NY: Orbis Books, 1988), 69.

8   Kevin Greeson, *The Camel: How Muslims Are Coming to Faith in Christ!*, rev. ed. (Monument, CO: WIGTake Resources, 2010), 199–200.

9   Scott Moreau, "Evangelical Models of Contextualization," in *Local Theology for the Global Church: Principles for an Evangelical Approach to Contextualization*, ed. Matthew Cook et al. (Pasadena, CA: William Carey Library, 2010), 169. He cites Stephen Bevans, *Models of Contextual Theology*, rev. and expanded ed. (Maryknoll, NY: Orbis Books, 2002), 37.

10   M. David Sills, *Reaching and Teaching: A Call to Great Commission Obedience* (Chicago: Moody, 2010), 195.

11   Scott Moreau, "Contextualization That Is Comprehensive," *Missiology* 34, no. 3 (2006): 325.

12   For examples, see Don Richardson, *Peace Child* (Glendale, CA: Regal Books, 1974); and Greeson, *The Camel*, 199–200.

13   Lesslie Newbigin, *The Gospel in a Pluralist Society* (Grand Rapids, MI: Eerdmans, 1989), 144 (cf. 189). Though not citing Newbigin, David Bosch concurs in *Transforming Mission: Paradigm Shifts in Theology of Mission* (Maryknoll, NY: Orbis Books, 1991), 297.

14   Baker, "Social Sciences," 75, italics mine.

15   Dean Flemming, *Contextualization in the New Testament: Patterns for Theology and Mission* (Downers Grove, IL: IVP Academic, 2005), 20.

16   Kevin Vanhoozer, "'One Rule to Rule Them All?': Theological Method in an Era of World Christianity," in *Globalizing Theology: Belief and Practice in an Era of World Christianity*, ed. Craig Ott and Harold Netland (Grand Rapids, MI: Baker Academic and Brazos Press, 2006), 100.

17   Wu, *Saving God's Face*, 10–33.

18   Ibid., 26.

19   Vanhoozer, "Theological Method," 116.

20   Bruce J. Nicholls, *Contextualization: A Theology of Gospel and Culture* (Vancouver, BC, Canada: Regent College, 2003), 25.

21   Also, this book does not affirm as good contextualization what often goes by the name "liberation theology," prominent in parts of Latin America.

22   David K. Clark, *To Know and Love God: Method for Theology* (Wheaton, IL: Crossway, 2003), 107.

23   Ibid., 50. He credits this term to Richard Lints, *The Fabric of Theology* (Grand Rapids, MI: Eerdmans, 1993), 8.

24   11/17/2014 11:17:00 AM"What is Everyday Theology?" in *Everyday Theology: How to Read Cultural Texts and Interpret Trends* (ed. Charles A. Anderson, Michael J. Sleasman, Kevin J. Vanhoozer; Grand Rapids, MI: Baker Academic, 2007), 36.

25   Various people have made similar comments, including Bevans, *Models of Contextual Theology*, 3; and Bosch, *Transforming Mission*, 423.

26   Sills, *Reaching and Teaching*, 198.

27   In chapter 5 I will show how we preach an "implicit gospel" that may have a more powerful influence on our listeners than we realize. This "implicit" message is shaped by our culture, even if we are explicitly talking about the Bible.

28   For a more detailed argument on related issues, see Wu, *Saving God's Face*, 193–292.

29   Dean Flemming, "Paul the Contextualizer," in Cook et al., *Local Theology*, 18–19.

30   John H. Walton, *The Lost World of Genesis One: Ancient Cosmology and the Origins Debate* (Downers Grove, IL: IVP Academic, 2009), 9.

31   To some measure, this happens regardless whether one knows it. Therefore it would be best to be intentional about the lens we use. I will address this issue in greater detail in the coming chapters. On the relationship between culture, interpretation, and hermeneutics, see Julian Ruth, "Ground Level Contextualization," in Cook et al., *Local Theology*, 57–89.

Chapter 2: A Common Problem

32   For a simple analogy, one could also imagine a family of five children. The mom gives one of the kids five cookies, which are to be shared with the other kids. Nevertheless the child still boasts, "Mom gave *me* five cookies and not to you!" Yes, this is true, but in a quite distorted and destructive sense.

33   C. S. Lewis, "To Dom Bede Griffiths" (23 April 1951), in *The Collected Letters of C. S. Lewis, Volume 3: Narnia, Cambridge, and Joy, 1950–1963*, ed. Walter Hooper (New York: HarperCollins, 2007), 111.

34   N. T. Wright, "Scripture, Exegesis, Dogma and Church: Some Pauline Proposals," in *Pauline Perspectives: Essays on Paul, 1978–2013* (Philadelphia: Fortress Press, 2013), 377.

35   John Piper, "Did Jesus Die for Us or for God?," Desiring God, 1 January 1995, http://www.desiringgod.org/resource-library/articles/did-christ-die-for-us-or-for-god (accessed 3 October 2012).

36   N. T. Wright, *Justification: God's Plan and Paul's Vision* (Downers Grove, IL: IVP Academic, 2009), 124.

37   For a scholarly review of the use of the word in ancient and biblical literature, see John Dickson, "Gospel as News —from Aristophanes to the Apostle Paul," *New Testament Studies* 51, no. 2 (2005): 212–30.

38   Evangelical theologians never mention the resurrection in Alliance of Confessing Evangelicals, "The Cambridge Declaration of the Alliance of Confessing Evangelicals," Center for Reformed Theology and Apologetics, 20 April 1996, http://www.reformed.org/documents/cambridge.html (accessed 25 October 2011). This was noted by Timothy Gombis, "The Gospel and Double Imputation," *Patheos* (blog), 25 October 2011, http://www.patheos.com/community/jesuscreed/2011/10/25/the-gospel-and-double-imputation/?utm_source= feedburner&utm_medium=feed&utm_campaign=Feed%3A+PatheosJesusCreed+%28Blog+-+Jesus+Creed%29 (accessed 25 October 2011, page discontinued). In the "Creation to Christ" story (C2C), only one line points to the resurrection: "On the third day Jesus rose from the dead and showed Himself to His followers" (in part 6)—Stephen R. Smith, "Gospel Presentations Used in T4T Packages," Training for Trainers, 2011, 6, http://t4tonline.org/wp-content/uploads/2011/02/3d-Gospel-Presentations-Used-in-T4T-Packages.pdf (accessed 21 February 2012).

39   For a succinct summary of the significance of ascribed honor for identity in a biblical, Jewish context, see David A. deSilva, *Honor, Patronage, Kinship and Purity: Unlocking New Testament Culture* (Downers Grove, IL: IVP Academic, 2000), 158–65, 206–12.

40   Seifrid even claims the biblical writers' "references to God's saving righteousness appear roughly four times as frequently as those to his retributive justice"—Mark Seifrid, *Christ Our Righteousness: Paul's Theology of Justification* (Downers Grove, IL: InterVarsity Press, 2000), 44.

41   For example, see Bruce Demarest, *The Cross and Salvation: The Doctrine of God* (Wheaton, IL: Crossway, 2006), 362–63.

42   This is a play on words that draws from a text with a bit different focus, namely the use of the OT in the NT. See G. K. Beale, ed., *The Right Doctrine from the Wrong Texts? Essays on the Use of the Old Testament in the New* (Grand Rapids, MI, MI: Baker, 1994).

Chapter 3: Pattern

43   For a few examples, see Greg Gilbert, *What Is the Gospel?* (Wheaton, IL: Crossway, 2010); Matt Chandler and Jared C. Wilson, *The Explicit Gospel* (Wheaton, IL: Crossway, 2012); Scot McKnight, *The King Jesus Gospel: The Original Good News Revisited* (Grand Rapids, MI: Zondervan, 2011); D. A. Carson, "What Is the Gospel?—Revisited," in *For the Fame of God's Name: Essays in Honor of John Piper*, ed. C. Samuel Storms and Justin Taylor (Wheaton, IL: Crossway, 2010), 147–70; John Piper, *God Is the Gospel: Meditations on God's Love as the Gift of Himself* (repr., Wheaton, IL: Crossway, 2011); N. T. Wright, *How God Became King: The Forgotten Story of the Gospels* (New York: HarperOne, 2012); Dickson, "Gospel as News."

44   For his ongoing series chronicling the various "gospel definitions," see Trevin Wax, "Results for 'Gospel Definitions,'" *Kingdom People* (blog), http://thegospelcoalition.org/blogs/trevinw ax/?s=%22gospel+definitions%22. For his list in PDF format, see Trevin Wax, "Gospel Definitions," *Kingdom People* (blog), June 2011, http://thegospelcoalition.org/blogs/trevinwax/2009/09/28/ gospel-definitions-pdf-format/ (accessed 26 December 2012).

45   For further explanation, see Trevin Wax, "3 Ways of Defining the Gospel," *Kingdom People* (blog), 22 February 2011, http://thegospelcoalition.org/blogs/trevinwax/2011/02/22/3-ways-of-defining-the-gospel/ (accessed 26 December 2012). He has even written his own book: Trevin Wax, *Counterfeit Gospels: Rediscovering the Good News in a World of False Hope* (Chicago: Moody, 2011).

46   Chandler and Wilson, *The Explicit Gospel*, 15.

47   Ibid., 16.

48   Gilbert, *What Is the Gospel?*, 103–7.

49   Ibid., 104. Gilbert seems to make a straw-man argument. While some would claim that Jesus can be Savior but not Lord, it's questionable how many people proclaim as the gospel that Jesus is Lord but not Savior.

50   Ibid., 103–4. Again, this seems to be a straw-man argument. Who preaches Jesus as Lord (not Savior) apart from the cross?

51   D. A. Carson and Timothy J. Keller, eds., *The Gospel as Center: Renewing Our Faith and Reforming Our Ministry Practices* (Wheaton, IL: Crossway, 2012). This paragraph draws from Wu, *Saving God's Face*, 19.

52   This number attempts not to count source citations, where these words are used in source titles.

53   McKnight, *The King Jesus Gospel*, 28–33.

54   Ibid., 14.

55   This line has been documented many places, including Ben Witherington, "Dialogue with Scot McKnight on 'King Jesus': Part One," *The Bible and Culture* (blog), 10 September 2011, http://www.patheos.com/blogs/bibleandculture/2011/09/10/dialogue-with-scot-mcknight-on-king-jesus-part-one-2/ (accessed 26 December 2012).

56   McKnight, *The King Jesus Gospel*, 51–52.

57   Trevin Wax, "Scot McKnight and the 'King Jesus Gospel' 2: Points of Concern," *Kingdom People* (blog), 14 September 2011, http://thegospelcoalition.org/blogs/trevinwax/2011/09/14/ scot-mcknight-and-the-king-jesus-gospel-2-points-of-concern/ (accessed 26 December 2012).

58   McKnight, *The King Jesus Gospel*, 133.

59   Ibid., 135.

60   Ibid., 117.

61   For a historical and empirical-based argument on this point, see Richard E. Nisbett, *The Geography of Thought: How Asians and Westerns Think Differently . . . and Why* (New York: Free Press, 2003).

62   In McKnight, *The King Jesus Gospel*, he directly states, "This Plan of Salvation is not the gospel" (38). By "this Plan," he refers to "how an individual gets saved, what God has done for us, and how we are to respond if we want to be saved" (37).

63   Gilbert, *What Is the Gospel?*, 26–27.

64   Ibid., 28, italics mine.

65   This paragraph's discussion of the Gospel Coalition's book comes from Wu, *Saving God's Face*, 18–19. "Gospel" language refers to the standard terminology that translates words like "gospel" or "to preach the gospel." In the NT the typical noun is εὐαγγέλιον; the verb is εὐαγγελίζω. The most common OT term is רשׂב. I do not suggest that one's understanding of the gospel should be restricted to such passages, yet one would expect them to carry great weight in how one formulates or frames the gospel.

66   Carson and Keller, *The Gospel as Center*.

67   Ibid., 243, 276. Page 243 uses 1 Corinthians 15:3 simply to explain the Lord's Supper.

68   Ibid., 141.

69   Bryan Chapell, "What Is the Gospel?," in Carson and Keller, *The Gospel as Center*, 115–34.

70   Chandler and Wilson, *The Explicit Gospel*, 15, 172.

71   For example, see ibid., 15, 136, 166–69.

72   For example, the book does not account for Acts 13–14 or key usages of "gospel" language in Isaiah 40:9 and 52:7. In a note given on p. 54, he mentions that the original Greek word εὐαγγέλιον means "good news," but Chandler does not talk more specifically about its historical usage and connotations.

73   By the phrase "more Jewish audiences," I refer also to those Gentiles who were "God fearers" or "proselytes," who would be more familiar with the Jewish Scripture than the average Gentile.

74   Two articles reviewing the way Paul presents his gospel in Acts include Dean Flemming, "Contextualizing the Gospel in Athens: Paul's Areopagus Address as a Paradigm for Missionary Communication," *Missiology: An International Review* 30, no. 2 (2002): 199–214; Atef M. Gendy, "Style, Content and Culture: Distinctive Characteristics in the Missionary Speeches in Acts," *Swedish Missiological Themes* 99, no. 3 (2011): 247–65.

75   To illustrate a point, the graph exaggerates the dichotomy between the legal motif and a given culture. I doubt anyone would ever separate the two so sharply. The ovals are meant to represent the most prominent themes within each sphere. Typically, Chinese culture, for example, is not said to be a "law-oriented" society but rather an "honor/shame" culture. Any culture will have features within it that resonate in some way with themes in the Bible.

76   Gilbert, *What Is the Gospel?*, 104–5.

77   Ibid., 102–3.

78   References to evangelicals can be found on pp. 103, 107, 109. He also adds, "The problem, though, is that creation-fall-redemption-consummation has been used wrongly by some as a way to place the emphasis of the gospel on God's promise to renew the world, rather than on the cross" (ibid., 106). Who are those people who wrongly de-emphasize the cross? It is unclear who he thinks does affirm the creation-fall-redemption-consummation paradigm without compromising the cross.

79   Sills, *Reaching and Teaching*, 198.

80   Gilbert, *What Is the Gospel?*, 105–6.

81   Ibid., 42–46. On p. 43 he contrasts God's love and righteousness when he says, "God's love does not cancel out his justice and righteousness."

82   Demarest, *The Cross and Salvation*, 362–63.

83   McKnight is both provocative and constructive when he distinguishes declarative and persuasive proclamation rhetoric. He says the latter describes evangelical gospel presentations and aims at creating a sense of "liminality." See Scot McKnight, "The Gospel and the Pastor" (lecture), Parchman Lectures, Truett Theological Seminary, Waco, TX, 12 October 2011), http://www.baylor.edu/truett/index.php?id=84799 (accessed 18 Oct 2011); cf. Scot McKnight, "Gospel and Rhetoric," *Jesus Creed* (blog), 7 November 2011, http://www.patheos.com/blogs/jesuscreed/2011/11/07/gospel-and-rhetoric/ (accessed 22 January 2013).

84   Although these three themes have long been prominent within biblical theology, I have not found any theologians or missiologists that directly make the claim I make here. That is, they do not explicitly utilize this threefold framework to explain the gospel as found in the Bible. Interestingly, these three themes are often implicit whenever biblical theologians summarize the gospel. For example, see Michael F. Bird, *Evangelical Theology: A Biblical and Systematic Introduction* (Grand Rapids, MI: Zondervan, 2013), 47–54. N. T. Wright also uses a similar framework when describing Second Temple Judaism as well as Paul's own theology. He lists monotheism, election, and eschatology. See N. T. Wright, *Paul and the Faithfulness of God* (Philadelphia: Fortress Press, 2013). His specific categories roughly correspond to my more general labels; respectively, creation, covenant, and kingdom.

Just before this book went to print, I found out that N. T. Wright briefly explains the gospel through the "themes of coronation, covenant, and creation." See N. T. Wright, *Simply Good News: Why the Gospel Is News and What Makes It Good* (San Francisco: HarperOne, 2015), 71–73, 98. Although he does not develop this train of thought in the way done in this book, his comments reinforce the presence of these three "framework themes."

85   For a scholarly review of the use of the word in ancient and biblical literature, see Dickson, "Gospel as News." Historically the word "gospel" primarily was a political/royal term, not a religious concept. A "gospel" announced the ascension, birth, or victory of a king. This is the meaning of the word in Greek culture during the time that the New Testament was being written. This usage is also consistent with the Old Testament, as will be seen. For a summary of his fuller argument, see John Dickson, *The Best Kept Secret of Christian Mission: Promoting the Gospel with More Than Our Lips* (Grand Rapids, MI: Zondervan, 2010), 111–40.

86   This was first shown to me in McKnight, *The King Jesus Gospel*.

87   For more on Paul's usage of creation, including the "cultural mandate" (Gen 1:26–28) in Colossians, see G. K. Beale, "Colossians," in *Commentary on the New Testament Use of the Old Testament*, ed. G. K. Beale and D. A. Carson (Grand Rapids, MI: Baker, 2007), 841–70.

88   This exact Greek wording only appears in Psalm 96:13. Instead of using the infinitive κρίνειν, the other verses use the future indicative κρινεῖ.

89   The meaning of Jewish monotheism and its theological implications have recently been summarized more thoroughly in Wright, *Paul*, 619–43.

90   What follows captures the essence of N. T. Wright's argument in N. T. Wright, *Climax of the Covenant* (Minneapolis: Fortress Press, 1993), 168–71. In short, verses 19,20 contrast the implications of Moses' mediatorship and God's promise concerning the nations (Gal 3:7–14). The second half of verse 19 acts as a *reductio ad absurdum*, assuming an absurdity in order to disprove it. Verse 20 points out the absurdity. The second part of verse 20 then overturns the absurdity. Put simply, the point of verses 19,20 is to explain the purpose of the law and argue that the law itself is not bad.

91   In agreement with others, I have argued elsewhere that Romans 2:14 is typically mistranslated and so obscures Paul's point. See Wu, *Saving God's Face*, 255–58. To rephrase the ESV, Romans 2:14 is better read, "For when Gentiles, who *by birth* do not have the law, do what the law requires, they are a law to themselves, even though they do not have the law."

Chapter 4: Priority

92   For a concise comparison between *mianzi* and *lian*, see Wu, *Saving God's Face*, 88–91. Lengthy articles include Hsien Chin Hu, "The Chinese Concepts of 'Face,'" *American Anthropologist* 46, no. 1 (March 1944): 45–64; David Yau-fai Ho, "On the Concept of Face," *American Journal of Sociology* 81, no. 4 (1976): 866–84.

93   See *SpreadTruth*, "The Story," http://viewthestory.com/ (accessed 26 July 2011).

94   Albert M. Wolters, *Creation Regained: Biblical Basics for a Reformational Worldview*, 2nd ed. (Grand Rapids, MI: Eerdmans, 2005).

95   Michael W. Goheen and Craig G. Bartholomew, *The Drama of Scripture: Finding Our Place in the Biblical Story* (Grand Rapids, MI: Baker Academic, 2004).

96   Alternatively, one might contrast chronology (God *first* saves humanity, then will restore creation) and teleology (ultimately, God glorifies himself by creating a new heaven and new earth).

97   In Paul's case, this meant his discerning Jesus' significance from the Old Testament. He did not have the "New Testament" in our present form. Today we could draw from the Old and New Testaments.

98   See Hays' discussion throughout his classic text, Richard B. Hays, *The Faith of Jesus Christ: The Narrative Substructure of Galatians 3:1–4:11*, 2nd ed. (Grand Rapids, MI: Eerdmans, 2002). He argues, "The framework of Paul's thought is constituted neither by a system of doctrines not by his personal religious experience but by a 'sacred story,' a narrative structure" (6). He frequently appeals to J. Christiaan Beker, "Contingency and Coherence in the Letters of Paul," *Union Seminary Quarterly Reveiw* 33 (1978): 141–51; also, Beker's *Paul the Apostle: The Triumph of God in Life and Thought* (Philadelphia: Fortress, 1980).

99   Notice that the writer of Psalm 104 interprets Genesis 1 by emphasizing the character of God.

100   For examples, see Glen Collins Li, *Sin, the Silent Killer* (Maitland, FL: Xulon Press, 2008), 96; Gilbert, *What Is the Gospel?*, 29–30. For a thought-provoking reflection on the matter, see McKnight, "Gospel and Rhetoric."

101   See Piper, *God Is the Gospel.*

102   For a defense of this point, see John Piper, *God's Passion for His Glory* (Wheaton, IL: Crossway, 1998). Piper's book contains a reprint of Jonathan Edwards' classic text *The End for which God Made the World.*

103   I purposely use "expression" in a vague sense. If one thinks "law" in Romans refers to the Jewish law, then breaking the Mosaic law is one means of sinning. If one thinks "law" is more general, referring to a law for all humanity, then "breaking the law" represents one metaphorical way of describing the human problem.

Others have highlighted the diverse ways of understanding sin. For example, see Richard Hibbert and Evelyn Hibbert, "Contextualising Sin for Cross-cultural Evangelism," *Missiology: An International Review*, vol 42, no. 3 (2014): 309–21; Mark E. Briddle, *Missing the Mark: Sin and Its Consequences in Biblical Theology* (Nashville, TN: Abington Press, 2005).

104   An excellent biblical theology that highlights this idea can be found in Scott J. Hafemann, *The God of Promise and the Life of Faith: Understanding the Heart of the Bible* (Wheaton, IL: Crossway, 2001).

105   For an excellent treatment of this idea, see James M. Hamilton Jr., *God's Glory in Salvation through Judgment: A Biblical Theology* (Wheaton, IL: Crossway, 2010).

106   For more extensive discussion on salvation in terms of honor and shame, see chapters 4–5 of Wu, *Saving God's Face.*

107   Kevin DeYoung and Greg Gilbert, *What Is the Mission of the Church? Making Sense of Social Justice, Shalom, and the Great Commission* (Wheaton, IL: Crossway, 2011), 110–11, italics in the original.

108   I italicize the word "that" to signify the content one is supposed to believe. In Mark 1:15 Jesus inserts "the gospel." I have simply interjected the condition clause to include the response within the gospel itself. Logically, Jesus' statement thus spirals into an infinite loop.

109   Consider an example from American history. Abraham's Lincoln's Emancipation Proclamation legally freed the slaves who lived in Confederate states. Lincoln, via executive order, *commanded* that there be a new reality. He was not merely giving information *about how* slaves could possibly be free.

110   Michael F. Bird, *Introducing Paul: The Man, His Mission and His Message* (Downers Grove, IL: IVP Academic, 2009), 81.

111   Martin Luther, "A Brief Instruction on What to Look for and Expect in the Gospels," in *Luther Works*, vol. 35, ed. J. Pelikan and H. T. Lehmann (Philadelphia: Fortress, 1960), 118–19. Cited in Bird, *Introducing Paul*, 78.

112   Paul is said to preach the gospel (εὐηγγελίζετο) in Acts 17:18.

113   Inexplicably, DeYoung and Gilbert add, "That's also why we never see the New Testament calling any *other* single promise of God to the redeemed 'the gospel.' For example, we never see the (*Mission of the Church*), 109. This claim directly contradicts the evidence shown here.

114   This is precisely what one finds when reading many gospel tracts or evangelical statements like the Alliance of Confessing Evangelicals' "Cambridge Declaration," which lays great stress on Jesus' death and our justification but omits any mention of the resurrection.

115   Timothy Gombis makes this argument more fully in "Racial Reconciliation and the Christian Gospel," *ACTS 3 Review* 15, no. 3 (2006): 117–28. He argues, "Racial reconciliation is not simply something nice that Christians should be doing, a sort of add-on to the gospel—nice, but not necessary. *It is at the very heart of the gospel*. Reconciliation *is* the gospel, and racial, or ethnic reconciliation" (117, italics in the original). DeYoung and Gilbert seem to disagree: "Or why does he never preach, 'The gospel is the good news that Jew and Gentile can be reconciled to one another through Jesus'? . . . Nor do we see reconciliation between humans called 'the gospel'"—*Mission of the Church?*, 107–8. However, in the context of Ephesians 3:1–10, Paul seems to make clear that human reconciliation is a part of a robust gospel announcement. Of course this blessing is not the entirety of the gospel's significance, but neither is forgiveness nor any other one blessing. They call forgiveness of sin the "fountainhead" of the gospel (p. 109). However, even if one agrees, a wellspring is a part of a spring, but one would never reduce the spring simply to its entry point.

116   Bird, *Introducing Paul*, 83.

117   Andrew Kipnis, *Producing* Guanxi: *Sentiment, Self, and Subculture in a North China Village* (Durham, NC: Duke University Press, 1997), 174.

118   In essence, first-century Christians were announcing, "Jesus is Lord"; thus, by inference, "Caesar is not." For a range of views and explanations on Christianity's relationship to the Roman Empire, see Scot McKnight and Joseph B. Modica, eds., *Jesus Is Lord, Caesar Is Not: Evaluating Empire in New Testament Studies* (Grand Rapids, MI: IVP Academic, 2013); N. T. Wright, "Paul's Gospel and Caesar's Empire," *Center of Theological Inquiry* (Princeton, NJ: T&T Clark) 2 (Spring 1999): 42–65; Richard A. Horsley, ed., *Paul and Empire: Religion and Power in Roman Imperial Society* (T&T Clark, 1997); Denny Burk, "Is Paul's Gospel Counterimperial? Evaluating the Prospects of the 'Fresh Perspective' for Evangelical Theology," *Journal of the Evangelical Theological Society* 51, no. 2 (June 2008): 309–37.

Chapter 6: Process

119   Campus Crusade for Christ (Cru), "Four Spiritual Laws," 2007, http://www.campuscrusade.com/fourlawseng.htm (accessed 26 July 2011) (updated website: http://www.crustore.org/fourlawseng.htm). For an analysis of its implied theology, see Wu, *Saving God's Face*, 139–40.

120   See chapter 3, which discusses specific biblical implications of monotheism. Training for Trainers, "Creation to Christ," http://t4tonline.org/wp-content/uploads/2011/05/creation-to-christ-oral-version-english.pdf (accessed 25 November 2013).

121   K. K. Yeo, *What Has Jerusalem to Do with Beijing: Biblical Interpretation from a Chinese Perspective* (Harrisburg, PA: Trinity Press, 1998), 5. For my own elaboration and defense of the use of contemporary culture to interpret the Bible, see chapter 10.

122   Elsewhere I have offered a more fully developed explanation on Romans 1:14,15, including its implications for ethnicity and the overall purpose of Paul's letter. See Jackson Wu, "Paul Writes to the Greek First and Also to the Jew: The Missiological Significance of Understanding Paul's Purpose in Romans," *Journal of the Evangelical Theological Society* 56, no. 4 (December 2013): 765–79.

123   I have given a detailed interpretation of these verses in Wu, *Saving God's Face*, 261–71.

124   Similar arguments could be made from Romans 3:1–5; 10:3 in their respective contexts.

Chapter 7: A Jewish Gospel among Gentiles

125   One could have drawn from any of the four Gospels. When considering Luke and John, which I cite, we should also remember that they were written with Gentile readers in mind.

126   Observe also that Paul uses the verb ὁρίζω, which echoes the noun ὅριον found in Deuteronmy 32:8.

Chapter 8: A Chinese Biblical Theology

127   Throughout this section, endnotes are used to express related ideas in Chinese characters.

128   For a sample of books and articles across disciplines, see Olwen Bedford and Kwang-Kuo Hwang, "Guilt and Shame in Chinese Culture: A Cross-cultural Framework from the Perspective of Morality and Identity," *Journal for the Theory of Social Behaviour* 33, no. 2 (June 1, 2003): 127–44; Daniel H. Bays, *A New History of Christianity in China* (Hoboken, NJ: Wiley-Blackwell, 2011); Chung-Ying Cheng, "The Concept of Face and Its Confucian Roots," *Journal of Chinese Philosophy* 13 (1986): 329–48; Ying-Yi Hong and Chi-Yue Chiu, "A Study of the Comparative Structure of Guilt and Shame in a Chinese Society," *Journal of Psychology* 126, no. 2 (March 1992): 171–79; Hu, "Chinese Concepts of 'Face'"; Dilin Liu, *Metaphor, Culture, and Worldview: The Case of American English and the Chinese Language* (Lanham, MD: University Press of America, 2002); Wenzhong Hu and Cornelius Lee Grove, *Encountering the Chinese: A Guide for Americans* (Yarmouth, ME: Intercultural Press, 1991); Kwang-Kuo Hwang, *Foundations of Chinese Psychology: Confucian Social Relations* (New York: Springer, 2012); Kipnis, *Producing* Guanxi; Li Liu, "Filial Piety, *Guanxi*, Loyalty, and Money: Trust in China," in *Trust and Distrust: Sociocultural Perspectives*, ed. Ivana Marková and Alex Gillespie (Charlotte, NC: Information Age Publishing, 2008), 51–73; Haihua Zhang and Geoffrey Baker, *Think Like Chinese* (Annandale, NSW, Australia: Federation Press, 2008). For explicitly Christian perspectives, see Richard R. Cook and David W. Pao, eds., *After Imperialism: Christian Identity in China and the Global Evangelical Movement* (Eugene, OR: Pickwick, 2011); Ralph Covell, *Confucius, the Buddha, and Christ: A History of the Gospel in Chinese* (Maryknoll, NY: Orbis Books, 1986); Enoch Wan, "Practical Contextualization: A Case Study of Evangelizing Contemporary Chinese," *Global Missiology* 1, no. 1 (October 2003): n.p.; Enoch Wan, "Critiquing the Method of Traditional Western Theology and Calling for Sino-Theology," *Global Missiology* 1, no. 1 (October 2003): n.p.

129   I have written in more detail about themes that both pervade Chinese culture and have particular relevance for a contextualized Chinese theology in Wu, *Saving God's Face*, 69–192.

130   For a brief introduction with reference to a biblical setting, see deSilva, *Honor*, 23–42, 158–65, 206–12; Halvor Moxnes, "Honor and Shame," *Biblical Theology Bulletin* 23, no. 4

(November 1993): 167–76. For a longer treatment, see Jerome H. Neyrey, *Honor and Shame in the Gospel of Matthew* (Louisville, KY: Westminster John Knox Press, 1998). For Chinese culture, see Ho, "Face," 870.

131 Hui Ching Chang and G. Richard Holt, "A Chinese Perspective on Face as a Interrelational Concern," in *The Challenge of Facework: Cross-cultural and Interpersonal Issues*, ed. Stella Ting-Toomey, Suny Series in Human Communication Processes (Albany: State University of New York Press, 1994), 122.

132 In Chinese, 枪打出头鸟 (qiāng dǎ chū tóu niǎo).

133 This ideal is captured by the phrase 传宗接代 (chuán zōng jiē dài).

134 Cf. Andrew M. Mbuvi, "African Theology from the Perspective of Honor and Shame," in *The Urban Face of Mission: Ministering the Gospel in a Diverse and Changing World*, ed. Manuel Ortiz and Susan S. Baker (Phillipsburg, NJ: P & R, 2002), 288–89. He suggests, "I am, because we are; and since we are, therefore I am."

135 See, for example, Christopher L. Flanders, "Shame," in *Global Dictionary of Theology*, ed. William A. Dyrness et al. (Downers Grove, IL: IVP Academic, 2010), 813–17; G. B. Funderburke, "Shame," in *The Zondervan Pictorial Encyclopedia of the Bible*, ed. Merrill C. Tenney (Grand Rapids, MI: Zondervan, 1975), 372–73; Robert Priest, "Shame," in *Evangelical Dictionary of World Missions*, ed. Scott Moreau (Grand Rapids, MI: Baker, 2000), 870–71; Wu, *Saving God's Face*, 148–53.

136 By necessity of space, the following rendering of the biblical story is broad. Many important ideas simply cannot receive the attention one would want to give them. The agenda of this chapter is broader than any single doctrine.

137 One might say, "欠神人情" (qiàn shén rén qíng), indicating that we have a relational debt to God, as a child to his or her parents. Cf. Romans 13:8.

138 The idiom in Chinese: 龙生龙凤生凤.

139 Perhaps a fitting line from Chinese poetry could be cited, "本是同根深相煎何太急," which roughly translates, "Those who come from the same root are eager to do harm to one another."

140 This is an implicit dynamic in *guanxi* cultures. Relationships are simply means to an end.

141 我们要神不知廉耻. In essence, we want God to become as us, being indifferent to so much of the shameful behavior done in the world.

142 The Chinese equivalent for this idiom says that a person "prefers to be the head of a chicken rather than the tail of a phoenix." In Chinese, "宁做鸡头也不做凤尾."

143 In Chinese, "face" can be translated two ways, *lian* and *mianzi*. Although they generally have the same meaning, there remains a subtle and important distinction. *Lian* is the kind of face that refers to our character, who we really are. It is precious and enduring. *Mianzi* is more circumstantial. It can simply refer to the general way that people respect or honor others. It could simply mean a person is famous. *Lian* is a kind of *mianzi*, but *mianzi* is not necessarily *lian*.

144 攀比; perhaps one could also say, "高攀" or "和人高攀."

145 In the standard Chinese Bible (和合本), the word for "sin" is 罪 (zui), meaning "crime."

146 China herself suffered under colonial imperialism during the "hundred years of humiliation."

147   This is an obvious adaption of Descartes' dictum, "I think, therefore I am." Mbuvi, "African Theology," 288–89.

148   In Chinese, this could be stated with subtle irony: 我们在神的脸上抹黑而无法抹掉这最根本的触犯. "抹黑" signifies "smearing" a black mark upon God's face, which we cannot "wipe away" (抹掉).

149   One should be keen to hear this from the perspective of someone living under the "one child" policy.

150   "礼仪" refers to the rituals and manners that distinctly mark the Chinese sense of propriety. Though out of use today, it still represents quintessential Chinese virtue. It is included among the "four social bonds" (礼义廉耻).

151   不要向世人掩面.

152   Rather than simply saying they were "不忠的," it may be better to say they "缺乏忠义" in order to connect with the righteousness theme found elsewhere in the Bible.

153   In Chinese, one might regard God as a "back door," through which one walks in order to get some benefit or favor; "人们算神为后台."

154   The Chinese language has a saying in which one grabs Buddha's feet in times of trouble (临时抱佛脚). Students might use this expression before an exam. We could adjust the phrasing such that a person grabs upon Jesus' feet merely in times of trouble (临时抱耶稣脚).

155   厚颜无耻.

156   The echo to China's name is obvious. In Chinese, "China" is literally translated "middle kingdom." Cf. Ezekiel 5:5,6, "Thus says the Lord GOD: This is Jerusalem. *I have set her in the center of the nations, with countries all around her.* And she has rebelled against my rules by doing wickedness more than the nations, and against my statutes more than the countries all around her; for they have rejected my rules and have not walked in my statutes."

157   他们宁死不活, 宁辱不荣耀神.

158   Once again, it might be appropriate to use 礼仪 rather than 律法 for "law."

159   洗雪他们的国耻.

160   Once again, Chinese can sympathize with Israel on these points.

161   William C. Callahan observes, "Indeed, the theme of [China's] 2004 National Defense Education Day was 'Never forget national humiliation, strengthen our national defense.'" William C. Callahan, "History, Identity, and Security: Producing and Consuming Nationalism in China," *BCAS* 38, no. 2 (June 2006): 180. See also his work, "National Insecurities: Humiliation, Salvation, and Chinese Nationalism," *Alternatives: Global, Local, Political* 29, no. 2 (March–May 2004): 199–218.

162   律法/礼仪的精髓.

163   洋鬼子 is a slanderous term used during the Mao period to refer to a foreigner.

164   最惠国的身份.

165   本是同根深相煎何太急.

166   六亲不认. For a thought-provoking essay that explores the subject of God's "one family" in the context of the book of Galatians, see N. T. Wright, *Pauline Perspectives: Essays on Paul, 1978–2013* (Minneapolis: Fortress Press, 2013), 510–47.

167   In Chinese, these four parts each use the *fu* sound as a way to alliterate the gospel (福音, *fuyin*). Each word represents Jesus' life, death, resurrection, and return respectively. The first of these four parts, 服侍 (fúshì), does not translate directly into English and has been adjusted accordingly.

168   The last section 复国 will be discussed at the end of the chapter rather than here.

169   犹太人要神为他们洗冤.

170   讨还血债.

171   Thus, we could say Jesus 传宗接代 (chuán zōng jiē dài).

172   In Greek, Romans 5:2 uses the typical word for "boast" (καυχάομαι), as in Romans 2:17,23; 5:3,11 (cf. 3:27; 15:17).

173   Conveniently, this sentence construction (以 A 为 B) can carry two meanings. First, it could mean to *regard* A *as* B. In this case, to regard what is shameful as glorious. Second, it means to *use* A *as* B. Thus, God can use what is "shameful" as something "glorious."

174   For this paragraph, cf. Matthew 22:1–14; Mark 12:1–9; Luke 14:7–14.

175   The word for "host" is 主人 (zhǔ rén). "Banquet" is 宴席 (yàn xí). By using these together, a fitting pun is made whereby God, as host of the banquet, is called "主席," which is the common name for "Chairman"—the title given to China's supreme leader. Thus, the gospel is proclaimed in a way that recalls the apostle's affirmation, "Jesus is Lord," thus implying that Caesar is not.

176   This idea has been echoed by many, including Bevans, *Models of Contextual Theology*, 3; Bosch, *Transforming Mission*, 423; Flemming, *Contextualization in the New Testament*, 298.

177   Richard Hays, *Echoes of Scripture in the Letters of Paul* (New Haven, CT: Yale University Press, 1989), 185, italics in the original.

178   Scot McKnight, "Mark 12:1–12" (sermon), Willow Creek Community Church, South Barrington, IL, https://itunes.apple.com/us/podcast/willow-creek-community-church/id468469977?mt=2 (accessed 4 February 2013).

Chapter 9: The Gospel with Chinese Characteristics

179   For a survey of different approaches, see Wu, *Saving God's Face*, 94–144.

180   For a critique of this tendency, see McKnight, *The King Jesus Gospel*.

181   For a sample of books and articles across disciplines, see Bedford and Hwang, "Guilt and Shame"; Bays, *A New History*; Cheng, "The Concept of Face"; Hong and Chiu, "Comparative Structure"; Hu, "Chinese Concepts of 'Face'"; Liu, *Metaphor*; Hu and Grove, *Encountering the Chinese*; Hwang, *Foundations of Chinese Psychology*; Kipnis, *Producing Guanxi*; Liu, "Filial Piety"; Zhang and Baker, *Think Like Chinese*. For explicitly Christian perspectives, see Cook and Pao, *After Imperialism*; Covell, *Confucius*; Wan, "Practical Contextualization"; Wan, "Critiquing."

182   Anne-Laure Monfret, *Saving Face in China: A First-hand Guide for Any Traveller to China* (Bloomington, IN: Xlibris, 2011), 12.

183   Mbuvi, "African Theology," 288–89.

184   This is the title of a book, unrelated to China, by Melissa Fay Greene, *There Is No Me without You: One Woman's Odyssey to Rescue Her Country's Children* (New York: Bloomsbury, 2007).

185   In fact, a well-known phrase used in China's past was "One more Christian, one less Chinese." The phrase is mentioned in many places, including John Promfret, *Chinese Lessons: Five*

Classmates and the Story of the New China (New York: Henry Holt, 2006), 198; Dong Long Yang, "Theological and Cultural Reflections on the Relationship between Church and Society in China," *Chinese Theological Review* (2003): 72.

186   For an introduction, see Liang Pan, "Op-ed: Here's a Correct Translation of the 'Chinese Dream,'" *Tea Leaf Nation*, http://www.tealeafnation.com/2013/05/op-ed-heres-a-correct-translation-of-the-chinese-dream/ (accessed 17 May 2013). Some argue that this dream has proven illusory. See Gerard Lemos, *The End of the Chinese Dream: Why Chinese People Fear the Future* (New Haven, CT: Yale University Press, 2012).

187   Li Wen, "Young Chinese Couples Face Pressure from '4-2-1' Family Structure," *People's Daily Online*, http://english.people.com.cn/90001/90782/7117246.html (accessed 19 April 2013).

188   For a broad survey concerning the state of the changing family, see the multiple articles in the *ChinaSource* edition on "The Changing Chinese Family" in *ChinaSource* 10, no. 3 (Fall 2008).

189   Brené Brown's insight is helpful, "We get sucked into perfection for one very simple reason: We believe perfection will protect us. Perfectionism is the belief that if we live perfect, look perfect, and act perfect, we can minimize or avoid the pain of blame, judgment, and shame. We all need to feel worthy of love and belonging, and our worthiness is on the line when we feel like we are never ___ enough (you can fill in the blank: thin, beautiful, smart, extraordinary, talented, popular, promoted, admired, accomplished)." Brené Brown, "Want to Be Happy? Stop Trying to Be Perfect," CNN, http://www.cnn.com/2010/LIVING/11/01/give.up.perfection/index.html (accessed 19 April 2013).

190   Han Chen tells of another consequence of the pressure related to the *gaokao*. In essence, college becomes anticlimactic and students pay little attention to their university education. Han Chen, "Translation: What's Wrong with Chinese Higher Education," *Tea Leaf Nation*, http://www.tealeafnation.com/2012/09/translation-whats-wrong-with-chinese-higher-education/ (accessed 19 April 2013).

191   As Nisbett points out, societies that depend on agriculture "need to get along with one another." Nisbett, *Geography of Thought*, 34.

192   Huo Shui, "China's Modern Family Problems," *ChinaSource* 10, no. 3 (2008): 11.

193   Antonio L. Rappa and Sor-Hoon Tan, "Political Implications of Confucian Familism," *Asian Philosophy* 13, no. 2/3 (2003): 90. Their article gives a broad but thorough introduction to the Chinese views on "family." Confucian familism centers upon the social relationships of men rather than women. For more on this, see N. H. Ko, "Familism in Confucianism" (paper), International Conference, Women's Global Connection, San Antonio, TX, 2004, http://wgc.womensglobalconnection.org/pdf/11naihuako.pdf (accessed 1 February 2011, page discontinued).

194   Fengyan Wang, "Confucian Thinking in Traditional Moral Education: Key Ideas and Fundamental Features," *Journal of Moral Education* 33, no. 4 (December 2004): 432. He quotes from P. S. Hu, Xiaojing Yizhu [translated notes on *The Book of Filial Piety*] (Beijing: Zhonghua Book Company, 1996), 1.

195   Rappa and Tan, "Political Implications," 93.

196   Jenny Yau, Judith Smetana, and Aaron Metzger, "Young Chinese Children's Authority Concepts," *Social Development* 18, no. 1 (2009): 211, 221, 224.

197   Kwang-Kuo Hwang, "*Guanxi* and *Mientze*: Conflict Resolution in Chinese Society," *Intercultural Communication Studies* 7, no. 1 (1997): 30.

198   I do not suggest that the child obeys whatever his parents command. Rather, the point is that, even in his rebellion, he will feel obliged to appear as if he is compliant to their wishes.

199   Hwang, *Foundations*, 284. The key distinction is between what one *positively* seeks to gain versus what one is merely obliged to maintain. In addition, Hwang says, "In Chinese parenting, parents usually encourage children to pursue highly socially approved 'vertical goals,' hoping to confirm a higher social status. However, for the 'horizontal goals' that the children personally feel interest, Chinese parents would not necessarily give the same support" (289).

200   Amy Chua, *Battle Hymn of the Tiger Mother* (New York: Penguin Press, 2011), 52.

201   This duty is called "a self-evident moral obligation" in Xinrui Yuan and Qing Wang, "A Tentative Study of Difference and Integration of Sino-Western Filial Piety Culture," *Asian Social Science* 7, no. 8 (2011): 100. Nietszche, in *On the Genealogy of Morals*, gives a negative assessment of societies that stress the debt of filial piety: "The conviction reigns that it is only through the sacrifices and accomplishments of the ancestors that the tribe *exists*—and that one has to *pay them back* with sacrifices and accomplishments: one thus recognizes a *debt* that constantly grows greater, since these forebears . . . accord the tribe new advantages and new strength." This is cited in Erin Khuê Ninh, *Ingratitude: The Debt-bound Daughter in Asian American Literature* (New York: New York University Press, 2011), 33.

202   This is rightly observed in Alvin M. Chan, "The Chinese Concepts of *Guanxi*, *Mianzi*, *Renqing*, and *Bao*: Their Interrelationships and Implications for International Business" (paper, Australian and New Zealand Marketing Academy Conference, Brisbane, Queensland, Australia, 2006), 3.

203   Kuang-Hui Yeh and Olwen Bedford, "Filial Belief and Parent-child Conflict," *International Union of Psychological Science* 39, no. 2 (April 2004): 141. Similarly, see Chang Hui-China and Holt G. Richard, "Debt-repayment Mechanism in Chinese Relationships: An Exploration of the Folk Concepts of *Pao* and Human Emotion Debt," *Research of Language and Social Interaction* 27, no. 4 (1994): 360.

204   Chua, *Battle Hymn*, 52–53.

205   Kwang-Kuo Hwang, "Two Moralities: Reinterpreting the Findings of Empirical Research on Moral Reasoning in Taiwan," *Asian Journal of Social Psychology* 1, no. 3 (1998): 232.

206   Ninh, *Ingratitude*, 38.

207   Ibid., 45–46.

208   Ibid., 46.

209   Ibid.

210   Chang and Holt, "Chinese Perspective," 122.

211   Lawrence Hsin Yang and Arthur Kleinman, "'Face' and the Embodiment of Stigma in China—The Cases of Schizophrenia and AIDS," *Social Science and Medicine* 67:3 (2008): 398–408.

212   Of course enforcement is difficult and doubtful. See Michelle FlorCruz, "Chinese Law Requires Children to Visit Elderly Parents," *International Business Times*, http://www.ibtimes.com/chinese-law-requires-children-visit-elderly-parents-987796 (accessed 13 May 2013). In Western history, laws concerning filial respect have also existed. See Patti Spencer, "Filial Support Laws: Am

I My Mother's Keeper?" Pennsylvania Fiduciary Litigation, 19 July 2009, http://www.pennsylva-niafiduciarylitigation.com/2009/07/articles/elder-law/filial-support-laws-am-i-my-mothers-keeper/ (accessed 13 May 2013).

213   It is noteworthy that Paul in Romans 6 says that everyone is a slave—either to sin or to righteousness.

214   At one level, parents say the added correction simply aims to help the child improve and keep them humble. This sounds reasonable. However, it is strangely convenient that so doing is highly beneficial for their own purposes and retaining some degree of control over the child. In addition, they don't do this in other relationships in the way they do it with their own children. Do they not love other people? Do they not want others humble as well?

215   We are all prone to compromise *best* things for the sake of merely *good* things. This exchange is the essence of idolatry.

216   Again, I refer to "cultural contextualization." For an example of "exegetical contextualiza-tion," where Scripture is interpreted through a cultural lens, see the previous chapter.

217   I especially refer to Romans 2, 4, and 6. They redefine what is honorable and shameful, who is a Jew "inwardly," an offspring of Abraham, and the meaning of freedom versus slavery. For a more detailed discussion on this point, see Wu, *Saving God's Face*, 250–80.

218   Many assertions in this section are defended more comprehensively in Wu, *Saving God's Face*, 193–292.

219   One of the most common ways Christians translate "God" (of the Bible) is *shang di*, 上帝, which depicts God as the highest emperor. The Chinese word for "emperor" is *huang di*. Perhaps this verbiage can be utilized to convey the point. Chinese Catholics have also emphasized God's role as ruler over the world. They have traditionally used the word *tian zhu* (天主), or "heavenly lord," to represent God.

220   Historically, Chinese thinkers and artists have drawn inspiration from the order and beauty of nature. It has been argued that Chinese people derive their moral philosophy from their view of nature. See Dora Shu-fang Dien, *The Chinese Worldview Regarding Justice and the Supernatural: The Cultural and Historical Roots of Rule by Law* (New York: Nova Science Publishers, 2007), 6.

221   It is noteworthy that China's leaders have traditionally taken a pragmatic approach to religion. Whether Buddhism, Daoism, Christianity, or another religion, emperors saw religion as a political tool to maintain social harmony. Although the Chinese Communist government in the past century has propagated atheism, modern political leaders echo these sentiments. In 1993 former Chinese President Jiang Zemin said the government should "actively lead religions to adjust to socialist society." Cited in Li Qiuling, "The Position of Religion in Chinese Society," in *Christianity and Chinese Culture*, ed. Mikka Ruokanen and Paulos Huang (Grand Rapids, MI: Eerdmans, 2010), 286. Similarly, Chinese scholar Zhibin Xie notes, "The chief moral role of religion lay not in its being a premise of ethical values, but in its assistance in the enforcement of the secular moral standards." Zhibin Xie, "Religious Diversity and the Public Roles of Religion in Chinese Society," in *Sino-Christian Studies in China*, ed. Huilin Yang and Xinan Yang (Newcastle, UK: Cambridge Scholars Press, 2006), 232, following C. K. Yang, *Religion in Chinese Society* (Berkeley: University of California Press, 1961), 286.

222   For a detailed, scholarly argument on this point, see Dickson, "Gospel as News." For a condensed summary, see John Dickson, "What Is the Gospel?", chap. 8 in *Best Kept Secret*. The "Son of God" title traces back to the Davidic covenant (2 Sam 7:14; cf. 1 Chron 17; Ps 2:2,6,7). In John 1:49, Nathaniel quite explicitly says to Jesus, "Rabbi, you are the Son of God! You are the King of Israel." In the ancient Mediterranean, deity and kingship were often linked such that a king of the nation was regarded as the son of that people's god.

223   Confucius, "The Analects," 15:23, see http://nothingistic.org/library/confucius/analects/analects28.html. Confucius, "The Analects," in *The Chinese Classics*, 15:11, trans. James Legge (1861), see: http://nothingistic.org/library/confucius/analects/analects07.html (accessed 16 May 2013).

224   For further elaboration on this debt theme, see Wu, *Saving God's Face*, 181–219.

225   The purpose of the people's offerings and sacrifices was to honor the Lord (1 Sam 2:29; 1 Chron 16:29; Ps 96:8; Isa 43:23). On offerings as a payment of reparations, see Numbers 5:5–10, where אָשָׁם, typically translated "guilt offering" or "compensation" (cf. Lev 5) is regarded as restitution: "And the Lord spoke to Moses, saying, 'Speak to the people of Israel, When a man or woman commits any of the sins that people commit by breaking faith with the Lord, and that person realizes his guilt, he shall confess his sin that he has committed. And he shall make full restitution [אָשָׁם] for his wrong, adding a fifth to it and giving it to him to whom he did the wrong. But if the man has no next of kin to whom restitution [הָאָשָׁם] may be made for the wrong, the restitution [אָשָׁם] for wrong shall go to the Lord for the priest, in addition to the ram of atonement with which atonement is made for him. And every contribution, all the holy donations of the people of Israel, which they bring to the priest, shall be his. Each one shall keep his holy donations: whatever anyone gives to the priest shall be his.'"

226   Thus, we can say God uses cursing for blessing, or *yi zhouzu lai zhufu* (以咒诅来祝福).

227   For a fuller exegetical discussion on this point, see chapters 2–3 of Gary A. Anderson, *Sin: A History* (New Haven, CT: Yale University Press, 2009).

228   K. K. Hwang discusses this idea in Hwang, *Foundations*, 335–36. In essence, one gains benefit from someone else's good face. There is no need to limit the use of the phrase to things like "name dropping." A mediator could use his "face" to reconcile two parties in conflict. Cf. ibid., 359–60; Chang and Holt, "Chinese Perspective," 116–20.

229   For a brief introduction, see China Media Project, "Eight Honors and Eight Disgraces," http://cmp.hku.hk/2007/07/05/425/ (accessed 9 May 2012).

230   In Chinese, the contrast is quite clear since the two phrases both use the number "eight." Each envisions the creation of an ideal society.

231   Kwame Bediako, *Theology and Identity: The Impact of Culture upon Christian Thought in the Second Century and in Modern Africa* (Oxford: Regnum, 1992), 39. In speaking of a "third" race, Tertullian makes a distinction from Jews and pagans.

Chapter 10: Contextualizing Our Ministry

232   A few introductory books on biblical theology include Michael Lawrence, *Biblical Theology in the Life of the Church: A Guide for Ministry* (Wheaton, IL: Crossway, 2010); James M. Hamilton Jr., *What Is Biblical Theology? A Guide to the Bible's Story, Symbolism, and Patterns*

(Wheaton, IL: Crossway, 2013). For an example of a biblical theology aimed at nonacademic readers, see Hafemann, *God of Promise*. At a more academic level, a few popular writers include Greg Beale, N. T. Wright, and Michael Bird, among others.

233   See Jackson Wu, "Are Missionaries Ashamed of the Language of Paul's Gospel?" (blog entry), 5 March 2013, http://jacksonwu.org/2013/03/05/are-missionaries-ashamed-of-the-language-of-pauls-gospel/ (accessed 19 December 2013).

234   This analogy comes from John Walton, who uses it in a different context to explain his interpretation of Genesis 1 as "an account of functional origins" rather than one of "material origins." He uses the "home" versus "house" contrast in various places, including John Walton, "Genesis through Ancient Eyes," Parts 1–4 (seminar), Evangelical Community Church, Bloomington, IN, 5–6 April 2013, http://eccbloomington.sermon.tv/9642072 (accesseed 20 December 2013). For the fuller context of his discussion, see Walton, *Lost World*.

Chapter 11: Cultural Lenses

235   A fantastic book on this subject is E. Randolph Richards and Brandon J. O'Brien, *Misreading Scripture with Western Eyes: Removing Cultural Blinders to Better Understand the Bible* (Downers Grove, IL: IVP Books, 2012).

236   Yeo, *Jerusalem*, 5.

237   See Wolters, *Creation Regained*, 87–113. I am not suggesting that general revelation is exactly equivalent to culture. Rather, culture is an imperfect carrier of general revelation via "creation structures."

238   To say "a means" does not imply the *only* means. Naturally, the interpretive process has a number of "checks" that guard against error, such as historical theology and biblical theology. Particularly important are the logic and grammar of the immediate context as well as the broader narrative of Scripture.

239   Ibid., 88.

240   Ibid., 87, italics in the original.

241   Newbigin, *Gospel*, 9–10.

242   For example, Ronald H. Nash, following Augustine, says, "Christians cannot accept the cyclical view of history because it contradicts the clear teachings of the New Testament," in *Life's Ultimate Questions: An Introduction to Philosophy* (Grand Rapids, MI: Zondervan, 1999), 164. Likewise, Danny Akin says, "A Christian philosophy of history has purpose and is linear; the Eastern religions have a cyclical view of history," in "Is Jesus the Only Way to God and How Do I Witness to Someone Involved in a Cult?" http://www.danielakin.com/wp-content/uploads/2008/04/5-is-jesus-the-only-way-to-god-and-how-do-i-witness-to-someone-involved-in-a-cult.pdf (accessed 25 September 2012).

243   See Ecclesiastes 1:3–11; 3:1–20; 4:1,7; 9:11.

244   G. K. Beale, *Handbook on the New Testament Use of the Old Testament: Exegesis and Interpretation* (Grand Rapids, MI: Baker, 2012), 21.

245   Rick E. Watts, "Mark," in *Commentary on the New Testament Use of the Old Testament*, ed. G. K. Beale and D. A. Carson (Grand Rapids, MI: Baker, MI: Baker, 2007), 136.

246   The references are too many. Specialized studies on the subject include Leland Ryken, James C. Wilhoit, and Tremper Longman III, eds., "Exodus, Second Exodus," in *Dictionary of Biblical Imagery* (Downers Grove, IL: InterVarsity Press, 1998), 253–55; Friedbert Ninow, *Indicators of Typology within the Old Testament: The Exodus Motif,* Friedensauer Schriftenreihe: Theologie, vol. 4 (Frankfurt: Peter Lang, 2001).

247   Craig L. Blomberg, "Matthew," in *Commentary on the New Testament Use of the Old Testament,* ed. G. K. Beale and D. A. Carson (Grand Rapids, MI: Baker, 2007), 7.

248   G. K. Beale, *Handbook on the New Testament Use of the Old Testament: Exegesis and Interpretation* (Grand Rapids, MI: Baker Academic, 2012), 65.

249   Wright, *How God Became King,* 72.

250   Examples of works that emphasize this individual focus include Mark Seifrid, "Unrighteousness by Faith: Apostolic Proclamation in Romans 1:18–3:20," in *Justification and Variegated Nomism: The Complexities of Second Temple Judaism,* ed. D. A. Carson, Mark A. Seifrid, and Peter T. O'Brien (Grand Rapids, MI: Baker Academic, 2004), 105–46; Campus Crusade for Christ, "Four Spiritual Laws." Also noteworthy is Campus Crusade for Christ (Cru), "The Theological Background of the Four Spiritual Laws," There Is Hope Ministries, November 2005, http://www. hope365.co.za/sites/hope365.co.za/files/i%20FN%201S01B%20$%20Theology%20of%20the%20 Four%20Spiritual%20Laws.pdf (accessed 21 February 2012, page discontinued).

251   For instance, see Seifrid, "Unrighteousness by Faith."

252   In Greek, καυχάομαι is typically translated "boasting" as in Romans 2:17,23; 1 Corinthians 1:29,31.

253   Many have argued this point. For examples, see Piper, *God's Passion* (which contains the republication of Jonathan Edwards' *The End for Which God Created the World*); Hamilton, *God's Glory.*

254   I have argued more extensively in Wu, *Saving God's Face.*

255   Herbert Fingarette, "Human Community as Holy Rite: An Interpretation of Confucius' Analects," *Harvard Theological Review* 59, no. 1 (January 1966): 54–55.

256   Nisbett, *Geography of Thought,* 154, 173–90.

257   Ibid., 182.

Appendix 2

258   For more information, see my blog: (1) "Do you want 'face'?" Online: http://jacksonwu. org/2014/08/13/do-you-want-face-2/ Published 13 Aug 2014; and (2) "How does God seek 'face'?" Online: http://jacksonwu.org/2014/09/02/how-does-god-seek-face/ Published 9 Sept 2014.

Bibliography

Akin, Danny. "Is Jesus the Only Way to God and How Do I Witness to Someone Involved in a Cult?" http://www.danielakin.com/wp-content/uploads/2008/04/5-is-jesus-the-only-way-to-god-and-how-do-i-witness-to-someone-involved-in-a-cult.pdf (accessed 25 September 2012).

Alliance of Confessing Evangelicals. "The Cambridge Declaration of the Alliance of Confessing Evangelicals." Center for Reformed Theology and Apologetics, 20 April 1996. http://www.reformed.org/documents/cambridge.html (accessed 25 October 2011).

Anderson, Gary A. *Sin: A History.* New Haven, CT: Yale University Press, 2009.

Ashford, Bruce Riley. "The Gospel and Culture." In *Theology and Practice of Mission: God, the Church, and the Nations,* edited by Bruce Riley Ashford, Kindle loc. 3099–492. Nashville: B & H Academic, 2011.

Baker, Susan S. "The Social Sciences for Urban Ministry." In *The Urban Face of Mission: Ministering the Gospel in a Diverse and Changing World,* edited by Manuel Ortiz and Susan S. Baker. Phillipsburg, NJ: P & R, 2002.

Bays, Daniel H. *A New History of Christianity in China.* Hoboken, NJ: Wiley-Blackwell, 2011.

Beale, G. K. "Colossians." In *Commentary on the New Testament Use of the Old Testament,* edited by G. K. Beale and D. A. Carson, 841–70. Grand Rapids, MI: Baker, 2007.

———. *Handbook on the New Testament Use of the Old Testament: Exegesis and Interpretation.* Grand Rapids, MI: Baker, 2012.

———, ed. *The Right Doctrine from the Wrong Texts? Essays on the Use of the Old Testament in the New.* Grand Rapids, MI: Baker, 1994.

Bedford, Olwen, and Kwang-Kuo Hwang. "Guilt and Shame in Chinese Culture: A Cross-cultural Framework from the Perspective of Morality and Identity." *Journal for the Theory of Social Behaviour* 33, no. 2 (June 1, 2003): 127–44.

Bediako, Kwame. *Theology and Identity: The Impact of Culture upon Christian Thought in the Second Century and in Modern Africa.* Oxford: Regnum, 1992.

Beker, J. Christiaan. "Contingency and Coherence in the Letters of Paul." *Union Seminary Quarterly Review* 33 (1978): 141–51.

———. *Paul the Apostle: The Triumph of God in Life and Thought.* Philadelphia: Fortress, 1980.

Bevans, Stephen. *Models of Contextual Theology,* rev. and expanded ed. Maryknoll, NY: Orbis Books, 2002.

Bird, Michael F. *Evangelical Theology: A Biblical and Systematic Introduction.* Grand Rapids, MI: Zondervan, 2013.

———. *Introducing Paul: The Man, His Mission and His Message.* Downers Grove, IL: IVP Academic, 2009.

Blomberg, Craig L. "Matthew." In *Commentary on the New Testament Use of the Old Testament,* edited by G. K. Beale and D. A. Carson, 1–110. Grand Rapids, MI: Baker, 2007.

Bosch, David. *Transforming Mission: Paradigm Shifts in Theology of Mission.* Maryknoll, NY: Orbis Books, 1991.

Briddle, Mark E. *Missing the Mark: Sin and Its Consequences in Biblical Theology.* Nashville, TN: Abington Press, 2005.

Brown, Brené. "Want to Be Happy? Stop Trying to Be Perfect." CNN, 1 November 2010. http://www.cnn.com/2010/LIVING/11/01/give.up.perfection/index.html (accessed 19 April 2013).

Burk, Denny, "Is Paul's Gospel Counterimperial? Evaluating the Prospects of the 'Fresh Perspective' for Evangelical Theology." *Journal of the Evangelical Theological Society* 51, no. 2 (June 2008): 309–37.

Callahan, William C. "History, Identity, and Security: Producing and Consuming Nationalism in China." *Critical Asian Studies* 38, no. 2 (June 2006): 179–208.

———. "National Insecurities: Humiliation, Salvation, and Chinese Nationalism." *Alternatives: Global, Local, Political* 29, no. 2 (March–May 2004): 199–218.

Campus Crusade for Christ (Cru). "Four Spiritual Laws." 2007. http://www.campuscrusade.com/fourlawseng.htm (accessed 26 July 2011).

———. "The Theological Background of the Four Spiritual Laws." There Is Hope Ministries, November 2005. http://www.hope365.co.za/sites/hope365.co.za/files/i%20FN%201S01B%20$%20Theology%20of%20the%20Four%20Spiritual%20Laws.pdf (accessed 21 February 2012, page discontinued).

Carson, D. A. "What Is the Gospel?—Revisited." In *For the Fame of God's Name: Essays in Honor of John Piper,* edited by C. Samuel Storms and Justin Taylor, 147–70. Wheaton, IL: Crossway, 2010.

———, and Timothy J. Keller, eds. *The Gospel as Center: Renewing Our Faith and Reforming Our Ministry Practices.* Wheaton, IL: Crossway, 2012.

Chan, Alvin M. "The Chinese Concepts of *Guanxi, Mianzi, Renqing*, and *Bao*: Their Interrelationships and Implications for International Business." Paper presented at the Australian and New Zealand Marketing Academy Conference, Brisbane, Queensland, Australia, 2006.

Chandler, Matt, and Jared C. Wilson, *The Explicit Gospel.* Wheaton, IL: Crossway, 2012.

Chang, Hui Ching, and G. Richard Holt. "A Chinese Perspective on Face: A Inter-relational Concern." In *The Challenge of Facework: Cross-cultural and Interpersonal Issues*, edited by Stella Ting-Toomey, 95–131. Suny Series in Human Communication Processes. Albany: State University of New York Press, 1994.

Chapell, Bryan. "What Is the Gospel?" In *The Gospel as Center: Renewing Our Faith and Reforming Our Ministry Practices*, edited by D. A. Carson and Timothy J. Keller, 115–34. Wheaton, IL: Crossway, 2012.

Chen, Han. "Translation: What's Wrong with Chinese Higher Education." *Tea Leaf Nation*, 3 September 2012. http://www.tealeafnation.com/2012/09/translation-whats-wrong-with-chinese-higher-education/ (accessed 19 April 2013).

Cheng, Chung-Ying. "The Concept of Face and Its Confucian Roots." *Journal of Chinese Philosophy* 13 (1986): 329–48.

China Media Project, "Eight Honors and Eight Disgraces 八荣八耻," http://cmp.hku.hk/2007/07/05/425/ (accessed 9 May 2012).

ChinaSource. "The Changing Chinese Family." *ChinaSource* 10, no. 3 (Fall 2008).

Chua, Amy. *Battle Hymn of the Tiger Mother.* New York: Penguin Press, 2011.

Clark, David K. *To Know and Love God: Method for Theology.* Wheaton, IL: Crossway, 2003.

Confucius. "The Analects." In *The Chinese Classics*, translated by James Legge (1861). http://ctext.org/analects (accessed 16 May 2013).

Cook, Matthew, Rob Haskell, Ruth Julian, and Natee Tanchanpongs, eds. *Local Theology for the Global Church: Principles for an Evangelical Approach to Contextualization.* Pasadena, CA: William Carey Library, 2010.

Cook, Richard R., and David W. Pao, eds. *After Imperialism: Christian Identity in China and the Global Evangelical Movement.* Eugene, OR: Pickwick, 2011.

Covell, Ralph. *Confucius, the Buddha, and Christ: A History of the Gospel in Chinese.* Maryknoll, NY: Orbis Books, 1986.

Demarest, Bruce. *The Cross and Salvation: The Doctrine of God.* Wheaton, IL: Crossway, 2006.

deSilva, David A. *Honor, Patronage, Kinship and Purity: Unlocking New Testament Culture.* Downers Grove, IL: IVP Academic, 2000.

DeYoung, Kevin, and Greg Gilbert. *What Is the Mission of the Church? Making Sense of Social Justice, Shalom, and the Great Commission.* Wheaton, IL: Crossway, 2011.

Dickson, John. *The Best Kept Secret of Christian Mission: Promoting the Gospel with More Than Our Lips.* Grand Rapids, MI: Zondervan, 2010.

———. "Gospel as News: —from Aristophanes to the Apostle Paul." *New Testament Studies* 51, no. 2 (2005): 212–30.

Dien, Dora Shu-fang. *The Chinese Worldview Regarding Justice and the Supernatural: The Cultural and Historical Roots of Rule by Law.* New York: Nova Science Publishers, 2007.

Fingarette, Herbert. "Human Community as Holy Rite: An Interpretation of Confucius' Analects." *Harvard Theological Review* 59, no. 1 (January 1966): 53–67.

Flanders, Christopher L. "Shame." In *Global Dictionary of Theology*, edited by William A. Dyrness and Veli-Matti Kärkkäinen, 813–17. Downers Grove, IL: IVP Academic, 2010.

Flemming, Dean. *Contextualization in the New Testament: Patterns for Theology and Mission.* Downers Grove, IL: IVP Academic, 2005.

———. "Contextualizing the Gospel in Athens: Paul's Areopagus Address as a Paradigm for Missionary Communication." *Missiology: An International Review* 30, no. 2 (2002): 199–214.

———. "Paul the Contextualizer." In *Local Theology for the Global Church: Principles for an Evangelical Approach to Contextualization*, edited by Matthew Cook, Rob Haskell, Ruth Julian, and Natee Tanchanpongs, 18–19. Pasadena, CA: William Carey Library, 2010.

FlorCruz, Michelle. "Chinese Law Requires Children to Visit Elderly Parents." *International Business Times*, 2 January 2013. http://www.ibtimes.com/chinese-law-requires-children-visit-elderly-parents-987796 (accessed 13 May 2013).

Funderburke, G. B. "Shame." In *The Zondervan Pictorial Encyclopedia of the Bible*, edited by Merrill C. Tenney. Grand Rapids, MI: Zondervan, 1975.

Gendy, Atef M. "Style, Content and Culture: Distinctive Characteristics in the Missionary Speeches in Acts." *Swedish Missiological Themes* 99, no. 3 (2011): 247–65.

Gilbert, Greg. *What Is the Gospel?* Wheaton, IL: Crossway, 2010.

Goheen, Michael W., and Craig G. Bartholomew. *The Drama of Scripture: Finding Our Place in the Biblical Story.* Grand Rapids, MI: Baker Academic, 2004.

Gombis, Timothy. "The Gospel and Double Imputation." *Patheos* (blog), 25 October 2011. http://www.patheos.com/community/jesuscreed/2011/10/25/the-gospel-and-double-imputation/?utm_source=feedburner&utm_medium=feed&utm_campaign=Feed%3A+PatheosJesusCreed+%28Blog+-+Jesus+Creed%29 (accessed 25 October 2011, page discontinued).

———. "Racial Reconciliation and the Christian Gospel." *ACTS 3 Review* 15, no. 3 (2006): 117–28.

Greene, Melissa Fay. *There Is No Me without You: One Woman's Odyssey to Rescue Her Country's Children.* New York: Bloomsbury, 2007.

Greeson, Kevin. *The Camel: How Muslims Are Coming to Faith in Christ!*, rev. ed. Monument, CO: WIGTake Resources, 2010.

Hafemann, Scott J. *The God of Promise and the Life of Faith: Understanding the Heart of the Bible.* Wheaton, IL: Crossway, 2001.

Hamilton, James M., Jr. *God's Glory in Salvation through Judgment: A Biblical Theology.* Wheaton, IL: Crossway, 2010.

———. *What Is Biblical Theology? A Guide to the Bible's Story, Symbolism, and Patterns.* Wheaton, IL: Crossway, 2013.

Hays, Richard B. *Echoes of Scripture in the Letters of Paul.* New Haven, CT: Yale University Press, 1989.

———. *The Faith of Jesus Christ: The Narrative Substructure of Galatians 3:1–4:11*, 2nd ed. Grand Rapids, MI: Eerdmans, 2002.

Hesselgrave, David J., and Edward Rommen. *Contextualization: Meanings, Methods, and Models.* Grand Rapids, MI: Baker, 1989.

Hibbert, Evelyn. Contextualising sin for cross-cultural evangelism," *Missiology: An International Review.* Vol 42, no. 3 (2014): 309–21.

Ho, David Yau-fai. "On the Concept of Face." *American Journal of Sociology* 81, no. 4 (1976): 866–84.

Hong, Ying-Yi, and Chi-Yue Chiu. "A Study of the Comparative Structure of Guilt and Shame in a Chinese Society." *Journal of Psychology* 126, no. 2 (March 1992): 171–79.

Horsley, Richard A., ed. *Paul and Empire: Religion and Power in Roman Imperial Society.* T&T Clark, 1997.

Hu, Hsien Chin. "The Chinese Concepts of 'Face.'" *American Anthropologist* 46, no. 1 (March 1944): 45–64.

Hu, P. S. Xiaojing Yizhu [translated notes on *The Book of Filial Piety*]. Beijing: Zhonghua Book Company, 1996.

Hu, Wenzhong, and Cornelius Lee Grove. *Encountering the Chinese: A Guide for Americans.* Yarmouth, ME: Intercultural Press, 1991.

Hui-China, Chang, and Holt G. Richard. "Debt-repayment Mechanism in Chinese Relationships: An Exploration of the Folk Concepts of *Pao* and Human Emotion Debt." *Research of Language and Social Interaction* 27, no. 4 (1994): 351–87.

Hwang, Kwang-Kuo. *Foundations of Chinese Psychology: Confucian Social Relations.* New York: Springer, 2012.

———. "*Guanxi* and *Mientze*: Conflict Resolution in Chinese Society." *Intercultural Communication Studies* 7, no. 1 (1997): 17–38.

———. "Two Moralities: Reinterpreting the Findings of Empirical Research on Moral Reasoning in Taiwan." *Asian Journal of Social Psychology* 1, no. 3 (1998): 211–38.

Kipnis, Andrew. *Producing* Guanxi: *Sentiment, Self, and Subculture in a North China Village.* Durham, NC: Duke University Press, 1997.

Ko, N. H. "Familism in Confucianism." Paper presented at the International Conference of Women's Global Connection, San Antonio, TX, 2004. http://wgc.womensglobalconnection.org/pdf/11naihuako.pdf (accessed 1 February 2011, page discontinued).

Lawrence, Michael. *Biblical Theology in the Life of the Church: A Guide for Ministry.* Wheaton, IL: Crossway, 2010.

Lemos, Gerard. *The End of the Chinese Dream: Why Chinese People Fear the Future.* New Haven, CT: Yale University Press, 2012.

Lewis, C. S. "To Dom Bede Griffiths" (23 April 23 1951). In *The Collected Letters of C.S. Lewis, Volume 3: Narnia, Cambridge, and Joy, 1950–1963,* edited by Walter Hooper, 111–12. New York: HarperCollins, 2007.

Li, Glen Collins. *Sin, the Silent Killer.* Maitland, FL: Xulon Press, 2008.

Lints, Richard. *The Fabric of Theology.* Grand Rapids, MI: Eerdmans, 1993.

Liu, Dilin. *Metaphor, Culture, and Worldview: The Case of American English and the Chinese Language.* Lanham, MD: University Press of America, 2002.

Liu, Li. "Filial Piety, *Guanxi,* Loyalty, and Money: Trust in China." In *Trust and Distrust: Sociocultural Perspectives,* edited by Ivana Marková and Alex Gillespie, 51–73. Charlotte, NC: Information Age Publishing, 2008.

Luther, Martin. "A Brief Instruction on What to Look for and Expect in the Gospels." In *Luther Works,* vol. 35, edited by J. Pelikan and H. T. Lehmann, 113–24. Philadelphia: Fortress, 1960.

Luzbetak, Louis J. *The Church and Cultures: New Perspectives in Missiological Anthropology.* Maryknoll, NY: Orbis Books, 1988.

Mbuvi, Andrew M. "African Theology from the Perspective of Honor and Shame." In *The Urban Face of Mission: Ministering the Gospel in a Diverse and Changing World,* edited by Manuel Ortiz and Susan S. Baker, 279–95. Phillipsburg, NJ: P & R, 2002.

McKnight, Scot. "Gospel and Rhetoric." *Jesus Creed* (blog), 7 November 2011. http://www.patheos.com/blogs/jesuscreed/2011/11/07/gospel-and-rhetoric/ (accessed 22 January 2013).

———. "The Gospel and the Pastor." Lecture, Parchman Lectures, Truett Theological Seminary, Waco, TX, 12 October 2011. http://www.baylor.edu/truett/index.php?id=84799.

———. *The King Jesus Gospel: The Original Good News Revisited.* Grand Rapids, MI: Zondervan, 2011.

———. *Kingdom Conspiracy: Returning to the Radical Mission of the Local Church.* Grand Rapids, MI: Baker, 2014.

———. "Mark 12:1–12." Sermon presented at Willow Creek Community Church, South Barrington, IL, 15 February 2012. https://itunes.apple.com/us/podcast/willow-creek-community-church/id468469977?mt=2 (accessed 4 February 2013).

———, and Joseph B. Modica, eds. *Jesus Is Lord, Caesar Is Not: Evaluating Empire in New Testament Studies.* Grand Rapids, MI: IVP Academic, 2013.

Monfret, Anne-Laure. *Saving Face in China: A First-hand Guide for Any Traveller to China.* Bloomington, IN: Xlibris, 2011.

Moreau, Scott. "Contextualization That Is Comprehensive." *Missiology* 34, no. 3 (2006): 325–35.

———. "Evangelical Models of Contextualization." In Local Theology for the Global Church:

Principles for an Evangelical Approach to Contextualization, edited by Matthew Cook, Rob Haskell, Ruth Julian, and Natee Tanchanpongs, 165–93. Pasadena, CA: William Carey Library, 2010.

Moxnes, Halvor. "Honor and Shame." *Biblical Theology Bulletin* 23, no. 4 (November 1993): 167–76.

Nash, Ronald H. *Life's Ultimate Questions: An Introduction to Philosophy.* Grand Rapids, MI: Zondervan, 1999.

Newbigin, Lesslie. *The Gospel in a Pluralist Society.* Grand Rapids, MI: Eerdmans, 1989.

Neyrey, Jerome H. *Honor and Shame in the Gospel of Matthew.* Louisville, KY: Westminster John Knox Press, 1998.

Nicholls, Bruce J. *Contextualization: A Theology of Gospel and Culture.* Vancouver, BC, Canada: Regent College, 2003.

Ninh, Erin Khuê. *Ingratitude: The Debt-bound Daughter in Asian American Literature.* New York: New York University Press, 2011.

Ninow, Friedbert. *Indicators of Typology within the Old Testament: The Exodus Motif.* Friedensauer Schriftenreihe: Theologie, vol. 4. Frankfurt: Peter Lang, 2001.

Nisbett, Richard E. *The Geography of Thought: How Asians and Westerns Think Differently . . . and Why.* New York: Free Press, 2003.

Pan, Liang. "Op-ed: Here's a Correct Translation of the 'Chinese Dream.'" *Tea Leaf Nation*, 14 May 2013. http://www.tealeafnation.com/2013/05/op-ed-heres-a-correct-translation-of-the-chinese-dream/ (accessed 17 May 2013).

Piper, John. "Did Jesus Die for Us or for God?" Desiring God, 1 January 1995. http://www.desiringgod.org/resource-library/articles/did-christ-die-for-us-or-for-god (accessed 3 October 2012).

———. *God Is the Gospel: Meditations on God's Love as the Gift of Himself.* Reprint, Wheaton, IL: Crossway, 2011.

———. *God's Passion for His Glory.* Wheaton, IL: Crossway, 1998.

Priest, Robert. "Shame." In *Evangelical Dictionary of World Missions*, edited by Scott Moreau, 870–71. Grand Rapids, MI: Baker, 2000.

Promfret, John. *Chinese Lessons: Five Classmates and the Story of the New China*. New York: Henry Holt, 2006.

Qiuling, Li. "The Position of Religion in Chinese Society," in *Christianity and Chinese Culture*, edited by Mikka Ruokanen and Paulos Huang, 276–86. Grand Rapids, MI: Eerdmans, 2010.

Rappa, Antonio L., and Sor-Hoon Tan. "Political Implications of Confucian Familism." *Asian Philosophy* 13, no. 2/3 (2003): 87–102.

Richards, E. Randolph, and Brandon J. O'Brien. *Misreading Scripture with Western Eyes: Removing Cultural Blinders to Better Understand the Bible*. Downers Grove, IL: IVP Books, 2012.

Richardson, Don. *Peace Child*. Glendale, CA: Regal Books, 1974.

Ruth, Julian. "Ground Level Contextualization." In *Local Theology for the Global Church: Principles for an Evangelical Approach to Contextualization*, edited by Matthew Cook, Rob Haskell, Ruth Julian, and Natee Tanchanpongs, 57–89. Pasadena, CA: William Carey Library, 2010.

Ryken, Leland, James C. Wilhoit, and Tremper Longman III, eds. *Dictionary of Biblical Imagery*. Downers Grove, IL: InterVarsity Press, 1998.

Seifrid, Mark. *Christ Our Righteousness: Paul's Theology of Justification*. Downers Grove, IL: InterVarsity Press, 2000.

———. "Unrighteousness by Faith: Apostolic Proclamation in Romans 1:18–3:20." In *Justification and Variegated Nomism: The Complexities of Second Temple Judaism*, edited by D. A. Carson, Mark A. Seifrid, and Peter T. O'Brien, 105–46. Grand Rapids, MI: Baker Academic, 2004.

Shui, Huo. "China's Modern Family Problems." *ChinaSource* 10, no. 3 (2008): 11.

Sills, M. David. *Reaching and Teaching: A Call to Great Commission Obedience*. Chicago: Moody Publishers, 2010.

Smith, Stephen R. "Gospel Presentations Used in T4T Packages." Training for Trainers, 2011. http://t4tonline.org/wp-content/uploads/2011/02/3d-Gospel-Presentations-Used-in-T4T-Packages.pdf (accessed 21 February 2012).

Spencer, Patti. "Filial Support Laws: Am I My Mother's Keeper?" Pennsylvania Fiduciary Litigation, 19 July 2009. http://www.pennsylvaniafiduciarylitigation.com/2009/07/articles/elder-law/filial-support-laws-am-i-my-mothers-keeper/ (accessed 13 May 2013).

SpreadTruth. "The Story." http://viewthestory.com/ (accessed 26 July 2011).

Training for Trainers. "Creation to Christ." http://t4tonline.org/wp-content/uploads/2011/05/creation-to-christ-oral-version-english.pdf (accessed 25 November 2013).

Vanhoozer, Kevin. "'One Rule to Rule Them All?': Theological Method in an Era of World Christianity." In *Globalizing Theology: Belief and Practice in an Era of World Christianity*, edited by Craig Ott and Harold Netland, 85–126. Grand Rapids, MI: Baker Academic and Brazos Press, 2006.

Walton, John H. "Genesis through Ancient Eyes," Parts 1–4. Seminar presented at Evangelical Community Church, Bloomington, IN, 5–6 April 2013. http://eccbloomington.sermon.tv/9642072 (accessed 20 December 2013).

———. *The Lost World of Genesis One: Ancient Cosmology and the Origins Debate.* Downers Grove, IL: IVP Academic, 2009.

Wan, Enoch. "Critiquing the Method of Traditional Western Theology and Calling for Sino-Theology." *Global Missiology* 1, no. 1 (October 2003): n.p.

———. "Practical Contextualization: A Case Study of Evangelizing Contemporary Chinese." *Global Missiology* 1, no. 1 (October 2003): n.p.

Wang, Fengyan. "Confucian Thinking in Traditional Moral Education: Key Ideas and Fundamental Features." *Journal of Moral Education* 33, no. 4 (December 2004): 429–47.

Watts, Rick E. "Mark." In *Commentary on the New Testament Use of the Old Testament*, edited by G. K. Beale and D. A. Carson, 111–250. Grand Rapids, MI: Baker, 2007.

Wax, Trevin. *Counterfeit Gospels: Rediscovering the Good News in a World of False Hope.* Chicago: Moody, 2011.

———. "Gospel Definitions." *Kingdom People* (blog), June 2011. http://thegospelcoalition.org/blogs/trevinwax/2009/09/28/gospel-definitions-pdf-format/ (accessed 26 December 2012).

———. "Results for '"Gospel Definitions."'" *Kingdom People* (blog). http://thegospelcoalition.org/blogs/trevinwax/?s=%22gospel+definitions%22.

———. "Scot McKnight and the 'King Jesus Gospel' 2: Points of Concern." *Kingdom People* (blog), 14 September 2011. http://thegospelcoalition.org/blogs/trevinwax/2011/09/14/scot-mcknight-and-the-king-jesus-gospel-2-points-of-concern/ (accessed 26 December 2012).

———. "3 Ways of Defining the Gospel." *Kingdom People* (blog), 22 February 2011. http://thegospelcoalition.org/blogs/trevinwax/2011/02/22/3-ways-of-defining-the-gospel/ (accessed 26 December 2012).

Wen, Li. "Young Chinese Couples Face Pressure from '4-2-1' Family Structure." *People's Daily Online*, 25 August 2010. http://english.people.com.cn/90001/90782/7117246.html (accessed 19 April 2013).

Witherington, Ben. "Dialogue with Scot McKnight on 'King Jesus': Part One." *The Bible and Culture* (blog), 10 September 2011. http://www.patheos.com/blogs/bibleandculture/2011/09/10/dialogue-with-scot-mcknight-on-king-jesus-part-one-2/ (accessed 26 December 2012).

Wolters, Albert M. *Creation Regained: Biblical Basics for a Reformational Worldview*, 2nd ed. Grand Rapids, MI: Eerdmans, 2005.

Wright, N. T. *Climax of the Covenant*. Minneapolis: Fortress Press, 1993.

———. *How God Became King: The Forgotten Story of the Gospels*. New York: HarperOne, 2012.

———. *Justification: God's Plan and Paul's Vision*. Downers Grove, IL: IVP Academic, 2009.

———. *The New Testament and the People of God*. Atlanta: Augsburg Fortress, 1992.

———. *Paul and the Faithfulness of God*. Philadelphia: Fortress Press, 2013.

———. "Paul's Gospel and Caesar's Empire." *Center of Theological Inquiry* (Princeton, NJ) 2 (Spring 1999): 42–65.

———. *Pauline Perspectives: Essays on Paul, 1978-2013*. Minneapolis: Fortress Press, 2013.

———. "Scripture, Exegesis, Dogma and Church: Some Pauline Proposals." In *Pauline Perspectives: Essays on Paul, 1978–2013*. Philadelphia: Fortress Press, 2013.

———. *Simply Good News: Why the Gospel is News and What Makes It Good* (HarperOne, San Francisco, Calif., 2015).

———. "Simply Jesus." Sermon, Willowcreek Community Church, South Barrington, IL, 6 November 2011. http://media.willowcreek.org/weekend/simply-jesus/.

Wu, Jackson. "Are Missionaries Ashamed of the Language of Paul's Gospel?" (blog entry), 5 March 2013. http://jacksonwu.org/2013/03/05/are-missionaries-ashamed-of-the-language-of-pauls-gospel/ (accessed 19 December 2013).

———. "Paul Writes to the Greek First and Also to the Jew: The Missiological Significance of Understanding Paul's Purpose in Romans." *Journal of the Evangelical Theological Society* 56, no. 4 (December 2013): 765–79.

———. *Saving God's Face: A Chinese Contextualization of Salvation through Honor and Shame*. Pasadena, CA: WCIU Press, 2013.

Xie, Zhibin. "Religious Diversity and the Public Roles of Religion in Chinese Society." In *Sino-Christian Studies in China*, edited by Huilin Yang and Xinan Yang, 230–44. Newcastle, UK: Cambridge Scholars Press, 2006.

Yang, C. K. *Religion in Chinese Society*. Berkeley: University of California Press, 1961.

Yang, Dong Long. "Theological and Cultural Reflections on the Relationship between Church and Society in China." *Chinese Theological Review* (2003): 64–75.

Yang, Lawrence Hsin, and Arthur Kleinman. "'Face' and the Embodiment of Stigma in China—The Cases of Schizophrenia and AIDS." *Social Science and Medicine* 67 (3) (2008): 398–408.

Yau, Jenny, Judith Smetana, and Aaron Metzger. "Young Chinese Children's Authority Concepts." *Social Development* 18, no. 1 (2009): 210–29.

Yeh, Kuang-Hui, and Olwen Bedford. "Filial Belief and Parent-child Conflict." *International Union of Psychological Science* 39, no. 2 (2004): 132–44.

Yeo, K. K. *What Has Jerusalem to Do with Beijing: Biblical Interpretation from a Chinese Perspective.* Harrisburg, PA: Trinity Press, 1998.

Yuan, Xinrui, and Qing Wang. "A Tentative Study of Difference and Integration of Sino-Western Filial Piety Culture." *Asian Social Science* 7, no. 8 (2011): 97–106.

Zhang, Haihua, and Geoffrey Baker. *Think Like Chinese.* Annandale, NSW, Australia: Federation Press, 2008.

Index

Scripture Index

Ps 62:12, 18
Ps 62:7, 64
Ps 68:11–14, 41
Ps 71:2, 40
Ps 74:12–17, 47
Ps 74:17, 119
Ps 89:2–3, 42
Ps 89:28–29, 42
Ps 89:35–36, 42
Ps 96:2, 46
Ps 96:6, 120
Ps 96:10, 46, 120
Ps 96:13, 46, 120
Ps 97:9, 120
Ps 98:6, 120
Ps 98:9, 46
Ps 104, 24
Ps 115:15, 61
Ps 118:22, 144
Ps 119:24, 168
Ps 119:47, 168
Ps 124:8, 61
Ps 143:1, 24
Ps 143:11, 24
Prov 24:12, 18
Isa 5, 144
Isa 11:6, 168
Isa 28:16, 64, 143, 168
Isa 29:13, 166
Isa 40–52, 68
Isa 40–66, 45
Isa 40:8–9, 14
Isa 40:9, 34, 41, 68, 118
Isa 40:9–10, 45
Isa 40:10–42:9, 41, 68
Isa 41, 68
Isa 41:8, 118
Isa 41:10, 68
Isa 41:21, 68

Isa 41:22–24, 68
Isa 41:25, 68
Isa 41:26–27, 68
Isa 42:5, 49
Isa 43:15, 45, 47, 68
Isa 45:8–9, 63
Isa 51:2, 118
Isa 52:7, 34, 41, 68, 118
Isa 60:6, 68
Isa 61:1, 68
Isa 63:16, 118
Jer 17:10, 18
Jer 31:31–34, 167
Dan 7:13, 24
Hos 11:1, 62
Hos 11:1–12, 62
Hos 13:4–5, 62
Amos 2:9–11, 62
Mal 1:6, 137

New Testament
Matt 3:2, 42
Matt 4:17, 42
Matt 5:3–10, 168
Matt 7:12, 162
Matt 9:35, 42
Matt 10, 159
Matt 10:7, 42
Matt 10:34–39, 159, 163
Matt 11:28–30, 168
Matt 12:48, 160
Matt 12:48–50, 80, 163
Matt 12:50, 159
Matt 14:13, 195
Matt 14:23, 195
Matt 15:8, 166
Matt 16:17, 18
Matt 19:29, 163
Matt 19:29–30, 142

Matt 20:25–28, 163
Matt 23:5–12, 166
Matt 24:14, 42, 45
Matt 25:31–46, 193
Matt 26:13, 45
Matt 28:18–20, 193
Mark 1:1, 139
Mark 1:14–15, 41
Mark 1:15, 39, 64
Mark 3:31–35, 163
Mark 3:32–35, 140
Mark 3:35, 159
Mark 7:6, 166
Mark 10:29–31, 163
Mark 10:42–45, 163
Mark 12:1–12, 144
Mark 14:9, 45
Mark 16:15, 45
Luke 4:18, 68
Luke 9:23–26, 165
Luke 11:43, 57
Luke 14:26, 184, 195
Luke 23:2–3, 117
Luke 24:44, 95
John 1:12–13, 167
John 1:49, 24, 42, 68
John 4:22, 51
John 5:23–24, 164
John 8, 163
John 8:23, 81
John 8:31, 160
John 8:31–58, 193
John 8:31–59, 160
John 8:33, 160
John 8:34–36, 160
John 8:39, 80
John 8:39–44, 80
John 8:39–47, 160
John 8:41, 160

John 8:48–51, 164
John 8:49–50, 161
John 8:54–56, 161
John 11:27, 42
John 12:32, 140
John 12:43, 166
John 17:3, 21, 51
John 17:14–16, 81
John 17:22, 73, 131, 141
John 17:22–23, 168
John 19:12, 117
John 20:31, 68
Acts 2:24, 165
Acts 2–4, 42
Acts 3:20, 68
Acts 3:25, 136
Acts 5:30, 70
Acts 5:42, 68, 70
Acts 7, 13
Acts 9:22, 68
Acts 9:4–5, 193
Acts 10, 115
Acts 10:36, 45, 68
Acts 10:42, 45
Acts 13, 42
Acts 13:17–41, 43
Acts 13:30–37, 70
Acts 13:32, 34, 39, 69
Acts 13:32–33, 44, 69
Acts 14, 35, 95, 115
Acts 14:7, 46, 69
Acts 14:15, 34, 39, 64, 66, 69
Acts 14:15–17, 45, 92
Acts 14:21, 46, 66, 69
Acts 14:22, 69, 92
Acts 15, 193
Acts 17, 35, 91, 95, 115–18, 121, 123–24
Acts 17:1–9, 117
Acts 17:3, 68